Frontispiece: Sculpture by Lehmbruck, Duchamp-Villon, Butler, Renoir, Lipchitz, Lachaise and Maillol in the Abby Aldrich Rockefeller Sculpture Garden of the Museum. Photo Alexandre Georges.

MASTERS OF MODERN ART

Edited by Alfred H. Barr, Jr.

THE MUSEUM OF MODERN ART NEW YORK

Distributed by Simon and Schuster   New York

PUBLISHED BY THE MUSEUM OF MODERN ART, 11 WEST 53 STREET, NEW YORK. PRINTED IN THE NETHERLANDS

CONTENTS

FOREWORD: THE COLLECTION OF THE MUSEUM OF MODERN ART

This book has been prepared by the Museum of Modern Art on the occasion of its Twenty-fifth Anniversary. Intended as a tribute to the art of our time, it deals with many branches of contemporary visual art produced in forty countries over the past seventy-five years. Obviously such a vast subject cannot be treated exhaustively in any one volume, but we believe that this book will serve its purpose if it conveys an idea of the variety, excellence of achievement, and vigor of modern art.

That it was possible to select the illustrations for this book entirely from the Museum's own collection is a matter of considerable pride to us. Twenty-five years is a short period in the history of most of the world's great art museums. Yet within that time the Museum of Modern Art has assembled great collections, some of them unsurpassed, in a variety of fields including painting, sculpture, prints, motion pictures, well-designed furniture and utensils, posters and photography.

Originally it was the Museum's stated policy to keep the collection fluid by passing on to other institutions even its best works as they matured and became 'classic'. Recently the Museum has adopted a radically new policy which will be implemented by the creation of a highly selective *permanent* collection of masterworks both by twentieth-century artists and their great nineteenth-century forerunners, particularly in painting. The selection and acquisition of these masterworks will be one of the major goals of the Museum, but the experimental collecting of new forms of art will continue in spite of the limited confines of our presently inadequate gallery and storage space.

The Museum's collection is a living testimony to the courage, the generosity, and the enthusiasm of the entire Museum community—its Trustees, its patrons, its staff. We are proud of past achievement but realize fully how much there is still to be done.

To help people enjoy, understand, and use the visual arts of **our time** is the stated purpose of the Museum of Modern Art. Particularly during a time when conformity enforced through authoritarian pressure is a constant threat to the development of a free society, it is most heartening to turn to the arts and to find in them the vitality and diversity that reflects freedom of thought and of faith. We believe that the collection of the Museum of Modern Art and this publication represent our respect for the individual and for his ability to contribute to society as a whole through free use of his individual gifts in his individual manner. This freedom we believe fundamental to democratic society.

JOHN HAY WHITNEY
Chairman of the Board of Trustees

PREFACE

The Museum of Modern Art was never intended to be merely a depository for artistic treasures. It was conceived as an institution that would work in and with the community, vigorously participating in its life.

Within the Museum's structure the collection is an intrinsic and important factor. It contributes constantly to all the Museum's varied and far-flung activities. As it grew in scope and excellence it became more and more capable of setting standards and providing a sense of continuity to the activities of the various departments of the Museum. By demonstrating the vast variety of styles and concepts so characteristic of modern art in the recent past, it makes for an open mind and helps keep the institution receptive to new trends. On the other hand, nearly all departmental activities contributed to the development of the collection. Not only did many works of art come to the Museum's attention through these activities, but the very existence of these activities has created a non-academic climate and kept the Museum close to the realities of today's art life.

Over the years the Museum has organized some 820 exhibitions in all branches of the modern visual arts and their relevant background. It has established a circulating service to bring these exhibitions to other cities in the United States and more recently it has embarked on a broad program of international interchange of exhibitions on a world-wide basis.

In order to give its work permanence and make it accessible to the widest possible public, the Museum has published an extended series of books on its various exhibitions and other subjects, some of which have been translated for distribution in foreign countries. The Museum has conducted competitions to fill specific needs in industrial and graphic design and has participated in the efforts of industry to raise the artistic standards of its products. It has served as an influential laboratory and clearing house in art education.

The Museum's library is more than just a collection of reference books. It has become a world center for bibliographic research in the Museum's field.

The Museum has done much to establish the artistic importance of photography and motion pictures and, through its film library, has rescued much valuable material from destruction. Most recently it has, in collaboration with the industry, embarked on a project in the field of television in the hope of rendering this newest medium of visual mass communications a service comparable to that rendered to the motion picture industry.

Thus the Museum during its twenty-five years of growth has played an important role in the cultural life of the city, the nation, and the world.

RENÉ D'HARNONCOURT
Director of the Museum

INTRODUCTION

Twenty-five years ago in the autumn of 1929, even before it opened its doors to the public, the Museum of Modern Art began to form its collection. Today in its manifold departments, the collection numbers many thousands of works of art. A few of the best or most characteristic are reproduced here, more to give pleasure than for any systematic exposition or record. Even more, this picture-book is an invitation to see the originals!

The words 'best' or 'most characteristic' immediately raise certain fundamental questions not only about this volume but about the collection it represents and, indeed, about the Museum itself. The Museum collects works radically different in purpose, medium, school and generation. Who is to say what is really important? The public is often slow to comprehend; critics and museum people are notoriously blind. Even the artist is no guide. Whistler's contempt for Cézanne was equalled only by Cézanne's contempt for Gauguin. Frank Lloyd Wright assails Le Corbusier. A leading authority on cubism still insists that a Mondrian is not a work of art at all; a devotee of Mondrian denounces the surrealism of Ernst and Dali as perversion of true art; a dadaist of 1920 finds the abstract expressionist of 1950 tedious; and the socialist realist cries a plague on all their bourgeois-bohemian houses. Artists and their champions may indeed seem a squabbling banderlog of isms. But, actually, they are not; their differences are real and significant, slowly developed, passionately believed in, and expressive not simply of artistic convictions but often of deeply-felt philosophies of life.

Even granting that the Museum should collect works of many kinds, there is still the problem of choosing the best of each. Quality, of course, should be and has been the first criterion. Yet the matter is not so simple. Picasso's *Three Musicians*, page 83, may be superior in quality to Picasso's *Demoiselles d'Avignon*, page 69, but the latter, with all its coarseness and experimental changes of mind may be equally important to the Museum: whatever its esthetic quality, it is a dramatic record of agonistic effort and the first detonation of a great historic movement.

Yes, it may be argued, but these two paintings are monumental achievements such as are essential to a collection's greatness. What about John Sloan's tiny etching, page 110, the Tiffany vase, page 215, the Olivetti typewriter, page 225, and Buster Keaton's obsessed slapstick, page 207—what place have they in the same collection? Taken together, an important place, for in spite of their smaller scale or 'humbler' medium, each is a work of exceptional distinction within the wide range of the visual arts of our period.

Of course many mistakes are made. No one connected with the Museum pretends to infallibility. Yet, if fifty years from now our errors should seem egregious, perhaps a hundred years hence some of our judgments may be justified. In any case, it is already clear that errors of omission are by far the most serious for they are usually irrevocable.

The Museum's Trustees, Committees and Staff are responsible for acquisitions to the collection (as well as for far more numerous rejections). Ordinarily the heads of the curatorial departments (pages 231-232) after consultation with the director of the collections make recommendations to the Committee on the Museum Collections, composed largely of Trustees. The Committee chairman then reports to the Board of Trustees. Anyone, however, may propose an acquisition for the collection, either as a gift or a purchase.

The Museum Collection has been a loyal collaboration. The long list of donors on pages 233-236 includes eight hundred names, among them some 200 corporations. A few individuals must be mentioned here for it is chiefly their generosity that has made the museum collections possible: Miss Lillie P. Bliss, the Museum's first vice-president, for her bequest of paintings; Mrs. John D. Rockefeller, Jr., after whom both the Museum's Sculpture Garden and Print Room are named, for her gifts of funds and her own collections; Mrs. Simon Guggenheim for her magnificently renewed purchase fund; A. Conger Goodyear, the Museum's first president, Stephen C. Clark, Nelson A. Rockefeller, for their gifts of funds and works of art. Of the architecture and design collections, Philip L. Goodwin, Philip C. Johnson and Edgar Kaufmann, Jr. have been the chief patrons; of the Print Room, Mrs. Rockefeller and her children, also Dr. F. H. Hirschland, Victor S. Riesenfeld; of the Film Library, Edward M. M. Warburg, John Hay Whitney, the Motion Picture Association, and the Rockefeller Foundation; of the photography collection, David H. Mc Alpin; of theatre design, Lincoln Kirstein. The various committees which have given such devoted service to the Museum Collections, present and past, are listed on page 231, and brief accounts of the curatorial departments, their patrons and their staffs on pages 231-36.

Among the staff who have rendered particularly valuable help in building up the collections are Iris Barry and Richard Griffith in the Film Library; Beaumont Newhall and Edward Steichen in photography; Mr. Johnson, Mr. Kaufmann, Mildred Constantine and Greta Daniel in the design collection; and William S. Lieberman in the Print Room. During their brief terms as Director of Painting and Sculpture, James Thrall Soby and James Johnson Sweeney each made notable accessions. As the writer can attest, they and Dorothy C. Miller, Curator of the Collections, have exerted influence upon the formation of the painting collection quite beyond their official roles in the Museum.

In the following text, the paragraphs initialed W. S. L. were written by William S. Lieberman, Curator of Prints.

ALFRED H. BARR, JR.
Director of the Museum Collections

An Index of Artists may be found on page 238. All works reproduced entered the collection, or were in negotiation, before 1954.

The small numbers [1] [2] [3] which appear in the text refer to the Bibliography, page 237, mostly selected from the Museum's own publications. A history and complete catalog is published in *Painting and Sculpture in the Museum of Modern Art* and its four supplements, bibl. 101, 101a, b, c, d. For general introductions to various fields of modern art see nos. 91, 98, 102, 105, 110-113.

PAINTINGS, SCULPTURE, DRAWINGS, PRINTS

ARTISTS OF THE PEOPLE

Depending on the stage of civilization, the bulk of the world's art may be distinguished as tribal or folk or popular. One of the greatest popular artists to have worked in our hemisphere was the Mexican engraver, José Guadalupe Posada.

Before his death in 1913 Posada may have made as many as fifteen thousand engravings for pamphlets and ballad broadsides. His fantastic, sometimes savage humor, enlivens his greatest series, the *calaveras*, those endless variations (so beloved by Mexicans) upon the dance of death, a medieval theme which Posada brings merrily up to date.

In his broadsides Posada often celebrated the Mexican victories over Maximilian's army, the army in which Henri Rousseau is said to have served. Rousseau's only print, *War*, is close to some of Posada's engravings in its popular allegorizing.

Like Posada, Rousseau was entirely, incorruptibly a man of the people yet his ambition was not to entertain or persuade but, simply, to be a great artist. In his own eyes he succeeded. Once, about 1908, he confided to Picasso: "We are the two greatest painters of our epoch, you in the Egyptian style, I in the modern style." Questions of "style" aside, when we stand before *The Sleeping Gypsy* and *The Dream* reproduced on the following pages (and, for that matter, certain works of Picasso, pages 69, 83, 93) Rousseau seems in this naive assertion almost as great a critic as he was a painter.

POSADA. *"Calavera"*: *Cyclists*. Engraving in type metal, $5\frac{7}{8} \times 10\frac{1}{8}''$. Purchase Fund, 1949. (Photo Soichi Sunami). José Guadalupe Posada. Mexican, 1851-1913. The Museum owns 433 prints by Posada, including 406 in a book.

"If I remember correctly 1897 is the year I saw the 'Bohémienne Endörmie' in the Salon des Indépendants. It was hung in the main *salle* opposite the entrance and as there was nothing of its *genre* nearby or in the room or in fact in the entire Salon it made it, one might say, the target of the Show, and everyone I came across in the ateliers or cafés enjoyed taking their shot at it . . . My own reaction was so hilarious that the police had to throw me out as I could not control my laughter. I have always excused myself on the ground that I was in my early twenties and studying with Raphael Collin." So wrote the late Frederic Clay Bartlett after seeing *The Sleeping Gypsy* in the Museum's galleries. A great connoisseur of modern painting, he was the ultimate purchaser of Seurat's *La Grande Jatte.*

Thadée Natanson, patron and friend of Lautrec, Vuillard, Bonnard, also saw *The Sleeping Gypsy* at the Indépendants of 1897. In *La Revue Blanche* he observed: "For the rest, it is necessary above all to speak of M. Henri Rousseau, whose incorruptible naiveté amounts to a style and whose stubborn and ingenuous simplicity makes one think, without the slightest intention on his part, of certain primitive works. His touching awkwardness deserves infinitely more attention than the mass of work in the big Salons . . ."

Rousseau himself so esteemed the picture that he offered it to Laval, his native town:

"Monsieur le Maire: I have the honor of sending you these few lines as a compatriot of yours who has become a self-taught artist and is desirous that his native city possess one of his works, proposing that you purchase from me a genre painting called *The Sleeping Gypsy* which measures 2.60 in width by 1.90 meters in height [including frame—Ed.]. A wandering Negress, playing the mandolin, with her jar beside her (vase containing drinking water) sleeps deeply, worn out by fatigue. A lion wanders by, detects her and doesn't devour her. There's an effect of moonlight, very poetic. The scene takes place in a completely arid desert. The Gypsy is dressed in Oriental fashion.

"I will let it go for 2,000 to 1,800 francs because I would be happy that the city of Laval possess a remembrance of one of its children.

"In the hope that my offer will be treated with favor, accept, Monsieur le Maire, the assurance of my distinguished consideration."

The Mayor referred Rousseau's offer to the Laval Museum but the picture itself disappeared for twenty years so that the cubist generation who came to admire Rousseau in his last years knew nothing of *La bohémienne endormie.* Shortly after the armistice of 1918 the picture reappeared. At that time Pierre Roché was acting as agent for the great New York collector, John Quinn. Roché reminisces in a recent letter:

"*The Sleeping Gypsy* was pointed out to me by Picasso as something for Quinn—it had just arrived at Kahnweiler's . . . I mailed a photo of it to Quinn and every day, almost, for a whole week, sent him a cable giving the exact opinions, for or against, of artists I had got to look at the picture . . . So, by the time Quinn got my letter he had already received 6 cables on the subject. He replied 'No money; buy nothing.' Nevertheless, he bought it right away and it was one of two or three pictures he had before his eyes upon his deathbed."

John Quinn died in 1925. When parts of his collection were sold at auction in Paris, the poet Jean Cocteau wrote for the catalog a two-page dithyramb on the picture which

ROUSSEAU. *The Sleeping Gypsy.* 1897. Oil, 51 × 79″. Gift of Mrs. Simon Guggenheim, 1939. Henri Rousseau. French, 1844-1910.

Rousseau himself had described modestly as a "genre painting":

"Why, you ask me, agree to write this preface? My reason is precise . . . the Quinn sale includes a phenomenon, a unique piece, the hub of the wheel, the dead center, the heart of the hurricane, the sleep of sleeps, the silence of silences: *La bohémienne endormie* of Henri Rousseau . . .

". . . This picture which surpasses painting, which soars above it, which compromises it . . . can rival the depth and maturity of surface of the Avignon primitives. We have here the contrary of poetic painting, of anecdote. One is confronted, rather, by painted poetry, by a poetic object . . . by a miracle of intuitive knowledge and sincerity.

". . . Perhaps, in fact, this lion and this river are the dream of the sleeper . . . It is probably not unintentional that the painter, who never forgot a detail, has put no imprints in the sand around those sleeping feet. The gypsy did not come there. She is there. She is not there. She is in no human place . . . She is the secret soul of poetry, an act of faith, a proof of love."

Yadwigha in a lovely dream,
Having most sweetly gone to sleep,
Heard the snake-charmer blow his flute,
Breathing his meditation deep.
While on the streams and verdant trees
Gleam the reflections of the moon,
And savage serpents lend their ears
To the gay measures of the tune.

These verses (translated,[59] as is the epitaph below, by Bertha Ten Eyck James) were written by Rousseau and attached to his last great canvas *The Dream* when he exhibited it at the Salon des Indépendants of 1910. On March 11th, a few days before the Salon opened, Rousseau wrote his friend and champion Guillaume Apollinaire: "I have sent my large picture—everybody likes it—I think you will deploy your literary talents and will avenge me for all insults and affronts received. I know, through Picasso, that it is in *L'Intransigeant* that you do art criticism."

Another critic, André Dupont, asked Rousseau why he put the couch in the jungle. Rousseau wrote him, April 1: "*Cher Monsieur:* I reply immediately to your kind letter in order to explain to you the reason for the whereabouts of the said couch in question. This woman asleep on the couch dreams that she has been transported into the forest, listening to the sounds of the enchanter's instrument. This is the reason the couch is in the picture."

Contradicting this circumstantial explanation, André Salmon reported that Rousseau confided to him that "the sofa is there only because of its glowing red color." One wonders. (The "glowing red" pigment is now much darkened.)

Ambroise Vollard, who bought *The Dream*, recalls in his *Souvenirs d'un marchand de tableaux* a conversation with Rousseau about his great picture:

"Tell me, M. Rousseau, how did you make so much air circulate among the trees and the moonlight look so real?"

"By studying nature, M. Vollard," replied the painter.

Thirty years later an American museum director wrote: "*The Dream* is a summation of all those qualities which make Rousseau inimitable. Its organization of spaces and complex tones (an artist counted over fifty variations of green alone) is equaled by its sentiment. The plane of reality (the figure on the sofa) is inventively joined to the plane of the dream (the jungle). In it appears, in heightened form, every symbol of the last ten years of Rousseau's life, redesigned and related with a free intensity. The nude figure surrounded by enormous lilies is one of Rousseau's most perfect realizations, while the leopards peering from the jungle leaves are full of his expressive mystery."—Daniel Catton Rich.[59]

On September 2nd, 1910, Rousseau died in poverty in a Paris hospital. Two months afterwards Rousseau was given a small memorial exhibition—his first one-man show anywhere—in Alfred Stieglitz' Photo-Secession Gallery at 291 Fifth Avenue, New York. The show comprised drawings and paintings owned by Rousseau's friend, Max Weber.

ROUSSEAU. *The Dream.* 1910. Oil, 80 × 118½″. Gift of Nelson A. Rockefeller, 1953. The Museum owns 3 oils and a print by Rousseau.

Robert Delaunay and Rousseau's landlord, M. Quéval, bought a stone for Rousseau's grave in the Bagneux Cemetery. On it Brancusi and Ortiz de Zarate engraved the Douanier's epitaph, written by Apollinaire:

> Hear us, kindly Rousseau.
> We greet you,
> Delaunay, his wife, Monsieur Quéval and I.
> Let our baggage through the Customs to the sky,
> We bring you canvas, brush and paint of ours,
> During eternal leisure, radiant
> As you once drew my portrait you shall paint
> The face of stars.

Joseph Pickett was a canal-boat builder, carpenter and, later in life, a storekeeper. During the summer he sometimes operated shooting galleries at country fairs and for these he painted landscape backgrounds. His few canvases date from the end of his life.

When Pickett's masterpiece, *Manchester Valley*, was put up at auction after the artist's death in 1918, his widow bought it in for a dollar and gave it to the school shown in the painting, the building with the flag. The train is said to be the first to come through the village of New Hope where Pickett lived.

In *Manchester Valley* Pickett enriches his paint with sand and suggests distance not by scientific perspective but by arranging his objects in tiers one above the other as in Oriental painting. *Manchester Valley* ranks high among twentieth-century American landscapes.

KANE. *Self Portrait*. 1929. Oil, 36⅛ × 27⅛".
Mrs. John D. Rockefeller, Jr. Purchase Fund,
1939. John Kane, American, 1860-1934. The
Museum owns 4 oils by Kane.

Scottish by birth, Kane worked in Pittsburgh as miner, laborer, carpenter, steel worker, construction foreman, and house painter. He was also a famous fist-fighter. "I began painting steel cars," Kane explained, "and in this way learned the use of paint . . . Carpentry has helped me with my art work . . . a painting has a right to be as exact as a joist . . ."

Rarely has an artist revealed himself so unflinchingly as has John Kane in his *Self Portrait*. Yet, by means of the arched canopy and the strange formality of the pose (as if he were a priest or a strongman or dead), the artist has given his lean, aging nakedness an austere and moving dignity. "With art," he once said, "comes goodness and beauty." This secular Ecce Homo is one of the unforgettable icons of the uncommon common man.

Opposite: PICKETT. *Manchester Valley.* 1914-18? Oil mixed with sand, 45 × 60".
Gift of Mrs John D. Rockefeller, Jr., 1939. Joseph Pickett. American, 1848-1918.

LOPEZ. *Adam and Eve and the Tree of Life* (detail). c. 1930. Cottonwood, figures 14″ high. Gift of Mrs. Meredith Hare, 1943. José Dolores Lopez. American, c. 1880-1939.

Posada, the big-city graphic artist, and Pickett, the village craftsman-painter, worked all their lives on the popular level as integrated members of society; Rousseau and Kane also were of the people in origin and in sentiment but entered the lists and held their own as artists against their countries' best professional painters.

John Wallace, on the contrary, was no self-taught naïf but a tribal artist, a master sculptor of the Haida nation of Northwest Coast Indians. Third in his line of totem pole carvers, he was still practicing his hereditary art as late as 1939 when, assisted by his son, he carved the Museum's totem pole. Its style is little changed from the high point of the tradition in the mid-nineteenth century. Its subject is a family legend telling how Raven dives to the sea-bottom home of Killer Whale and brings back a totem pole.[71]

José Dolores Lopez of New Mexico was also a craftsman who, among other hereditary trades, worked as a *santero*, a maker of saints. His religious images or *bultos* are in the provincial tradition of the Spanish colonial frontier, but they are carved and joined with an imaginative power and sense of form far beyond that of the ordinary folk artist.

Left: WALLACE. *Totem Pole.* 1939. Red cedar, polychrome, 32′ high. Extended loan from the Indian Arts and Crafts Board, U.S. Department of the Interior, 1940. (Photo Soichi Sunami). John and Fred Wallace. Haida Indians, British Columbia, Canada. John Wallace was born about 1860; Fred is his son.

IMPRESSIONISM TRANSFORMED

"Monet is only an eye—but what an eye!" exclaimed Cézanne, praising his impressionist colleague with faint damnation.

Yet, freshly examined, Monet's *Poplars at Giverny* is far more than an optical exercise. The public had been correct in finding Monet's forms fuzzy, vague, his colors unnatural; but wrong in assuming at first that these heresies were a denial of art, and later, in being reconciled to them by quasi-scientific explanations about light and vision. For Monet was an artist as well as an eye. Having, perhaps unintentionally, helped liberate form and color from visual facts, he was in the late 1880s moving toward an art of semi-abstraction in which the important reality would be his surface textures and shimmering color.

MONET. *Poplars at Giverny, Sunrise.* 1888. Oil, $29\frac{1}{8} \times 36\frac{1}{2}''$. Gift of Mr. and Mrs. William B. Jaffe, 1951. Claude Monet. French, 1840-1926.

CÉZANNE. *Still Life with Apples*. 1890-1900. Oil, 27 × 36½". Lillie P. Bliss Collection, 1934.

Nevertheless, before 1888, not only Cézanne but Renoir too and even Pissarro had found impressionism wanting. It was too unsure in contour, too soft and spineless in structure, too casual in composition. Cézanne, even while painting as an impressionist, was haunted by what he called "the art of the museums."

The seventeenth-century composition of the Museum's great *Still Life with Apples* calls to mind Maurice Denis' assertion that "Cézanne is the Poussin of the still life"—but Poussin would not have understood his modeling in color; nor would he have granted that painting apples and a jug could be a problem worthy of a great master.

"Cézanne is not an impressionist," Pissarro once explained to the youthful Matisse, "because all his life he has been painting the same picture. He has never painted sunlight; he always paints grey weather."[41]

CÉZANNE. *Pines and Rocks*. 1895-1900. Oil,
32 × 25¼". Lillie P. Bliss Collection, 1934.
Paul Cézanne. French, 1839-1906. The
Museum owns 4 oils by Cézanne, 6 watercolors, 2 drawings and 25 prints.

At first glance, the *Pines and Rocks* seems impressionist but upon study it takes on a
profound sense of stability and permanence. Yet its stability appears mysteriously weightless, a structure without mass achieved in space; and its air of permanence seems an affair
less of the sensual, material world than of the spirit.

Recently Matisse, looking back fifty years to his talk with Pissarro, remarked that while
an impressionist landscape is a moment of nature, "a Cézanne is a moment of the artist."

Matisse believes that when Pissarro referred to a picture that Cézanne had been painting "all his life" he had in mind Cézanne's endless series of bathers. Typical is the lithograph below with its clumsy studio figures awkwardly disposed in a landscape which seems a bit too small for them. The lithograph, though Cézanne drew it on the stone in 1899, is actually a variant of a composition of 1876. The central standing bather is closely related to the figure in the Museum's canvas *The Bather* painted a dozen years later.

Both figures have their source in a photograph recently found pasted on the back of a Cézanne drawing, and now in the Museum's possession. It is published here for the first time not as a curiosity or historical document but because it reveals Cézanne's greatness as few of the numerous photographs of his landscape motifs can.

Cézanne, a very shy man with more than his share of nineteenth-century inhibitions, could rarely endure working directly from the nude model. Furthermore the living model could probably not have endured Cézanne who tyrannically insisted upon even his portrait subjects' keeping as "still as an apple" through a hundred sittings. So Cézanne sometimes depended upon photographs of professional models.

Photograph of model. Gift of Curt Valentin.

This slightly ridiculous image of a naked young man with a mustache Cézanne transforms into one of his most monumental paintings of the single figure. Cézanne generalizes somewhat, suppressing the idiosyncrasies of the model but without idealizing. Indeed the original humility of the individual is curiously preserved yet modified by Cézanne's intuitive sense of human dignity. Academically the drawing is poor, the right knee inexcusable, but seen as a whole the figure stands firm as a stone. In fact, it rises before one like a colossus who has just bestrode mountains and rivers—for Cézanne, adapting a landscape from another picture, has again fumbled his naturalistic scale while achieving artistic grandeur.

Opposite: CÉZANNE. *The Bather.* c. 1885-90. Oil, 50 × 38⅛″. The Lillie P. Bliss Collection, 1934.

CÉZANNE. *The Bathers.* 1899, after a composition of 1876. Lithograph, 16¼ × 19⅞″. Mrs. John D. Rockefeller, Jr. Purchase Fund, 1953. There is also an edition with color added by the lithographer Clot reproducing watercolor added by Cézanne to a proof of the original black and white lithograph. The Museum owns a trial proof of the colored edition.

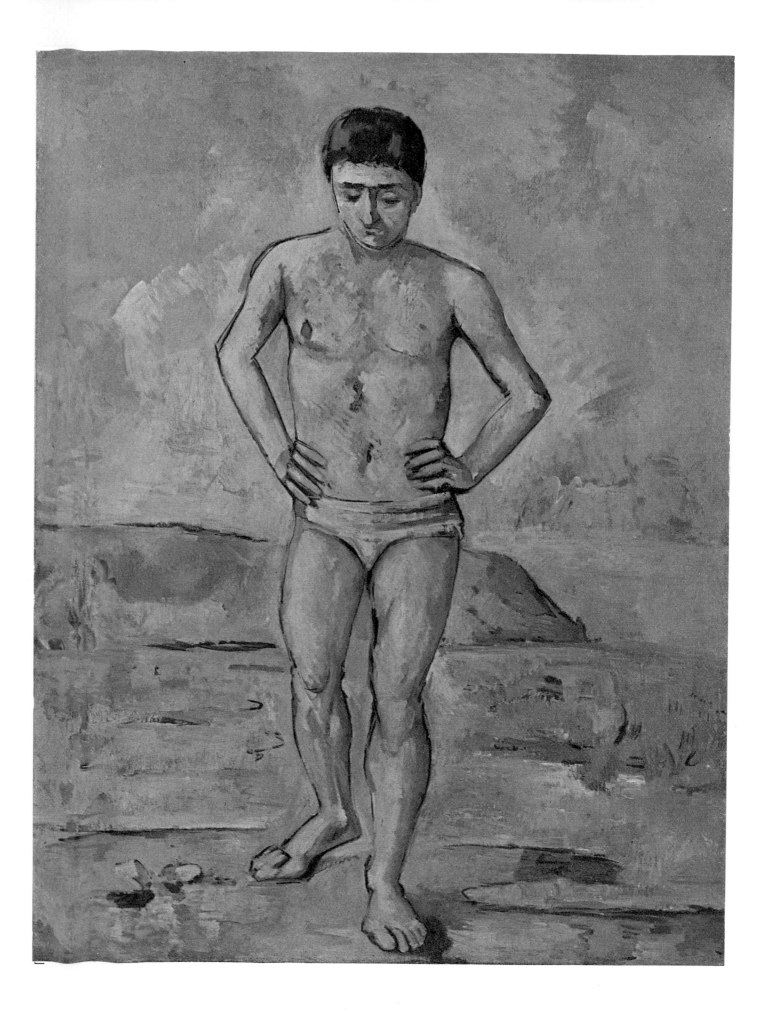

One contemporary critic wrote of Seurat's paintings such as *The Fishing Fleet at Port-en-Bessin* that he was "the first to render the feeling which the sea inspires on a calm day." Another was moved by these "really beautiful seascapes, canvases enveloped in a grey dust of light . . ." But Seurat answered: "Certain critics do me the honor of crediting me with poetry. But I paint according to my method, caring for nothing else."—John Rewald, *Seurat*, New York, 1946.

Seurat's preparatory research for *A Sunday Afternoon on the Island of La Grande Jatte*, one of the great achievements of European painting, involved thirty oil sketches and some twenty-five drawings in conté crayon. Among the drawings one of the most beautiful is the Museum's *Seated Woman*. Usually Seurat refined and simplified his studies when translating them to the final composition, but the superb and subtle silhouette of the *Seated Woman* seems to have satisfied the artist from the first. She reappears almost unaltered in the big canvas (now in the Art Institute of Chicago).

La Grande Jatte was the last of Seurat's great out-of-doors figure compositions. Thereafter his figures appear in the studio or, more commonly, in cabarets and circuses. Perhaps the best known of his theatre drawings is the Museum's crayon study made in the music hall called *Le Concert Européen*. Again, as in the *Seated Woman*, Seurat transmuted temporary eccentricities of fashion into forms of classic dignity.

SEURAT. *Fishing Fleet at Port-en-Bessin.* 1888? Oil, 21½ × 25½″. Lillie P. Bliss Collection, 1934.

Seurat's method! No painter since Uccello and his "dear perspective" had ever sacrificed so constantly, so passionately to a method—the little dots of primary colors each an act of calculation sanctioned by the physicists, the lines and tones of the composition systematically related to a scheme of emotional responses.

Seurat's art: the oval patches of grass in the foreground of the *Port-en-Bessin* announce the counterpoint played between the small, sharply-angled white sails and the gentle ovals of cloud shadows as they move together (*diminuendo poco a poco*) into the distance until they are resolved by the horizon.

VAN GOGH. *Sorrow.* 1882. Transfer lithograph, $15\frac{1}{8} \times 11\frac{1}{4}''$. Inscribed lower left, below design, *épreuve d'essai.* Purchase, 1951. Vincent van Gogh. Dutch, born 1853; died in France, 1890. The Museum owns 1 oil, 1 gouache, 1 drawing and 2 prints by van Gogh.

"Today I mailed you a drawing;" van Gogh wrote[118] his brother Theo from the Hague in April 1882, "the best figure I have drawn as yet . . . and as it was for you, who understands these things, I did not hesitate to make it rather melancholy." Later, he explained: "In that pale, slender woman's figure . . . I wanted to express something of the struggle for life. Or rather, because I tried to be faithful to nature as I saw it before me without philosophizing about it, involuntarily something of that great struggle is shown."

The drawing was inscribed with the word "Sorrow"; the model had been the destitute streetwalker whom van Gogh had cared for during the previous winter.

So important did this drawing in the "English" style seem to him that in the fall he drew a variant of it for the second of his nine extremely rare lithographs. "You will receive," he wrote Theo, November 14, 1882, "the *very first* print of *Sorrow.*" He mentions sending two other proofs "but the very first I marked as a trial copy." Only three proofs are now known – and the Museum's copy is in fact inscribed, apparently in van Gogh's own hand, "*épreuve d'essai.*"

Six years later, in 1889, van Gogh entered the hospital of Saint Pol at Saint-Rémy near Arles in southern France. He had just recently suffered serious mental attacks. For a time he seemed much better but soon his attacks began to recur. By May 1890, he wrote[118] Theo from the hospital: "My surroundings here weigh on me more than I can express . . . I need air, I feel overwhelmed with boredom and depression." It was perhaps in this mood that he had painted the interminable vistas of the *Hospital Corridor at Saint-Rémy.*

Nevertheless it was at Saint-Rémy that van Gogh painted several of his greatest pictures, among them the Museum's *Starry Night*, done in June 1889, only a month or so after he had entered the sanitarium.

Van Gogh's *Starry Night* is a work of crucial importance. Not only is it one of the artist's most moving and beautiful paintings but its style marks a turning point in his art, its subject was of special symbolic significance to the artist, and the struggle, internal and external, which involved the picture throws a clear light upon one of the fundamental conflicts which have engaged the artists of the past hundred years. This is the conflict between fact and feeling, between prose and poetry, between realism and imaginative vision.

VAN GOGH. *Hospital Corridor at Saint-Rémy*. 1889-1890. Gouache and watercolor, $24\frac{1}{8} \times 18\frac{5}{8}''$. Bequest of Mrs. John D. Rockefeller, Jr., 1948.

In the late 1880s the impressionists, for all their free use of color, followed the factual or realist tradition in painting the everyday world around them. Opposed to them were van Gogh's friends, Gauguin and Emile Bernard, who insisted upon the right of the artist to express his feelings both in style and in subject. Theo van Gogh, though he was Gauguin's loyal and tolerant dealer, tended to side with the impressionists. We can follow the conflict in Vincent's letters to Theo van Gogh [118] and Emile Bernard.[22] From Arles in April 1888 van Gogh writes to Bernard: "The imagination is certainly a faculty which we must develop and it alone can bring us to creation of a more exalting and consoling nature . . . A star-spangled sky, for instance, that's a thing I would like to try to do . . . But how can I manage unless I make up my mind to work . . . from imagination?" A month later he writes again: "I wonder when I'll get my starry sky done, a picture that haunts me always." Within six months in a letter to Theo, Vincent repeats his argument: "To express hope by a star, the eagerness of the soul by a sunset radiance. Certainly there is nothing in that of . . . realism, but is it not something that exists?"

But later in September, the realist (or impressionist) point of view reasserts itself and he writes Theo: "The problem of painting night scenes . . . on the spot and actually by night interests me enormously." Before the end of the month he had done a canvas of a "starry sky painted actually at night under a gas jet." This first version of a starry night he describes to Theo with an almost Whistlerian esthetic detachment: "The town is blue and violet, the gas is yellow . . . On the blue-green field of the sky the Great Bear sparkles, its discreet pallor contrasting with the brutal gold of the gaslight." But in the same letter, after speaking of the difficulty of painting a street scene in the spirit of the realistic novelists, Zola and Flaubert, he confesses: "That does not prevent me having a terrible need of—shall I say the word—of religion. Then I go out at night to paint the stars . . ." The influence of Gauguin and Bernard was at work. The two had spent the summer together in Brittany developing their "Synthetist" principles which were already tinged with the anti-realism of the Symbolist poets, particularly Mallarmé. Late in the fall of '88, while Gauguin is visiting him in Arles, Vincent writes Theo: "Gauguin gives me courage to imagine things." And, finally, summoning this new courage, he painted some six months later his second and great *Starry Night*.

On June 19, 1889, he writes from Saint-Rémy to Theo announcing the new picture: "I have a landscape with olive trees and also a new study of a starry sky. Though I have not seen either Gauguin's or Bernard's last canvases I am pretty well convinced that these two studies are parallel in feeling . . . When you have looked at these two studies for some time it will give you some idea, better than words could, of the things Gauguin and Bernard and I used to talk about."

But Theo after he had received the new picture was still unconvinced. He replied, October 1889: "I find that you are at your best when you do realistic things. I understand what preoccupies you in these new canvases like the village in the moonlight and the mountains, but I think these stylized researches weaken the feeling of reality. In the last lot of pictures from Gauguin I find the same preoccupation . . ."

Theo had liked the earlier night canvas with its placid feeling and impressionist technique; he had even sent it to a public exhibition. But the new *Starry Night* and the other pictures from Saint-Rémy had passed beyond his impressionist taste.

For it was in the Saint-Rémy pictures with their flamboyant cypresses, twisted olive trees and heaving mountains that van Gogh was finally able to free his art from the objective realistic vision of the impressionists. The surging lines not only bind the composition into active rhythmic unity—they express magnificently the vehemence and passion of van Gogh's spirit.

VAN GOGH. *The Starry Night*. 1889. Oil, 29 × 36¼″. Acquired through the Lillie P. Bliss Bequest, 1941.

The *Starry Night* goes further: it is fundamentally an imaginative invention. The cypress and the distant hills, it is true, occur in other Saint-Rémy pictures. But thc village with its northern church—is it English or Dutch?—seems remote from Provence. And the sky, the dazzling moon, the Milky Way turned to meteors, the stars like bursting bombshells —this is the unique and overwhelming vision of a mystic, a man in ecstatic communion with heavenly powers.

IMPRESSIONISM REJECTED

As in the fairy tale of *Goldilocks and the Three Bears* the objects in this still life by Gauguin come by threes—three puppies, three blue goblets, three apples—and the innocent sentiment of the subject is matched by the simplicity of the style. Curiously, Gauguin may have owed something of both sentiment and style to Kate Greenaway, the English illustrator of children's books which he admired for their flat-patterned, nursery primitivism.

Gauguin himself was however far from innocent, either as a man or as an artist. For a dozen years he had been painting as a junior colleague of the impressionists and then, like Cézanne and Renoir, had grown dissatisfied. He tried briefly to follow Cézanne's profound effort "to make of impressionism something solid and enduring"—and won Cézanne's contempt. He flirted very briefly with Seurat's elaborate Neo-Impressionist discipline. In Brittany, perhaps with the help of Emile Bernard, he found his own style, based upon the definite outlines, flattened perspective and often "unnatural" color which he discovered variously in Egyptian and medieval painting, Japanese prints, Breton peasant art and last (and perhaps least) Miss Greenaway's picture books.

That was about 1888, the year he painted the *Three Puppies* and the year he declared that "painting is an abstraction," a remark which anticipated by two years the often quoted injunction of his follower, Maurice Denis: "Remember that a painting—before being a war horse, a nude woman, or some anecdote or other—is essentially a plane surface covered by colors arranged in a certain order."

With his escape to Tahiti, Gauguin considered his break with convention complete. The essential change in his art, however, was in subject matter rather than style.

GAUGUIN. *Women at the River (Auti te pape)*. 1891-93. Color woodcut, 8 × 14″. Gift of Mrs. John D. Rockefeller, Jr., 1940.

The woodcut offered Gauguin a medium which, by its very directness, was particularly suited to the primitive attitude he wished to assume. In *Women at the River* light areas such as the rocks and banks of either shore were gouged out with a knife. The flowing river and the dark seated figure, areas where the surface of the block was less touched, offer a rhythmic contrast to the boldness of his carving and the roughness of the wood. Gauguin's exploitation of the very texture of the wood itself established a tradition characteristic of the woodcut today.—W. S. L.

GAUGUIN. *Still Life with Three Puppies*.
1888. Oil on wood, $36\frac{1}{8}$ × $24\frac{5}{8}$″.
Mrs. Simon Guggenheim Fund, 1952.
Paul Gauguin. French, born 1848;
South Seas, 1891; died in The Mar-
quesas, 1903. The Museum owns 2 oils
and 25 prints by Gauguin.

TOULOUSE-LAUTREC. *Hanging Man.* 1895. Lithograph, printed in black and green, 30¼ × 22″. Purchase, 1949. Henri de Toulouse-Lautrec-Monfa. French, 1864-1901. The Museum owns 67 lithographs by Toulouse-Lautrec.

Although its early masters had been painters, lithography in the mid-nineteenth century gradually lapsed into the control of commercial printers. In the 1890s, however, lithography as a creative medium was revived by French painter-lithographers who to a great extent initiated to-day's extraordinary renaissance in printmaking.

The color lithographs reproduced here were both printed in Paris in the 1890s. The poster has been chosen from the Museum's collection of sixty-seven prints by Toulouse-Lautrec. The lithograph at the right by Edvard Munch was commissioned by Ambroise Vollard whose publications helped to establish the standards of modern printmaking.

Between 1892 and 1900 Toulouse-Lautrec produced over 360 lithographs. More than any painter of his time he realized the full possibilities of the medium. Unlike his more familiar subjects the *Hanging Man*, printed somberly in black and green, seems close in spirit to Munch's *Anxiety*. Both scenes are affected by a macabre sentiment that fevers the *fin de siècle*.

In any summary of modern art it is difficult to place the solitary figure of Edvard Munch. The foremost painter Scandinavia has yet produced, he was a contemporary of the post-impressionists in France and knew their achievements. Like James Ensor, however, he worked far into the twentieth century and died in 1944 only a few years before the Belgian painter and printmaker.

Since Munch's paintings are seldom seen in America, the Museum is fortunate to possess fifteen of his rare prints of the 1890s, his best period. In lithography and woodcut Munch's neurotic melancholy finds its clearest expression. His prints influenced a younger generation of artists and, more than any other figure, he is the father of expressionism in Germany.

MUNCH. *Anxiety*. 1896. Color lithograph, $16\frac{1}{8} \times 15\frac{1}{8}$". Purchase, 1940. Edvard Munch. Norwegian, 1863-1944. The Museum owns 20 prints by Munch.

In *Anxiety* Munch exploits the sinuous, curvilinear style of the Art Nouveau to express a state of mind. The vertical silhouettes of the figures merge into the flowing lines of the landscape. These solid blacks contrast with the ominous red rhythms of the clouds. The atmosphere is charged, even disquieting in its intensity. The pulsating lines emphasize the feeling of unrest and expectancy suggested by the stark, scarcely delineated features of the waiting crowd.—W. S. L.

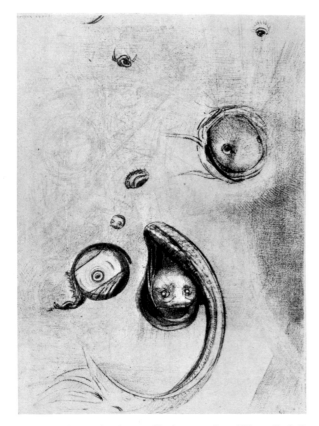

REDON. "... *a formless world where eyes floated like mollusks*". From the portfolio *The Temptation of St. Anthony.* 1896. Lithograph, $12\frac{1}{4} \times 8\frac{7}{8}$". Gift of Mrs. John D. Rockefeller, Jr., 1940.

REDON. *The Day.* 1891. Lithograph, $8\frac{1}{4} \times 6\frac{1}{8}$". From the portfolio *Dreams.* Lillie P. Bliss Collection, 1934. Odilon Redon. French, 1840-1916. The Museum owns 2 oils by Redon, 2 pastels, 1 drawing and 58 prints, including 29 in 2 portfolios.

"My originality," wrote Redon, "consists in putting the logic of the visible to the service of the invisible." Apparitions haunt his obscure world of dream and night. In *The Day*, through a barred window set in the restless darkness of a room, an ordinary tree is touched by mystery and enchantment.

Much of Redon's inspiration was literary and three series of lithographs, his most ambitious graphic work, illustrate Flaubert's Symbolist drama *The Temptation of St. Anthony*. The disquieting image at the left is a literal accompaniment to a line of Flaubert's text. The strange floating microcosm, however, emerges from the shadows of Redon's own vision.

Redon turned to lithography to increase the distribution of his work, and until 1900 he drew exclusively in black and white. For twenty years he had found the rich blacks of charcoal and the lithographic crayon best suited to his fantasies. "Black is the most essential color," he explained. "It is the agent of the mind far more than the most beautiful color of the palette or prism."—W. S. L.

Though he died only in 1949 James Ensor, the foremost Belgian painter since the time of Rubens, was born three years before Toulouse-Lautrec and only a year later than Seurat. Like Redon he worked at first in a realistic style but during the 1880s he and Redon took their places at the extreme left of the modern movement as the two great masters of imaginative freedom.

Ensor lived all his very long life at Ostend but by 1887, when he painted his *Tribulations of St. Anthony*, he was already familiar with the work of the Paris vanguard through the annual exhibitions of the Brussels *Société des XX*, at that time the most progressive art society in the world.

In the Museum's *St. Anthony* Ensor went beyond the impressionists and flatly rejected the scientifically rational theory and technique of Seurat's Neo-Impressionism which was then the last word in Paris. He was half English and probably knew Turner's luminous reds and yellows and bold handling of light. In the *St. Anthony* he uses any color he pleases and his brush swirls and slashes over his canvas with a freedom which matches the audacity of his imagination. Indeed, at this moment in his career, Ensor was possibly the boldest living painter. Gauguin was still painting semi-impressionist pictures and only in the following year, 1888, was van Gogh, under the burning sun of Arles, able to free himself from impressionism.

Ensor's *St. Anthony* of 1887 points the way not only toward the unfettered humor and fantasy of Klee and the surrealists, Miro, Ernst and Masson, but also toward the abstract expressionism of Kandinsky and his descendants among the younger artists of the mid-twentieth century.

ENSOR. *Tribulations of St. Anthony.* 1887. Oil, $46\frac{1}{8} \times 66''$. Purchase, 1940. Baron James Ensor. Belgian, 1860-1949. The Museum owns 2 oils and 16 prints by Ensor.

In its general subject and composition, Ensor's *St. Anthony* was directly inspired by an engraving of about 1635 by Jacques Callot who in turn looks back past the Bruegels to the great late Gothic fantast, Jerome Bosch. At the left sits the Saint surrounded by his immediate temptations one of whom, as in old pictures of the same subject, is a beautiful woman. To the right the fiery mouth of hell belches a swarm of evil phantasms which fill air, land, and sea. The Saint seems dismayed by this cataract of nightmares but legend reassures us: he was staunch against their devilish assaults.

THE IMPRESSIONIST TRADITION

When Mallarmé translated Whistler's *Ten O'Clock*, Seurat read it with enthusiastic approval. Yet, though Whistler was the most famous American artist throughout the world, it was Mary Cassatt who held the firmer place in the esteem of the great French impressionists, particularly Degas who was her chief mentor. Her color prints show his influence and that of the Japanese; they are masterly in their highly personal technique of etched line and aquatint.

Maurice Prendergast was born the same year as Seurat and left Boston to study in Paris the year *La Grande Jatte* was exhibited. Neo-Impressionism, particularly that of Signac, certainly affected his later work but it was to Cézanne he gave his chief admiration and loyalty. Cézanne was first made known to many artists in America through Prendergast.

CASSATT. *Under the Horse-chestnut Tree*. Color aquatint and drypoint, $15\frac{7}{8} \times 11\frac{1}{4}''$. Gift of Mrs. John D. Rockefeller, Jr., 1940. Mary Cassatt. American, 1845-1926; lived in France. The Museum owns 3 prints by Cassatt.

PRENDERGAST. *Orange Market*. c. 1900. Monotype, $12\frac{1}{2} \times 9\frac{1}{8}''$. Gift of Mrs. John D. Rockefeller, Jr., 1945. Maurice Brazil Prendergast. American, 1859-1924. The Museum owns 1 oil, 5 watercolors and 2 monotypes by Prendergast.

PRENDERGAST. *Acadia.* 1922. Oil, $31\frac{1}{4} \times 37\frac{1}{2}''$. Mrs. John D. Rockefeller, Jr. Purchase Fund, 1945.

The *Orange Market* is one of a series of monotypes done in Italy at the end of the '90s. Prendergast's late style is seen at its best in *Acadia.* Girls moving among park benches and trees with sailboats in the distance are thoroughly impressionist in subject but, like his younger contemporary Bonnard, Prendergast transmutes these pleasant commonplaces into richly-worked surfaces and lyrical color; such is the poetic sentiment of *Acadia* that it might well have been titled *Arcadia.*

Bonnard and Vuillard, like Prendergast, worked during the 1890s more or less in reaction against impressionism. The two young Frenchmen were in fact members of the avant-garde Nabi group who looked to Gauguin for guidance but were influenced more than he by Japanese prints.

Bonnard's four-paneled screen of lithographs, page 215, with its daring, asymmetric voids, makes very clear why he was called "the very Japanese Nabi." Yet, already by 1900, both Bonnard and Vuillard had deserted the decorative flat patterns and sinuous lines of the Art Nouveau for a return to a more impressionist style. In Vuillard's intimate *Mother and Sister of the Artist* the figures are seen in perspective while the sister's plaid dress is played boldly and tartly against the dazzle of the wallpaper in contrast to the mother's sober black against monochromes.

Three decades later, Bonnard's *Breakfast Room* is still "Intimist" in spirit, still impressionist in style, but the artist's palette is now fully matured. The objects on the table, the figure at the left cut by the edge of the picture, the view of the garden are all seen in the shimmering glory of Bonnard's color.

BONNARD. *The Breakfast Room.*
c. 1930-31. Oil, $63\frac{1}{4} \times 44\frac{1}{8}''$.
Given anonymously, 1941.
Pierre Bonnard. French,
1867-1947. The Museum owns
2 oils by Bonnard and 211 prints,
including 177 in 2 illustrated
books, 4 in a decorative screen
and 5 posters.

RODIN. *The Dancer*. Watercolor and pencil, 16¼ × 11⅞″. Purchase, 1946. Auguste Rodin. French, 1840-1917. The Museum owns 1 watercolor and 2 drawings by Rodin.

SCULPTORS OF THE IMPRESSIONIST GENERATION

The Museum, to make a paradox of its poverty, has no paintings by the painter Renoir and no sculpture by the sculptor Rodin, both among the greatest artists of their generation. Yet there is some slight comfort to be found even in these unhappy circumstances.

During the early years of our century when the supremacy of Rodin's sculpture began to be challenged, his drawings continued to rise in esteem because of their revelation of movement and wonderfully spontaneous silhouette. In *The Dancer* the model is seen falling forward while she kicks high above her head.

The grandeur of Renoir's late forms may be felt in his sculpture and lithographs even though the saturated opulence of his color must be foregone; and, one might add, even though his sculpture was produced under perhaps the most curious circumstances in the history of art. Except for some casual essays during a visit of Maillol, Renoir in 1914, at the age of seventy-five, had never shown any interest in sculpture. Furthermore his hands were seriously crippled by arthritis. Yet his dealer Vollard insisted that he attempt sculpture and provided him with a skillful but entirely docile young Italian modeler. Thus equipped with one man's initiative and another's hands, Renoir produced a series of admirable bronzes, among them the magnificent figure humbly entitled the *Washerwoman*.

RENOIR. *The Washerwoman.* 1917. Bronze, 48″ high. A. Conger Goodyear Fund, 1953. (Photo Soichi Sunami). Pierre-Auguste Renoir. French, 1841-1919. The Museum owns 1 sculpture and 5 prints by Renoir.

MAILLOL. *Desire.* c. 1904. Plaster, 47 × 45″. Gift of
the sculptor, 1930. (Photo Soichi Sunami.) Aristide
Maillol. French, 1861-1944. The Museum owns
7 sculptures by Maillol, 1 drawing and 104 prints,
including 89 in 2 illustrated books.

"Art is complex, I said to Rodin who smiled because he felt I was struggling with nature.
I was trying to simplify, whereas he noted all the profiles, all the details . . .

"The particular does not interest me; what matters to me is the general idea.

"One must synthesize . . . I should make better Egyptian sculpture than modern, and
better gods than men."— Maillol to Judith Cladel.[105]

At the Salon d'Automne of 1905 Maillol exhibited for the first time his most famous
figure, *The Mediterranean,* listed in the catalog as *Femme accroupie.* Maurice Denis, by then
grown conservative but still perhaps the most influential French art critic between Baude-
laire and Apollinaire, reviewed the Salon for *L'Ermitage.* At the end of his long article in
which, among other controversial matters, he chides the fauve Matisse for being too abstract
and systematic, he concludes:

"Here is a fine statue by Maillol—the *Femme accroupie* . . . Although some sculptors
protested against its anatomical liberties or against the seductiveness of such lovely forms,
the public was unanimous. Here at last, after so many attempts either incomplete or

disconcerting, was a finished work, not created to astound anyone, not meant to satisfy a coterie of esthetes; here was a noble figure, at once expressive and harmonious, simple and grand as the works of the antique. Maillol has created it without a system, with his genius alone, aided perhaps by that sentiment for generalization of which Félibien speaks and which in Maillol is instinctive. In any case, it is this classic sculpture which is the most novel work of art in the entire Autumn Salon. Let us admire it; and let us learn from it the vacuity of subtleties."

MAILLOL. *The Mediterranean.* c. 1901. Bronze, 41″ high. Gift of Stephen C. Clark, 1953. (Photo Soichi Sunami.)

Its daring instability of pose combined with its dynamic torsion make *The River* unique in Maillol's sculpture. Maillol's characteristic figures such as *The Mediterranean* are calm, reposeful, static. Even when they represent muscular strain, there is little movement; the action is self-contained. Maillol was aware of his avoidance of movement, and remarked upon it as late as 1937. Nevertheless, within a year or so afterwards he had conceived *The River*, a work of astonishing, almost reckless movement such as had not appeared in his work since his canvases of women tumbling in the waves done long before in the 1890s while he was still a painter.

Begun before the war, probably late in 1938 or early 1939, *The River* was originally commissioned as a monument to the famous writer and pacifist Henri Barbusse —a project which was abandoned when the war started.

In composing *The River*, Maillol began with various elements of an earlier figure, *The Mountain*, which he had completed in 1937. Much of the work on the plaster model was carried out, following Maillol's instructions, by the sculptor Couturier, his friend and disciple. The figure, an entirely new conception, was apparently finished late in 1943 when Maillol gave final approval to the work a few months before his death at the age of eighty-two.

The River is probably Maillol's last completed work, a final magnificent flowering of bold invention and creative energy on the part of a man who was, in his generation, the world's greatest sculptor.

Despiau's few large figures are less heroic than Maillol's but their natural grace, sensitive modeling and modesty of style give them a distinction which lifts them above the conventional figures turned out by the hundreds in the academic studios of Europe and America. However, Despiau's fame rests primarily upon his portrait busts which are unrivaled in recent French sculpture.

DESPIAU. *Assia*. 1938. Bronze, 6′$\frac{3}{4}$″ high. Gift of Mrs. Simon Guggenheim, 1939. (Photo Ansel Adams.) Charles Despiau. French, 1874-1946. The Museum owns 6 sculptures, 4 of them portraits, 2 drawings and 1 print by Despiau.

Opposite: MAILLOL. *The River.* c. 1939-43. Lead, 7′6″ long. Mrs. Simon Guggenheim Fund, 1949. (Photo Soichi Sunami.)

45

THE FAUVE GENERATION

"What is presented to us here—apart from the materials employed—has nothing to do with painting: some formless confusion of colors; blue, red, yellow, green, the barbaric and naive sport of a child who plays with the box of colors he has just got as a Christmas present." Thus did a newspaper critic greet the gallery in the Autumn Salon of 1905 where the earliest wave of twentieth-century innovators, later called the fauves, was scandalizing the Paris public.

Matisse was the greatest artist and the dominant personality among them, but his leadership, though accepted by his disciple Derain, was contested by his rival Vlaminck and ignored by his friend Rouault. In the following year, 1906, the group received its name les fauves, "the wild beasts," and reached the zenith of its influence; but before the

DERAIN. *Blackfriars Bridge, London.* 1906. Oil, 26 × 39″. Gift of Mr. and Mrs. Charles Zadok, 1952. André Derain. French, born 1880. The Museum owns 11 oils by Derain, 1 watercolor, 1 drawing, and 114 prints, including 105 in 4 books.

end of 1907 the "color-mad" fauves were beginning to submit to the disciplinary influence of Cézanne, who had just died, and the structural innovations of the youthful Picasso who had just completed *Les Demoiselles d'Avignon*, page 69.

Looking at Derain's *Blackfriars Bridge, London* one can easily understand why fauve color seemed so shocking. Cézanne, Monet, van Gogh, Gauguin had all in their various ways and for differing purposes departed from "natural" color, but fauve color was far brighter and far more boldly independent of the "normal" color of the objects and even of their shapes. Yet in *Blackfriars Bridge* a reaction toward a more solid structure within a deeper picture space has already set in.

The Museum has sculpture, prints and drawings of Matisse's fauve period but as yet no paintings.

MATISSE. *Figure Study.* c. 1907. Ink, 10⅛ × 8″. Gift of Captain Edward Steichen, 1952. Henri Matisse. French, born 1869. The Museum owns 7 oils by Matisse, 10 sculptures, 7 drawings, 419 prints, including 262 in illustrated books, 30 in 2 portfolios and 1 poster, 4 maquettes of cut-and-pasted paper for vestments, stained glass and book jackets; also 1 stained glass window, 1 silk chasuble (page 227) with 4 ancillary vestments, and 1 rug after his designs.

From Paris early in 1908 Edward Steichen (page 186) wrote Alfred Stieglitz who had just opened his gallery at 291 Fifth Avenue with a show of Rodin drawings:

"My dear A. S.—I have another cracker-jack exhibition for you that is going to be as fine in its way as the Rodins are . . . Drawings by Henri Matisse the most modern of the moderns . . . they are to the figure what the Cézannes are to the landscape. Simply great. Some are more finished than Rodin's; more of a study of form than movement—*abstract* to the limit . . . Hastily—Steichen"

The exhibition—Matisse's first one-man show outside of Paris—opened April 6 (and included the Museum's drawing, above). The New York critics outdid the French: "ugliness that is most appalling and haunting . . . artistic degeneration . . . subterhuman hideousness . . ." Even the sophisticated Huneker denounced Matisse's honest studies as "memoranda of the brothel and gutter . . . With three furious scratches he can give you the female animal in all her shame and horror."[41]

But Bernard Berenson, who knew Matisse's work through Leo and Gertrude Stein, writing with all the authority of a great art historian and connoisseur, defended Matisse in the New York *Nation:*[41] "I have the conviction that he has, after twenty years of very earnest searching, at last found the great highroad traveled by the best masters of the visual arts for the last sixty centuries at least. Indeed he is singularly like them in every essential respect. He is a magnificent draughtsman and a great designer . . ."

Five years or so after the breakup of the fauve movement, Dufy painted the *Sailboat at Sainte-Adresse*. Here his angularity of style superficially suggests cubism but is perhaps closer to Gothic woodcuts. The tall houses too seem curiously Gothicized by comparison with those of Dufy's many later paintings of the same seaside resort. The intense color, vigorous brushing and dense composition (so different from Dufy's later calligraphy) make this picture one of the artist's strongest works.

Matisse was forty-two in 1911 when he painted the *Red Studio*. He was then the most famous painter of the modern movement though Picasso and the cubists were already surpassing the older artist in influence. And he had left behind him the tentative but exciting trial-and-error of his fauve period to perfect his own flat, two-dimensional style, based it is true on his studies of such predecessors as Gauguin, page 31, and the painters of the Near East, but now completely assimilated and mastered.

DUFY. *Sailboat at Sainte-Adresse*. 1912. Oil, 35 × 45½″. Gift of Mr. and Mrs. Peter A. Rübel, 1953. Raoul Dufy. French, 1877-1953. The Museum owns 2 oils, 1 watercolor by Dufy, and 29 prints including 16 in 2 portfolios.

MATISSE. *The Red Studio*. 1911. Oil, 71¼ × 86¼". Mrs. Simon Guggenheim Fund, 1949. The white plaster profile at the right is *Jeannette, IV*, see next page.

At first glance the scattering of little shapes in this wonderfully gay and courageous composition seems haphazard. There is no clearly symmetrical division of spaces. On the contrary the design seems centrifugal, without anchor or axis, until one begins to notice the unobtrusive outline of the grandfather's clock which stands like a one-eyed monitor regulating a calculated informality. Around this slight but effective median the other objects float on their rust-red sea like bright islands for the eye.

For half a century Matisse has been curiously diffident about his sculpture. His two most extraordinary achievements in that medium, the series of heads called *Jeannette*, 1910-11, and the three great reliefs of a woman's back, 1910-29, were never shown in their entirety until 1950 so that it was only then that Matisse took his place as one of the major living sculptors.

Jeannette I and *II* (the latter not reproduced) are portraits modeled from nature. "The model must impress you," Matisse told his students in 1908, "awaken in you an emotion, which in turn you seek to express. You must forget all your theories, all your ideas before the subject."

Jeannette III, IV and *V*, however, were not done from a model but are free variations inspired by the two original portraits: *III* is pear-shaped, with heavy features and bulging eyes; *IV* is aquiline, hollow-cheeked, with cornice-like eyelids and hair rising like a cluster of toy balloons. In *Jeannette V* Matisse has lopped off the hair or, rather, forced the hair and the cranium into a bilobate structure. More striking still is the left eye, flattened into a single plane like a monocle or patch. *Jeannette V* is bolder than any cubist sculpture of the period. Indeed it anticipates Picasso's big post-cubist heads of 1932.

MATISSE. *Jeannette, I, III, IV, V* (four versions of a portrait of Jeanne Vaderin). 1910-11. Bronze, 13″, 23¼″, 24⅛″, 22⅞″ high, respectively. Acquired through the Lillie P. Bliss Bequest, 1952. (Photo Soichi Sunami.)

MATISSE. Three versions of *The Back*. *I*, c. 1909-10; *II*, c. 1914?; *III*, 1929? Bronze, each about 6'2" × 44". Mrs. Simon Guggenheim Fund, 1952. Photographed by Soichi Sunami in the Abby Aldrich Rockefeller Sculpture Garden.

Matisse's three *Backs* form a theme-and-variations which moves more clearly than the *Jeannette* series toward radical simplification. Matisse once enjoined his students in sculpture: "Express by masses in relation to one another . . . the legs work up into the torso, which clasps down over them. It must have a spinal column. One can divide one's work by opposing lines (axes) which give the direction of the parts and thus build up the body . . ."—Noted by Sarah Stein, 1908[41]

The Back I, done only a couple of years after these precepts were laid down, may be interpreted as a study in the dynamic balance of forms on either side of the spinal axis which is emphasized by a deep furrow. Shoulders and arms are exaggerated and the neck muscles recall those of Barye's *Jaguar* from which principally, over a period of two years study, Matisse had learned the art of sculpture.

The Back II, done about 1914, suggests Matisse's newly awakened interest in cubism, especially in the angular handling of scapula and hip. As in *Jeannette V*, hair and bony structure are combined, here to create a kind of external spine or fulcrum about which the other forms are balanced.

In *The Back III*, Matisse rounds and simplifies the roughhewn planes of the second version to create a kind of monumental columnar architecture in human form.

During the years 1914 to 1916 Matisse was seriously depressed by the World War and at the same time, though on another plane, preoccupied with cubism which previously he had largely ignored. These factors more or less affected his painting, which passed through a time of disciplined sobriety both in color and structure.

The *Piano Lesson* of 1916 is one of the most important compositions of the period. The artist's son Pierre sits practicing on the Pleyel in the living room of the villa near Paris. At the left, a big window with open casements looks on the garden.

Two works by Matisse, the painted female figure, clothed and Gothicly rigid in the upper right-hand corner, and the sculptured female figure, nude and relaxed, at the lower left, wittily complement each other. Similarly, the vertical green wedge of the garden at the upper left balances the complementary pink of the horizontal piano top, lower right; and the black scrolling of the music rack in the foreground is echoed by the slower arabesque of the wrought-iron window grill beyond. Only the metronome (*pace* Einstein!) seems solidly three-dimensional.

There are some cubist vestiges in the *Piano Lesson* but no cubist ever surpassed the beautiful divisions, the grave and tranquil elegance of this big picture. Nor did Matisse himself.

Of the Museum's 264 lithographs by Matisse the two reproduced below suggest the range of his graphic art. The *Nude, Face Partly Showing* well demonstrates the artist's mastery of spontaneously sweeping line and his skillful placing of the design upon the sheet. In *Nude in an Armchair*, Matisse's capital lithograph of the mid-1920s, the artist uses the maximum degree of high-relief modeling in rendering a figure pose which appears again and again in paintings, drawings and even a bronze of the same period.

Opposite: MATISSE. *Piano Lesson.* 1916. Oil, 8′½″ × 6′11¼″. Mrs. Simon Guggenheim Fund, 1946.

Right: MATISSE. *Nude, Face Partly Showing.* 1914. Lithograph, 19¼ × 12″. Frank Crowninshield Fund, 1945.

Far right: MATISSE. *Nude in an Armchair.* 1925. Lithograph, 25⅛ × 18⅞″. Purchase, 1953.

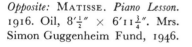

To represent the collection of illustrated books in the Abby Aldrich Rockefeller Print Room a double page spread from the great Matisse-Skira edition of Mallarmé's poems is reproduced below. In designing his etchings, Matisse's goal was not simply a visual balance: "The problem," he explains, "was to balance the two pages—one white, with the etching, and the other one comparatively black with the printing. I achieved my purpose by modifying my design in such a way that the spectator should be interested as much by the white page as by the expectation of reading the text."[41]

The Museum owns no recent painting by Matisse but opposite is one of the best of his series of large, vigorous brush-and-ink still lifes done in 1947-48 when he was approaching his seventy-eighth birthday. A still more recent work is the original chasuble, page 227, in silk appliqué made for the chapel of the Dominican nuns at Vence following Matisse's design in cut paper. The silk was too heavy for use in the liturgy so the nuns consented to exchange it for a lighter replica.

MATISSE. Pages 132-133 of the *Poésies de Stéphane Mallarmé*, with an etched portrait of Poe by Matisse, illustrating the poem *Tombeau d'Edgar Poe*. Page size, 13 × 9¼″. Lausanne, Albert Skira, 1932. Mrs. John D. Rockefeller, Jr. Purchase Fund, 1951.

MATISSE. *Dahlias and Pomegranates*. 1947. Brush and ink, $30\frac{1}{8} \times 22\frac{1}{4}''$. Mrs. John D. Rockefeller, Jr. Purchase Fund, 1950.

"Why is it that at the sight of certain works of art we are aware of receiving 'an immortal wound'? Rouault's painting is purely painting, totally intent on a passionate research for the requirements of pictorial matter, on the sensitivity of the eye, and on the most refined and shrewd accuracy of technical means. And at the same time it lives on the internal universe of the soul, on the depths of inner vision and poetic intuition, obscurely grasping in emotion both the subjectivity of the painter and the mystery of the visible world. Here is Rouault's great lesson.

"Those who have followed him through the various phases of his untiring effort have not been surprised at seeing this art of unbridled violence, so concerned with the atrocious contours of sin and human ferocity, but also, and more and more, imbued with unspeakable pity, attain at last a summit of religious and hieratic painting, where suffering and peace are expressed together in a new harmony and nobility of form."

—Jacques Maritain[58]

"For five years, from 1922 to 1927, in obsession, delight and despair, he worked at perfecting the *Miserere* plates, usually afternoons and evenings, sometimes three full days a week; the rest of the time he continued his painting . . .

"What Rouault has now given to us and to posterity is a set of magnificent plates, an album, with no text save a brief foreword by himself and a caption for each plate. There is a tradition in Catholicism and in the cultural history of Europe for such unliterary books, intended for the edification and uplift of those who could read only a little, or not at all. Inheriting the spirit and iconography of the late middle ages, this album takes its place in the first rank of twentieth-century art; and in the particular category of modern religious art, it is perhaps the greatest single work."

—Monroe Wheeler[56]

ROUAULT. "*The just, like sandalwood, perfume the axe that strikes them.*" From *Miserere*. 1926. Aquatint and drypoint over heliogravure, $23\frac{1}{4} \times 16\frac{1}{4}''$. Purchase, 1949. Georges Rouault. French, born 1871. The Museum owns 4 oils, 5 gouaches and watercolors and 168 prints by Rouault.

ROUAULT. *Three Judges.* 1913. Gouache and oil on cardboard, $29\frac{7}{8} \times 41\frac{5}{8}''$. Sam A. Lewisohn Bequest, 1952.

Venality, arrogance, stupidity: Rouault, capable of moral indignation over and beyond his religious convictions, here assaults the corruption of the law courts at their worst, hewing out the brutal planes of his three jurists' faces as if his brush were an avenging axe. The sombre color admirably supports the drawing: there is about this painting a "sultriness," as the late donor once expressed it, "that has the menacing feeling of an approaching thunderstorm."

The *Three Judges* is one of the great works of Rouault's middle period when hatred of evil seems to have been a stronger incentive in his art than piety or pity.

BARLACH. *Head* (detail, War Monument, Güstrow Cathedral). 1927. Bronze, 13½" high. Gift of Edward M. M. Warburg, 1941. (Photo Soichi Sunami.) Ernst Barlach. German, 1870-1938. The Museum owns 2 sculptures by Barlach, 1 drawing and 78 prints, including 63 in 2 illustrated books and 2 portfolios.

NOLDE. *Three Kings.* 1913? Color lithograph, 25¼ × 21". Purchase, 1951. Emil Nolde. German, born 1867. The Museum owns 2 watercolors, 1 drawing and 28 prints by Nolde.

THE GERMAN EXPRESSIONISTS

Though admiration for the great nineteenth-century French masters was earlier and more general in Germany than in France itself, the best German art of the early twentieth century remained strikingly national.

Born about 1870, the expressionists Barlach and Nolde were of the same generation as Bonnard, Matisse and Rouault in France, John Marin and John Sloan in our own country. Ensor and Gauguin and the Japanese printmakers are among Nolde's forebears, but his gestures are wilder, his contours shaggier, his spirit Gothic, in both senses of the word. Barlach admired Millet and van Gogh; his sculpture is earthy, close to peasant wood carvings, emotional and religious in spirit. The Museum's *Head* is from the great bronze angel of death which hung suspended, high in a chapel of the Cathedral of Güstrow as a war memorial. Hitler removed it as subversive and un-German in spite of its resemblance to the tragic faces of certain German crucifixes of the Ottonian period.

Lovis Corinth, a dozen years older than Nolde and Barlach, was born in the generation of Seurat, Maillol and our own Prendergast. But that is also the generation of Sargent, Zorn, Boldini, the showy virtuosi of the slashing brush. Corinth's early work is distinguished from theirs chiefly by a certain coarse vitality of subject matter but in his later years, perhaps under the influence of his juniors, the expressionists, his art deepened. Painted in modest tans and greys, the *Self Portrait*, done the year before his death, suggests a profound, almost Rembrandtesque feeling for the human personality rare in our century's art.

CORINTH. *Self Portrait*. 1924. Oil, 39⅛ × 31⅝". Gift of Curt Valentin, 1950. Lovis Corinth. German, 1858-1925. The Museum owns 1 painting and 27 prints by Corinth.

KIRCHNER. *Two Ladies in the Street*. 1922. Color woodcut, $27\frac{1}{4} \times 15''$. Purchase, 1945. Ernst Ludwig Kirchner. German, 1880-1938. The Museum owns 3 oils by Kirchner, 1 drawing and 29 prints, including 5 in a book.

"Did you know that as far back as 1900 I had the audacious idea of revitalizing German art? Indeed I did, and the impulse came to me while looking at an exhibition of the Munich Secessionists . . . Indoors were hung these anemic, bloodless, lifeless studio daubs. Outside was life, noisy and colorful, pulsating . . .

"First of all I tried to find a method whereby I could seize the effect of motion . . . how to arrest a movement in a few bold strokes, catching the passing moment and finding new forms . . .

"My sense of design was simplified and strengthened by the fact that I had learned to make woodcuts from my father when I was only fifteen years old. So armed, I arrived in Dresden and during my studies there I was able to arouse my friends' enthusiasm over my new ideas.

"My goal was always to express emotion and experience with large and simple forms and clear colors."
— Kirchner to Curt Valentin, 1937

In Dresden in 1905 three young students, Kirchner, Heckel and Schmidt-Rottluff, banded together to form the first group of German expressionists, *Die Brücke—* The Bridge. They were joined by Nolde and later by other painters; but until the First World War dissolved the group, the founding trio remained its core.

The formation of the *Brücke* coincides with the looser association of the fauves in France. Both groups of painters had been deeply influenced by the post-impressionists and by primitive art. Both also exploited unnatural color and bold distortion in their drawing. But the more intimate, even daily association of the German artists gave the *Brücke* cohesion as a brotherhood. They constituted the avant-garde reaction against impressionism growing academic by 1905.

From the outset printmaking was as important as painting in the program of the *Brücke*. In the woodcut they found a medium which naturally combined strength and decoration. Although their intensity of emotion seems essentially Germanic, their direct cutting continues a tradition established a decade before by Gauguin, page 30.

In retrospect Kirchner emerges as the dominant personality of the *Brücke*. In his color woodcut reproduced here, the angular violence of the design transforms a moment of everyday life into a dramatic study in arrested movement. Heckel's portrait, perhaps his own, offers a more reflective analysis. The brooding introspection, so characteristic of the expressionists, reveals a debt greater to Munch than to van Gogh or Gauguin.

The three kings of Schmidt-Rottluff may be compared with the three magi of Nolde, page 58. But in contrast to the other two woodcuts on these pages, the Schmidt-Rottluff seems less sensitive, more arbitrary in pattern and distortion. His heads are unabashedly derived from African masks; yet the general effect recalls those primitive German woodcuts with which the history of prints begins. — W. S. L.

HECKEL. *Portrait of a Man.* 1919? Woodcut, printed in color, $18\frac{1}{4} \times 12\frac{1}{4}''$. Purchase, 1950. Erich Heckel. German, born 1883 The Museum owns 1 oil, 1 watercolor and 31 prints by Heckel.

SCHMIDT-ROTTLUFF. *The Three Kings.* 1917. Woodcut on linden wood, printed in black through rubbing, $19\frac{1}{2} \times 15\frac{1}{8}''$. Purchase, 1945. Karl Schmidt-Rottluff. German, born 1884. The Museum owns 1 watercolor and 15 prints by Schmidt-Rottluff.

"It is the quest of our ego that drives us along the eternal and never ending journey we must all explore . . . What am I? This is the question that constantly persecutes and torments me."

As if in search of answer, the most constant theme in the art of Max Beckmann is his own image which he drew and painted over and over again. On this page are three self-portraits printed from copper, wood and stone. The delicate impressionistic drypoint at the left reveals a young man of thirty, brooding and intense. The vigorously carved woodcut suggests a character much more certain and assured. The latest of the three, a lithograph, was drawn in 1946, four years before Beckmann's death at the age of sixty-five.

—W. S. L.

Departure, Beckmann's great triptych, was painted in Frankfort during the early years of the Nazi tyranny. When it was shipped from Germany in 1937 it was labeled "Scenes from Shakespeare's *Tempest*" in order to mislead Hitler's inspectors. The Nazis had already purged Beckmann's subversive *kunstbolschewistische* paintings from no less than fifteen German museums.

BECKMANN. *Self Portrait*. 1914. Drypoint, $9\frac{1}{8} \times 7''$. Gift of Paul J. Sachs, 1929.

Self Portrait. 1922. Woodcut, $8\frac{1}{4} \times 6\frac{1}{8}''$. Given anonymously.

Self Portrait. 1946. Lithograph, $12\frac{1}{2} \times 10\frac{1}{8}''$. Purchase, 1947.

BECKMANN. *Departure*. 1932-35. Oil, center panel $84\frac{1}{4} \times 45\frac{1}{8}''$; side panels each $84\frac{1}{4} \times 39\frac{1}{4}''$. Given anonymously, 1942. Max Beckmann. German, born 1884; died in New York, 1950. The Museum owns 3 oils by Beckmann, 4 gouaches, 1 bronze, 1 drawing, and 143 prints, including 54 in 4 portfolios, 19 in 3 illustrated books.

"The picture speaks to me of truths impossible for me to put into words and which indeed I did not even know before.

"It can speak only to people who consciously or unconsciously already carry within themselves a similar metaphysical code.

"Departure, yes departure, from the illusions of life toward the essential realities that lie hidden . . .

"It is to be said that 'Departure' bears *no* tendentious meaning—it could well be applied to any period." —Beckmann to Curt Valentin, 1938

Yet, *Departure* seems to be an allegory of good and evil, of light against darkness, of foul passions and sadistic brutalities between which the human spirit, serene, upright, undaunted, crowned like a king, embarks on a triumphant voyage in the bright light of noon.

"All art is measure. Measure set against measure, that is all. Measure or, in figures, proportion, determines the impression, determines the effect, determines the expression of the body, determines the line, the silhouette—everything. Therefore a good sculpture must by treated like a good composition, like a building, where measure is weighed against measure, and so it is impossible to negate detail, for detail is the small measure for the whole.—Lehmbruck[105]

". . . Lehmbruck's departure from realism in physical form suggests at once his preoccupation with the spiritual . . . There is, accordingly, in Lehmbruck's sculpture more of the quality of an action relative to a mental state—a moving tenseness born of the man himself, for the nervous tensity of a life that ended in tragedy goes into Lehmbruck's work . . . there must always be for him in his sculpture something which commands, 'think!'—not *of* it but *with* it. Something which evades us but holds us, a strange rapport between a thing lifeless, yet *knowing*, and ourselves." —Jere Abbott[37]

"Lehmbruck, probably the greatest sculptor Germany has produced in this century, admired both Maillol and Rodin. His *Standing Woman* of 1910 is still close to the former. Within one year he turned from the poised, compact Mediterranean calm of this figure to the *Kneeling Woman* of 1911 . . . Elegance and lyrical tenderness are the qualities that are most appealing in his *Kneeling Woman*. The exquisite relationships of the several parts of the figure, the inevitability of its proportions, are what make this one of the masterpieces of twentieth-century sculpture. His *Standing Youth* is a monumental companion figure." —Andrew Carnduff Ritchie[105]

LEHMBRUCK. *Standing Woman*. 1910. Bronze, 6'4" high. Given anonymously, 1930. (Photo Peter Juley.) Wilhelm Lehmbruck. German, 1881-1919. The Museum owns 5 sculptures, 1 drawing and 17 prints by Lehmbruck.

Lehmbruck gallery. *Standing Youth*. 1913. Cast stone, 7'8" high. Gift of Mrs. John D. Rockefeller, Jr., 1936. *Kneeling Woman*. 1911. Cast stone, 69½" high. Mrs. John D. Rockefeller, Jr. Purchase Fund, 1939. (Photo Soichi Sunami).

KOKOSCHKA. *Portrait of Dr. Tietze and His Wife.* 1909. Oil, $30\frac{1}{8} \times 53\frac{5}{8}''$. Mrs. John D. Rockefeller, Jr. Purchase Fund, 1939. Oskar Kokoschka. Austrian, born 1886; since 1909 has lived in Berlin, Dresden, Prague, London, Switzerland. The Museum owns 2 oils by Kokoschka, 1 watercolor, 1 drawing and 60 prints, among them 37 in 5 books or portfolios.

"I never intended to entertain my contemporaries with the tricks of a juggler, in the hope of being recognized as an original . . . I consider myself responsible, not to society, which dictates fashion and taste suited to its environment and its period, but to youth, to the coming generations, which are left stranded in a blitzed world, unaware of the Soul trembling in awe before the mystery of life."[33]

Thus wrote Oskar Kokoschka in 1948 looking back upon his turbulent career. A great European and the foremost painter in the history of Austrian art, he grew to maturity in the Vienna of Freud, Strzygowski, Schnitzler, Klimt, Mahler, whose widow encouraged him, Hoffmann of the *Wiener Werkstätte* where he worked as a youth, and Adolf Loos who advised him to leave, for Vienna was also the ultra-conservative city of the aged Emperor Franz Joseph. Unfortunately the Museum owns none of his great landscapes or figure compositions from his later expatriate periods but many lithographs and two of his early portraits are some compensation since they are among his finest works.

The double portrait of the distinguished historians of Venetian painting, Dr. and Mrs. Hans Tietze, was commissioned for an overmantel in their house in Vienna. Notable are the subtle relationship between the two figures, the sensitive drawing of faces and hands, the mysterious graffiti in the background.

THE CUBIST GENERATION IN PARIS

Cubism, the first of the three great innovating movements in twentieth-century art, begins in 1907 with Picasso's *Les Demoiselles d'Avignon* and ends, some say, about 1921. Actually cubist principles and devices continue down to the present in the art of such masters as Picasso and Braque. Under the above heading, *The Cubist Generation in Paris*, are grouped their works early and late, cubist and non-cubist, together with those of their major colleagues, Gris, Léger, Lipchitz and others, lesser or more marginal. A few—Duchamp, Malevich, Mondrian, Rivera—who left the movement to help generate other revolutions are reproduced on other pages.

Unfortunately, the Museum has no pre-cubist paintings by Picasso and Braque. Moscow is far richer in Picasso's Blue, Rose, and "Negro" periods (though long hidden from public view as subversively "formalist"); Basel probably surpasses us in analytical cubism, Philadelphia in cubist collages, the Solomon R. Guggenheim Museum here in New York, in paintings by Delaunay, Gleizes and Metzinger; and the Paris Musée d'Art Moderne in the work of the past decade in which the Museum is deficient. Nevertheless the cubist generation, by and large, is more comprehensively represented in the Museum than in any other public collection in the world.

Of these riches, because of limitations of space and color plates, the following pages can offer only a sampling: for instance, two of eight oils by Braque, two of ten by Léger, eight of sixteen by Picasso, two of eight by Gris, three of eight sculptures by Lipchitz.

In 1904 Picasso was living in an ancient wooden tenement on Montmartre among poverty-stricken poets, actors, clerks and laundresses. A little earlier, he himself had known starvation so that the *Frugal Repast* is based on firsthand experience.

Avoiding sentimentality which had softened some of his "Blue" canvases he draws the woman and her blind companion with their wine and crust of bread. Their emaciation seems appropriate but it is largely a matter of mannered style, and so is the elaborately studied composition of the hands (which may be compared to Kokoschka's, opposite).

Picasso was twenty-two at the time and the *Frugal Repast*, technically a tour de force, was his first major etching. It remained perhaps his greatest, certainly his most ambitious, print until the *Minotauromachy* of 1935 (page 92).

PICASSO. *The Frugal Repast*. Paris, 1904. Etching on zinc, $18\frac{1}{8} \times 14\frac{7}{8}''$. Gift of Mrs. John D. Rockefeller, Jr., 1940. Pablo Ruiz Picasso. Spanish, born in Malaga 1881; Barcelona 1896-1903 with sojourns in Paris where he has lived since 1904. The Museum owns 16 oils by Picasso, 4 watercolors and gouaches, 1 sculpture, 1 collage, 12 drawings, 362 prints, including 158 in 13 books, 4 posters, 1 copper plate and a rug from his design.

Possibly the mannered attenuations of Picasso's *Frugal Repast* were inspired by El Greco. In any case, two years later on a summer's trip to Spain in 1906 Picasso renewed an early enthusiasm for the great sixteenth-century Mannerist. During the same year Picasso had been stirred by Spanish art of a much earlier period, pre-Christian "Iberian" sculpture; and he had been deeply impressed by the memorial exhibition of Cézanne's work.

Picasso and Matisse had already met at Leo and Gertrude Stein's apartment and were beginning to feel that rivalry, alternately friendly and jealous but always implicitly flattering, which they were to maintain for decades. Matisse had shown his very large and controversial *Joy of Life* at the Salon des Indépendants in the spring of 1906, an event which may well have excited Picasso to emulation. In any event, Leo Stein (who was the first to see that they were the two foremost painters of our time) remembers visiting Picasso's studio that fall and finding there a huge canvas which, before he had painted a stroke, the artist had had expensively lined as if it were already a classic work. Picasso was marshaling his creative energies for a great effort.

PICASSO. *Man's Head*. Study for *Les Demoiselles d'Avignon*. 1907. Watercolor, $23\frac{1}{4} \times 18\frac{1}{2}''$. A. Conger Goodyear Fund, 1952.

For months that winter Picasso worked on dozens of figure and composition studies. In the spring of 1907 he began to paint. The picture was probably finished by autumn but it was given no name for a dozen years thereafter. About 1920 a literary friend of Picasso christened it with the romantic title *Les Demoiselles d'Avignon*, an ironic reference to the "damsels" of a house on Avignon Street in Barcelona.

The title was however more than a joke, for Picasso had originally planned the picture as an allegory or charade of the wages of sin in which a sailor was to be seen surrounded by women, flowers and fruit, while at the left a warning figure enters bearing a skull as a *memento mori*. The Museum's watercolor, *Man's Head*, is a study for this last figure. But in the final composition one of the women has taken his place, the sailor and the flowers are gone, leaving behind some fruit and five of the least seductive female nudes in the history of art. Obviously Picasso was interested in other than homiletic problems.

He was interested in the jagged highlights of El Greco's skies and draperies, the compact composition of angular planes and the flattening of pictorial space in the late work of Cézanne, page 21, the eyes, ears and rigid figures of archaic Iberian sculpture. All these passed through the alchemical laboratory of Picasso's mind into the big canvas.

The process was no easy one. Signs of intense and sometimes unresolved struggle appear everywhere on this rectangular battlefield. As the eye moves from left to right the background changes in style as well as in color, the heads of the figures are painted in four different ways—those at the right were probably done, or redone, after Picasso had discovered West African Negro masks (though the artist has denied this).

Yet, while *Les Demoiselles* is a problematic and transitional work, it has justly been considered the first cubist picture. Though never exhibited until thirty years had passed, it influenced the "cubist generation" as did no other single work. It can fairly be called epoch making; and beyond its historical importance it remains one of Picasso's most courageous and challenging achievements, a work of formidable genius.

PICASSO. *Les Demoiselles d'Avignon.* 1907. Oil, 96 × 92″. Acquired through the Lillie P. Bliss Bequest, 1939.

color of both the *Woman in a Chair* and *"Ma Jolie"* is limited principally to austere greys and tans.

Cubist abstraction went little further but it changed character. In the collage, *Man with a Hat* (below) head, eyes, mouth, ear, shoulders are diagrammed with an absolute modicum of detail and no sense of depth or substance. Yet external reality, thus almost banished, returns paradoxically in the rectangles of newsprint, blue, and black paper pasted over or under the drawing.

PICASSO. *Woman in a Chair.* 1909. Oil, $28\frac{1}{4} \times 23\frac{5}{8}''$. Gift of Mr. and Mrs. Alex L. Hillman, 1953.

PICASSO. *Man with a Hat.* Paris, December, 1912. Pasted paper, charcoal, ink, $24\frac{1}{2} \times 18\frac{5}{8}''$. Purchase, 1937.

When Picasso drew the head of his central "demoiselle" full face and her nose sideways (previous page) he was taking a step toward cubism more important though less obvious than the angular drawing of the figures or the jagged planes of the whole composition. Two and a half years later, in the *Woman in a Chair* (above) such dislocation occurs again and again. The faceted planes of the face and figure begin to slip, the weight and solidity of the body to disintegrate.

Later still in *"Ma Jolie"* (opposite) the figure has almost disappeared into an elaborate congeries of flat, straight-edged, transparent planes. Vestiges of "reality" can be found, fingers for instance, and the sign of a treble stave beside the affectionate title of a popular song. But new pictorial reality has almost completely superseded the reality of ordinary experience. The

"The fact that for a long time cubism has not been understood and that even today there are people who cannot see anything in it, means nothing. I do not read English, an English book is a blank book to me. This does not mean that the English language does not exist, and why should I blame anybody else but myself if I cannot understand what I know nothing about?

"Many think that cubism is an art of transition, an experiment which is to bring ulterior results. Those who think that way have not understood it. Cubism is not either a seed or a foetus, but an art dealing primarily with forms, and when a form is realized it is there to live its own life . . .

"Mathematics, trigonometry, chemistry, psychoanalysis, music and what not, have been related to cubism to give it an easier interpretation. All this has been pure literature, not to say nonsense, which brought bad results, blinding people with theories.

"Cubism has kept itself within the limits and limitations of painting, never pretending to go beyond it. Drawing, design and color are understood and practiced in cubism in the spirit and manner that they are understood and practiced in all other schools . . . We have kept our eyes open to our surroundings, and also our brains." —Picasso to Marius de Zayas in *The Arts*, 1923[49]

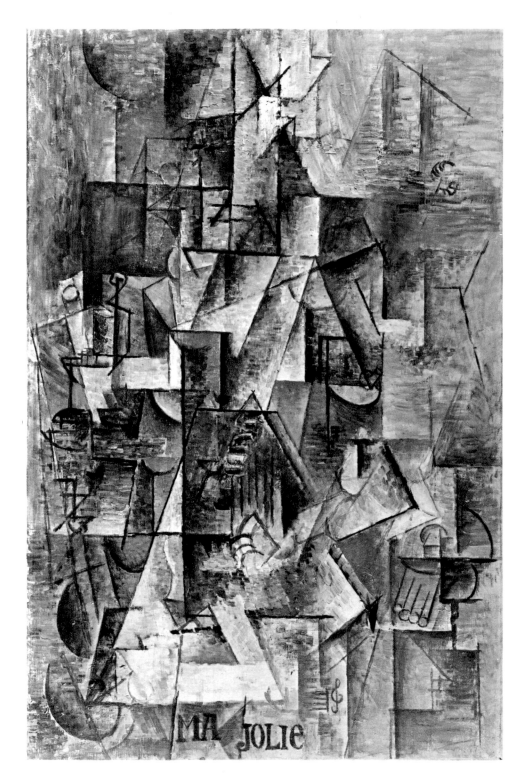

Picasso. *"Ma Jolie"* *(Woman with a Guitar)*. 1911-12. Oil, $39\frac{1}{8} \times 25\frac{1}{4}$". Acquired through the Lillie P. Bliss Bequest, 1945.

BRAQUE. *Man with a Guitar*. 1911. Oil, $45\frac{1}{4} \times 31\frac{7}{8}''$. Acquired through the Lillie P. Bliss Bequest, 1945. Georges Braque. French, born 1882. The Museum owns 8 oils and 34 prints by Braque.

Though it is very difficult at times to distinguish between the work of Braque and Picasso done in 1911-1912, the paintings of Juan Gris differ markedly from those of both his elders. Gris' work is further removed from impressionism's freedom of composition and brush-stroke. And he is much more systematic. In *Guitar and Flowers*, for instance, he uses an obviously geometric scheme of design through which the composition is given an initial order by dividing the canvas in half four ways: vertically, horizontally and twice diagonally. He then proceeds to adorn and partially to conceal his geometry by means of the consistently fragmented images of a table cover, fruit, a guitar, a vase of flowers and a curtain, drawn aside at the right. The paint is laid on in regular strokes, the color restrained.

The result may seem calculated and rather cold. Yet, when the painting is studied, its clarity and sustained intensity of rhythm put it on a par with the diametrically different Braque, opposite, with all its good taste and sense of masterly improvisation.

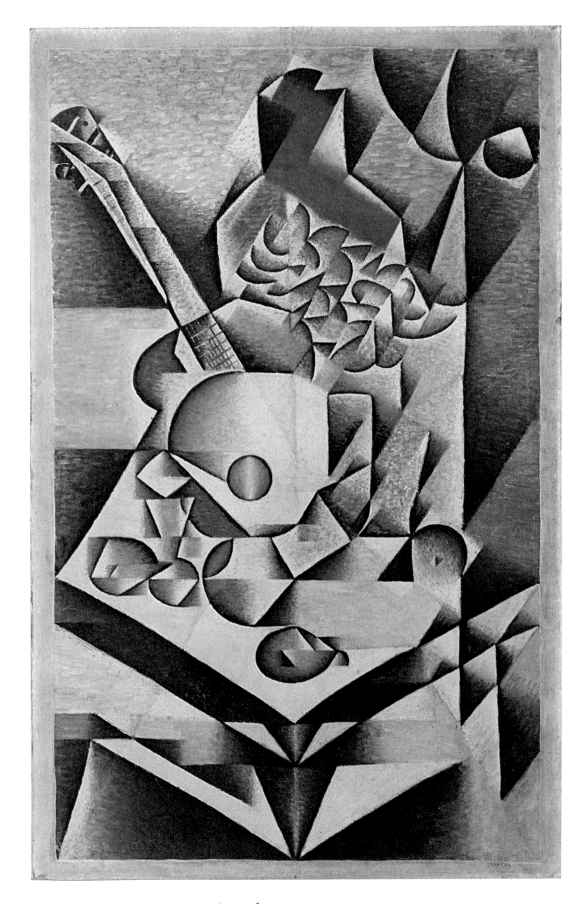

GRIS. *Guitar and Flowers*. 1912. Oil, $44\frac{1}{8} \times 27\frac{5}{8}''$. Bequest of Anna Erickson Levene in memory of her husband, Dr. Phoebus Aaron Theodor Levene, 1947. Juan Gris (José Gonzalez). Spanish, born 1887; worked in Paris 1906, until his death, 1927. The Museum owns 7 oils by Gris, 1 collage, 1 drawing and 10 prints, including 4 in an illustrated book.

In 1908 at Le Mans, where La Fresnaye was born, Wilbur Wright made his famous record-breaking flight. But in his masterpiece, *The Conquest of the Air*, La Fresnaye does not insist upon technological triumphs—though the abstract parallels in the right foreground possibly refer to a biplane. Instead the air is gently conquered by a sailboat, the French tricolor and, in the distant empyrean, a balloon. Perhaps the chief conquest takes place in the minds of the men at the table who, with cubist indifference to gravity, float high above the roofs of the village.

La Fresnaye was not one of the inner circle of cubists. Indeed, *The Conquest of the Air* seems remote from the typical cubist pictures of 1913 with their patient dissections of models, guitars and decanters. There is less sense of experiment than of completion in this spacious canvas. Its grandeur of scale, its charm of color and its serene and noble rhetoric make it one of the monuments of modern French art.

Between 1891 and 1910 Jacques Villon produced over two hundred etchings and lithographs. Although these early prints offer an engaging picture of Paris at the turn of the century, they give no hint of the rapid redirection of his art under the impact of cubism.

In 1911 Villon abandoned his successful, illustrative style to concentrate on painting. A dozen prints, however, mirror his development as a painter between 1911 and 1914.

With a point, fine and sharp, Villon has cut *The Dinner Table* into the copper surface. The still life is elaborate and the carafes, glasses and china seem obviously suited to cubist analysis. Villon's treatment is sustained but not schematic. He displays the classic refinement and sense of decoration as typical of his art as they are characteristic of a tradition particularly French. —w. s. l.

Opposite: LA FRESNAYE. *Conquest of the Air.* 1913. Oil, 7'8⅞" × 6'5". Mrs. Simon Guggenheim Fund, 1947. Roger de La Fresnaye. French, 1885-1925. The Museum owns 2 oils, 1 drawing and 1 print by La Fresnaye.

VILLON. *The Dinner Table.* 1913. Drypoint, 11⅛ × 15". Purchase, 1935. Jacques Villon. French, born 1875. The Museum owns 2 oils, 2 watercolors by Villon, and 95 prints, including 11 in 2 books.

GRIS. *Breakfast*. 1914. Pasted paper, crayon and oil on canvas, $31\frac{7}{8} \times 23\frac{1}{2}''$. Acquired through the Lillie P. Bliss Bequest, 1948.

Meanwhile, cubist collage (paper pasting), comparatively simple in Picasso's *Man with a Hat* of 1912, page 70, was developing a high degree of virtuosity. In Gris' *Breakfast* of 1914, the table is represented by two shades of imitation wood-grain paper, the newspaper by a fragment of newspaper (with the artist's name), the wall paper by wall paper; the folds and string of the tobacco packet are crayon but the stamp is real. Space is flattened almost against the plane of the canvas but the coffee cups are modeled in high relief to give an illusion of solid actuality only to be sliced as if they were butter not china. And fragments of the *faux-bois* table top become transparent as the egg cup and parts of the coffee pot sink beneath its surface.

Thus does Gris, the metaphysician, juggle density and opacity, texture and color, genuine and counterfeit, flatness and relief, integrity and analysis, space and time, truth and fact. What is the nature of experience, he asks, what is reality—yet he does not press these questions. For Gris, the artist, their resolution lies in his picture, its paradoxical wit, its poetry and its harmony

Robert Delaunay had never been an orthodox cubist, often preferring Gothic stone and structural steel to studio subject matter, and bright color to greys and tans. Then, in 1912, his heresy ran riot. Rebelling against intricate cubist scholasticism, he began to paint brilliant, completely abstract compositions inspired by the physics of light as analyzed by Isaac Newton and his nineteenth-century followers. *Disks* is his capital essay in what Apollinaire promptly labeled Orphism.

"In pure color painting," Delaunay explained,[114] "it is color itself . . . which forms the structure of the rhythmic development and not the collaboration of ancient means such as geometry. Color is *form and subject*." *Disks*, painted in pure prismatic colors, is a radiant hymn to the sun.

Opposite: DELAUNAY. *Disks*. 1913. Oil, $53\frac{1}{4}''$ diameter. Mrs. Simon Guggenheim Fund, 1953. Robert Delaunay. French, 1885-1941. The Museum owns 1 oil, 1 gouache, 2 drawings and 2 prints by Delaunay.

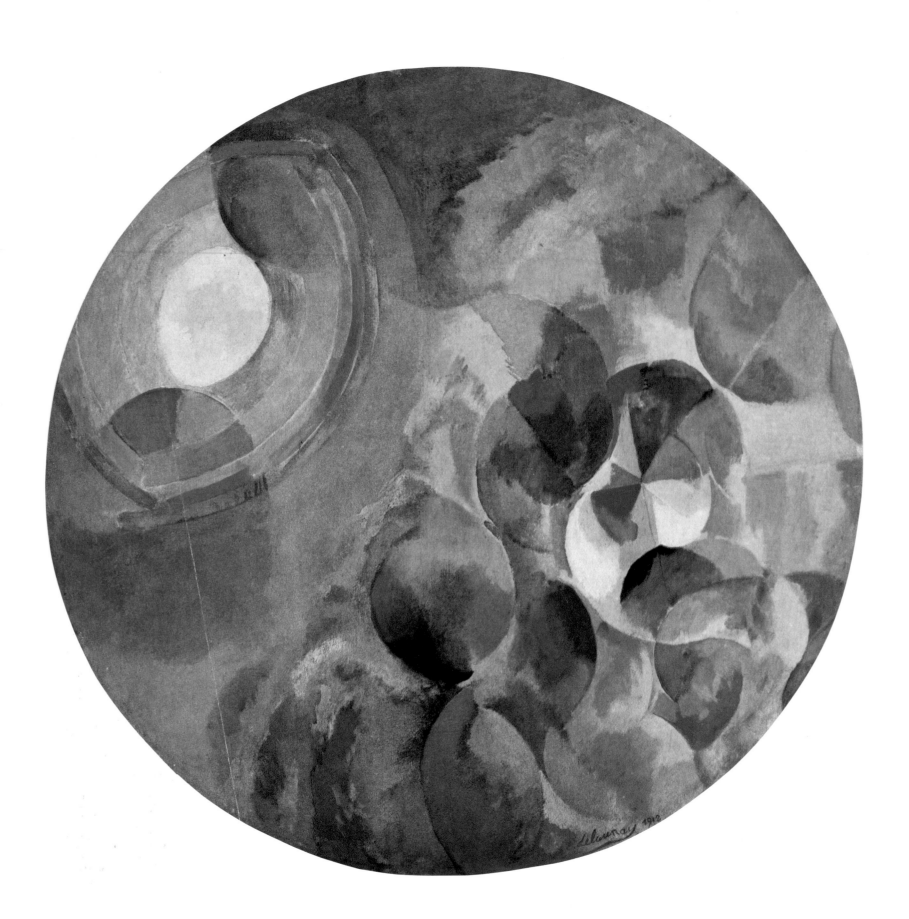

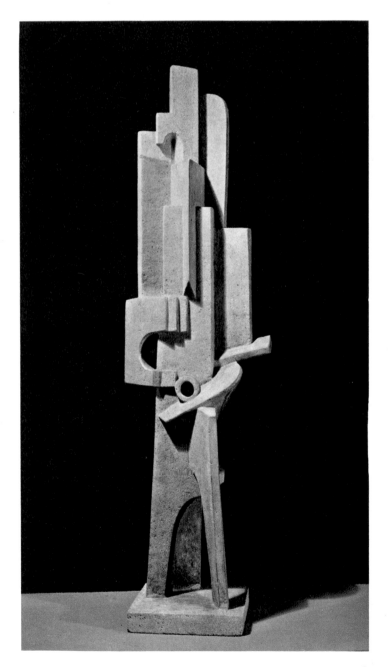

"... Cubism ... was not a school, an aesthetic, or merely a discipline—it was a new view of the universe. Cubism sought a new way to represent nature, a manner adequate to the age. Cubism was essentially a search for a new syntax. Once this was arrived at there was no reason for not employing it in the expression of a full message."—Lipchitz to James Johnson Sweeney.[80]

Unlike Duchamp-Villon, the younger cubist sculptors Lipchitz and Laurens frequently adapted both the style and the static subject matter of the cubist painters, Gris, Braque and Picasso. Laurens even perfected a polychrome cubist relief which combined painting and sculpture in one piece. His *Head*, a construction in painted wood, is more original. In it he achieves a grotesque vividness quite surpassing his usual style.

Lipchitz, in his *Man with a Guitar*, builds up his interlocking, interpenetrating slabs and prisms into a monumental composition which survives viewing from almost all angles. His straight lines are relieved by occasional curves, notably the round sound-hole of the guitar which with exceptional formal humor the sculptor carries all the way through the musician's body.

DUCHAMP-VILLON. *The Horse*. 1914. Bronze, 40" high. Posthumous cast enlarged from the original model according to the artist's instructions by his brother, Jacques Villon, and Albert Pommier. Van Gogh Purchase Fund, 1937. (Photo Herbert Matter.) Raymond Duchamp-Villon. French, 1876-1918. The Museum owns 2 sculptures by Duchamp-Villon.

Duchamp-Villon's bronze *Horse* is conceived as a great animal-machine: he tosses his head sidewise; the fore and hind feet, ready for the leap, are gathered beneath him into one great hoof; his legs are joined to his body as the pistons of a locomotive are connected with the reciprocal eccentrics. Thus the sculptor has suggested in one powerful figure a fusion of organic and mechanical dynamics.

The Horse is perhaps the greatest piece of cubist sculpture though in various ways Duchamp-Villon had been anticipated by the Spanish Picasso, the Russian Archipenko and the Italian Boccioni.

Having been the chief leader of the cubists, Picasso, ten years later, lent his already great prestige to the general reaction against radical experimentation which swept over Western art after the armistice of 1918. Shortly before then he had made precise, comparatively realistic drawings of ballet dancers and pencil portraits of his friends. These he followed by a few studies of peasants of which the *Sleeping Peasants* is the most notable. The distortions, particularly in the arms and throat of the woman, and possibly the astringent color, are inspired by Ingres; but Picasso's drawing is more vigorous, his composition more ingeniously, even humorously, compact.

The gigantism of the *Sleeping Peasants* grows to Roman proportions in the colossal *Three Women at the Spring,* opposite. Painted in browns and stone greys, this composition is like a high relief of poured-concrete figures each weighing tons. Only the skillful play of hands seems to link such mannerism of mass with the mannerism of attenuation seen in the *Frugal Repast,* page 67.

PICASSO. *Sleeping Peasants.* 1919. Gouache, 12¼ × 19¼″. Mrs. John D. Rockefeller, Jr. Purchase Fund, 1951.

Although Picasso upset some of his fellow cubists and other vanguardians by his revival of the style and subject matter of Greco-Roman antiquity, he himself simultaneously continued to develop cubism. In the same year that he produced the *Three Women at the Spring*, previous page, he painted the *Three Musicians*.

During his long career as a painter Picasso has periodically concentrated his energies to produce a single canvas which sums up a whole period of his work. The *Three Musicians* is such a picture.

And not only is the *Three Musicians* one of Picasso's climactic achievements, it is perhaps the culminating work of cubism, the most important movement in the art of the first quarter of our century.

Cubism had begun with another great Picasso canvas, *Les Demoiselles d'Avignon* of 1907, page 69. It developed during the following five years as an art of austere analysis, of breaking up the shapes of objects into angular fragments and cross sections, turning them about, making them transparent and then reintegrating them, transmuting them into a new form or construction, pages 70-74.

About 1913 the cubists turned toward a simpler, flatter and more decorative style often called "synthetic cubism" (page 76) and magnificently demonstrated eight years later by Picasso's *Three Musicians* of 1921.

In the *Three Women at the Spring* Picasso gave his figures a sense of maximum volume, mass and density. The figures in the *Three Musicians* are the same size but by contrast are weightless, disembodied, almost two dimensional. Yet, as presences, they are equally "real" and even more impressive.

In 1920 Picasso had designed costumes for *Pulcinella*, a ballet based on the old Italian *Commedia dell'Arte*. The following year, in the *Three Musicians*, the traditional *Commedia* characters appear again as musicians seated around a table: Pierrot in white at the left playing a recorder, Harlequin in the center with a guitar, and at the right a strange figure in a domino or monk's black habit, singing behind his veiled mask while he holds his music on his knees. Beneath Pierrot's chair sprawls a dog.

The subject of the *Three Musicians* is traditionally gay; but by means of the monumental size of the picture, its sombre background and mysterious masks Picasso transforms the three music-making comedians into a solemn and majestic triumvirate.

Now, after these observations, let the reader be warned by Picasso's words to Zervos: "People who try to explain pictures are usually barking up the wrong tree. Gertrude Stein joyfully announced to me the other day that she had at last understood what my picture of the three musicians was meant to be. It was a still life!"

PICASSO. *Three Musicians.* 1921. Oil, 6'7" × 7'3¼". Mrs. Simon Guggenheim Fund, 1949.

During the post-World-War I period, when Matisse had turned back to a kind of decorative realism, and Picasso was balancing late cubism against neo-classic revival, two painters, Ozenfant and Jeanneret (the architect, Le Corbusier), were systematically trying to reassert the importance of the objective world without sacrificing the formal discoveries of the cubists. Their compositions, as in Ozenfant's drawing below and Le Corbusier's painting on page 219, do indeed preserve the integrity of everyday objects or at least their silhouettes. Their still lifes are remarkable for their compactness, economy, and precision. They called their program Purism.

Influenced perhaps by the Purists but a greater painter than they, Léger turned from his own highly abstract style to produce one of his masterpieces, the *Three Women*. (This English title is the Museum's; Léger's original title, *Le grand déjeuner*, is awkward, to say the least, if literally translated.)

Léger's *Three Women* was painted the same year as Picasso's *Three Women at the Spring* and *Three Musicians*, pages 81 and 83. Léger says that he intended no conscious emulation but his picture is not only comparable in subject matter but is painted on the same over-life-size scale so that it does constitute a challenge, and a highly successful one, to Picasso's greatest works of the period.

Curiously, Léger's *Three Women* in its distance from "nature" stands midway between Picasso's two big canvases. Léger's women are more abstract and more absorbed into their surroundings than are Picasso's sculpturesque giantesses. At the same time they, their breakfast table and utensils, and their cat, all preserve their integrity of shape and three-dimensional volume more completely than do Picasso's musicians, their table and instruments, and their dog.

Yet, in his *Three Women* Léger keeps many of the characteristics of his previous more abstract style in which technological forms predominate. Léger's love of the beauty of machinery survives even in this picture of a domestic interior. The impassive women,

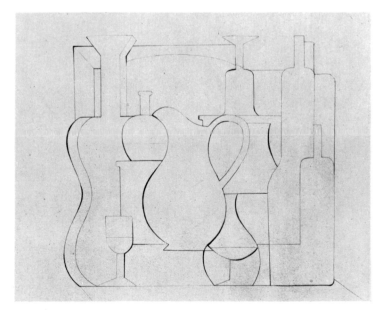

OZENFANT. *Fugue.* 1925. Pencil, 18 × 22″. Gift of the artist, 1942. Amédée Ozenfant. American, born in France, 1886; in New York since 1938. The Museum owns 1 oil, 1 drawing and 1 print by Ozenfant.

LÉGER. *Three Women (Le grand déjeuner)*. 1921. Oil, 6'¼" × 8'3". Mrs. Simon Guggenheim Fund, 1942. Fernand Léger. French, born 1881. The Museum owns 10 oils by Léger, 1 gouache, 1 watercolor, 4 drawings, including a ballet design, and 80 prints, including 72 in 3 illustrated books.

their belongings and surroundings, are all drawn, modeled and, as it were, polished as if they were an assembly of crank shafts, cylinders, casings and instrument boards. The color, too, seems inspired by the paints used on pipes, ducts and machine housings to differentiate the functions of the equipment in a factory or on the deck of a freighter.

Esthetically, the *Three Women* may be compared to the beauty of a superb motor running smoothly, powerfully, all of its complex parts moving in silent rhythmic perfection. Socially, perhaps metaphysically, his painting has another value: Léger has been attacked by several varieties of "humanists" for "dehumanizing" art by mechanizing his figures; but has he not at the same time helped to humanize the machine by rendering it esthetically assimilable?

Loyal to his youth, Lipchitz insists "I am always a cubist." But for him, page 78, "cubism was essentially a search for a new syntax." Picasso, on the other hand, remarks "to search means nothing in painting. To find is the thing . . . Many think that cubism is an art of transition, an experiment which is to bring ulterior results. Those who think that way have not understood it."

To Picasso, its principal inventor, cubism was "no different from any other school of painting"; it was equipped "to live its own life." Both are right. For Lipchitz, looking back, cubism was indeed a syntax to be studied and mastered. But it was also a liberation, "a new view of the universe."[105]

Without cubism Lipchitz' *Figure* would not have existed, in the sense that van Gogh's *Starry Night*, page 29, would not have been possible without impressionism. But, if we compare the *Figure* begun in 1926 with the *Man with Guitar* of 1915 (page 78), we can see that the great bronze reproduced here is indeed post-cubist. Its strict, bilateral symmetry is non-cubist; its structural elements, influenced perhaps by Negro and South Pacific sculpture, seem organic rather than geometric, the product of growth rather than of analysis and reintegration. Psychological or dramatic effects such as those in Picasso's *Three Musicians* are incidental, perhaps accidental, but in Lipchitz' magnificent *Figure* there is a hieratic, awe-inspiring power such as one might expect but rarely finds in primitive cult images.

Picasso's *Studio*, opposite, with its two-dimensional space, sparse rectilinear design and dislocation of detail suggests cubist compositions such as the *Man with a Hat* of 1912, page 70, but the careful isolation of the objects shown, the sense of structural rigidity rather than of overlapping, shifting planes, is post-cubist. Or perhaps it illustrates Picasso's ironic concession: "If cubism is an art of transition I am sure that the only thing that will come out of it is another form of cubism."

LIPCHITZ. *Figure*. 1926-30. Bronze, 7'1¼" high. Van Gogh Purchase Fund, 1937. (Photo Soichi Sunami.)

PICASSO. *The Studio*. 1927-28. Oil, 59 × 91″. Gift of Walter P. Chrysler, Jr., 1935.

At the left stands the painter before his canvas, one hand holding his brush, the other his palette, represented only by the thumb-hole. To the right is a table with a still life comprising a bowl of fruit and a plaster bust, its eyes and mouth arranged in a vertical row as are those of the artist. In the background are a mirror, a framed picture and a door or window.

What are the values in such a picture? First of course there is the esthetic value of the taut, finely constructed design, the *quality* of the relationships between lines, shapes, colors. Then there is the artist's extraordinary power of abstracting, simplifying and combining the images of objects in a consistent and harmonious style without destroying their identity. Thus, though the picture seems highly abstract at first glance, Picasso by making identification possible, maintains a tenuous, but tense and important connection between the real objects he saw and the painted forms we see.

In the spring of 1932 Picasso, with a creative energy astounding even for him, produced a long series of spectacular canvases of women, mostly seated or asleep. He was to have his first great retrospective exhibition early that summer. The previous June, in the same galleries, Matisse had had his first large Paris retrospective so that Picasso may well have felt, and not for the first time, a strong desire to surpass his ancient rival even in Matisse's own special field of color.

In all this brilliant series, the *Girl before a Mirror* is the most elaborately designed and the most sumptuously painted. Its magnificent color, heavy dark lines, and diamond-patterned background recall Gothic stained glass. Some of Matisse's *odalisques* of the late 1920s come to mind, too, but though more subtle they lack the density and power of Picasso's picture.

"The *Girl before a Mirror* is unique, too, in its psychological implications. The intricate metamorphosis of the girl's figure—'simultaneously clothed, nude and x-rayed'—the further transformation of her image in the mirror, the paradoxical tension between a contemplative subject and a composition of maximum activity in color and design, all suggest poetic and metaphysical reverberations rare in Picasso's art of this rather objective period."[49]

Since his *Three Women* of 1921, page 85, Léger's vigorous art had moved between complete abstraction and, more frequently, a concentrated interest in the "sensible appearance of things." In the ink drawings below he intensifies the images of the objects by simplification, elimination of any competing background, and a coarse, emphatic technique. The two drawings were mounted by the artist in the same frame, and so demonstrate one of the esthetic problems which have often interested Léger, that of contrasting balancing groups of organic and inorganic forms.

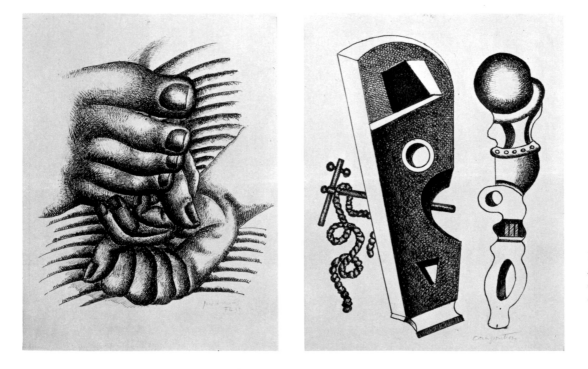

Léger. *Hands and Foot. Composition.* 1933. Two ink drawings on one mount $12 \times 9\frac{1}{4}$″ each. Purchase, 1935

PICASSO. *Girl before a Mirror*. March, 1932. Oil, $63\frac{1}{4} \times 51\frac{1}{4}''$. Accessioned in 1938, this was the first purchase made with the Mrs. Simon Guggenheim Fund.

GONZALEZ. *Head.* 1935? Wrought iron, 17¼" high. Purchase, 1937. (Photo Herbert Matter.) Julio Gonzalez. Spanish, born 1876; Paris, 1900, until his death, 1942. The Museum owns 2 sculptures and 1 print by Gonzalez.

"The age of iron began many centuries ago by producing very beautiful objects, unfortunately, for a large part, arms. Today, it provides as well, bridges and railroads. It is time this metal ceased to be a murderer and the simple instrument of a super-mechanical science. Today the door is wide open for this material to be, at last, forged and hammered by the peaceful hands of an artist . . .

"Only a cathedral spire can show us a point in the sky where our soul is suspended!

"In the disquietude of the night the stars seem to show to us points of hope in the sky; this immobile spire also indicates to us an endless number of them. It is these points in the infinite which are precursors of the new art: '*To draw in space.*'

"The important problem to solve here is not only to wish to make a work which is harmonious and perfectly balanced— No! But to get this result by the marriage of *material* and *space*. By the union of real forms with imaginary forms, obtained and suggested by established points, or by perforation—and, according to the natural law of love, to mingle them and make them inseparable, one from another, as are the body and the spirit."—Gonzalez[105]

Julio Gonzalez, five years older than Picasso, had known his more famous compatriot since their early years in Barcelona during the 1890s. Though trained originally as a metal craftsman Gonzalez gave most of his energies to painting until about 1930 when Picasso began to take lessons from him in ironsmithery. They worked together with great excitement— Picasso learning to master a new medium, Gonzalez learning a new imaginative freedom and a new approach to form.

In his *Head*, wrought about 1935, Gonzalez rivals Picasso in the extreme liberties he takes with the features: the eyes are seen as a double prong springing from a point in the brain or core of the head; below is the mouth with teeth; above, the hair parted in the middle. Since the *Head* was purchased by the Museum in 1937, the interlaced metal disk and the sickle-shaped skull have influenced younger American sculptors.

The *Woman Combing her hair* is another and much more important of Gonzalez' variations upon human forms. Here stance and gesture are suggested in wrought iron which maintains a sense of metallic hardness beneath a rich warm patina.

GONZALEZ. *Woman Combing her Hair*. 1936. Wrought iron, 52″ high. Mrs. Simon Guggenheim Fund, 1953. (Photo Soichi Sunami.)

Look, the Minotaur! He advances, his huge right hand raised against the candle held high by the little girl. Flowers in her hand, she confronts the monster fearlessly. Between the two staggers a horse, his intestines hanging from a rent in his belly. A female matador collapses across his back, her breasts bared, her *espada* held so that the hilt seems almost in the grasp of the Minotaur, the point aimed at the horse's head or the flower girl. A bearded man in a loin cloth climbs a ladder to safety, looking over his shoulder. In a window above, two girls watch two doves on the sill. Beyond, at the right, the sea fills the background, a single sail in the far distance.

The *Minotauromachy* tempts the interpreter. But explanation, whether poetic or psychoanalytic, would be subjective. All during the mid-1930s Picasso was obsessed by the Minotaur—triumphant, lecherous, ingratiating, wounded, pathetically blind. Here, the ancient, dreadful myth which, along with the bull ring itself, originated in Crete, is obviously interwoven with the modern Spanish tauromachy. To these he has added certain motifs used by him in his theatre pictures and, significantly, in his *Calvary* of 1930.

Picasso has not, probably cannot, put into words the meaning of this dramatic charade of the soul. But the allegory, though ambiguous, bites deep. No other work of Picasso is so complex in its moral implications, yet so saturated with emotion.

PICASSO. *Minotauromachy*. 1935. Etching, $19\frac{1}{2} \times 27\frac{1}{8}''$. Purchase, 1947.

PICASSO. *Night Fishing at Antibes*. August, 1939. Oil, 6′9″ × 11′4″. Mrs. Simon Guggenheim Fund, 1952.

In the *Night Fishing at Antibes* we see two men spearing fish by the light of large lanterns. One of them, in a striped jersey, with a four-tined spear pierces a sole (most Picassoid of fishes!) lying on the bottom. The other fisherman leans over the side of the boat as refraction bends the shaft of his spear. His face, close to the water, is tense with eagerness and anxiety. At the right, on the stone sea wall, two girls stand watching, one with a bicycle and a double ice cream cone. The rocky shore to the left is surmounted by the two towers of the town. Above, the shining moon casts its spiral reflection on the water. All these circumstantial details, including grotesquely distorted figures, are subordinated to the romantic mood and to a resonant color harmony perhaps unsurpassed in Picasso's art.

This nocturne is the largest and possibly the most important canvas painted by Picasso during the decade following the *Guernica* mural of 1937. It was completed a month before World War II began.

In 1946 Picasso returned to Antibes and there painted over twenty pictures which together with a wealth of his own ceramics he gave to the town. The "Musée Picasso" is housed in the Grimaldi Castle, the tower of which we can see at the extreme left in *Night Fishing at Antibes*.

BRAQUE. *Woman with a Mandolin.* 1937. Oil, $51\frac{1}{4} \times 38\frac{1}{4}''$. Mrs. Simon Guggenheim Fund, 1948.

"What seduces us at first glance is . . . his coloring, exact and sober and of a ravishing delicacy . . . this same sure instinct is to be observed in . . . his handling of textures . . . the word for it is the one which the critic now hesitates to use: beauty. Braque's painting is beautiful painting."—Jean Cassou[4]

Lipchitz' first designs for the *Mother and Child* were studies of a woman's torso drawn in Paris during 1939-40, the period of the static war. The idea was carried further in southern France and then in New York, where Lipchitz came as a refugee in 1941. It was only some time after he began these studies of a woman's torso that he suddenly recognized in them a resemblance to the head of a bull. He developed the bull's head further until he achieved the balanced double image which then took final form in the sculpture.

Halfway through this development he also recognized the probable source of the woman's figure. Once, several years before, on a rainy night, he had heard the loud, hoarse voice of a woman singing. When he came nearer he saw her in the light of a street lamp. She had lost both legs so that her torso rose directly from a little cart. She was singing with her arms outstretched, her face raised to the light and her long hair hanging wet in the rain. The almost apparitional figure of this indomitable beggar woman impressed Lipchitz deeply.

The double image of the woman-and-bull's-head Lipchitz associates with the myth of Europa and the Bull and interprets as an expression or symbol of the mixed despair and hopeful energy of conquered Europe during the dark years of occupation. Whatever its symbolic meaning, Lipchitz has made of his double image an unforgettable work of sculpture.

LIPCHITZ. *Mother and Child, II.* 1941-45. Bronze, 50″ high. Mrs. Simon Guggenheim Fund, 1951. (Photo Herbert Matter.)

During World War II Léger lived in the United States, mostly in New York but traveling widely and getting to know the country intimately, visually speaking. One of his best American paintings is *Big Julie* in which he once more attacks one of his favorite problems, the balancing of human and machine forms as he had in the drawings, page 88.

LÉGER. *Big Julie (La grande Julie)*. 1945. Oil on canvas, 44 × 50⅛". Acquired through the Lillie P. Bliss Bequest, 1945.

"For me," Léger explained[80] to James Johnson Sweeney in 1946, "the contrast in the United States between the mechanical and the natural is one of great anti-melodic intensity. But bad taste is also one of the valuable raw materials for the country. Bad taste, strong colors—it is all here for the painter to organize and get the full use of its power. Girls in sweaters with brilliant colored skin; girls in shorts dressed more like acrobats in a circus than one would ever come across on a Paris street. If I had only seen girls dressed in 'good taste' here I would never have painted my *Cyclist* series, of which *La Grande Julie* in the Museum was the culmination.

"I always hate to see 'good taste' come to the people. For painters like me who are robust it is very dangerous to frequent the *beau monde*, ballets and the like. French 'taste' is a pitfall for the creative artist . . . In Paris the 'Casino de Paris' represents 'taste'; the same sort of taste has taken the vitality out of the musical shows in New York. Even burlesque shows are infected by 'good taste.' Still there is no need yet to worry. One only has to study the hand-painted ties on Broadway—a locomotive and four pigeons on a violet and black ground, or a buxom nude on a saffron ground—to realize there is still a vigorous survival."

In the past decade, far more than ever before, the leading masters of the School of Paris have produced original prints remarkable for their boldness of scale and frequent use of color. Of them all, Picasso has been the most prolific. The Museum unhappily has no post-war paintings by Picasso but the Print Room owns fifty of approximately two hundred single prints he has done since 1945. Most of these are lithographs in which Picasso, always eager to exploit the possibilities of any medium, has worked in a great variety of techniques. One of the most arresting of his recent prints, however, is the large aquatint *Girl at a Window* of 1952. In this print Picasso uses one of the least familiar of the intaglio media, a technique which he learned in 1936—the sugar process or "lift ground" method of aquatint. He draws directly in black rather than building up from light to dark. The process allows much freedom and, what particularly appealed to Picasso as a painter, the aquatint may be directly applied in brush strokes. —w. s. l.

PICASSO. *Girl at a Window.* 1952. Aquatint, $32\frac{1}{4} \times 18\frac{5}{8}$". Purchase, 1952.

ITALIANS: THE OLDER GENERATION

In 1910 five young Italian artists published their *Manifesto of the Futurist Painters* in Milan. They proposed to "exalt every form of originality . . . to rebel against the tyranny of the words 'harmony' and 'good taste' . . . to glorify the life of today, incessantly and tumultuously transformed by the victories of science . . ."[106]

Yet when he composed *The City Rises*, an ardent hymn to industrial Milan, Boccioni, the leader of the Futurists, painted immense draft horses—an old-fashioned romantic symbol. Only in the background can one discern such modernisms as a puffing locomotive and a street car. But what horses these are! The men who toil beside them can scarcely control their power.

CARRÀ. *Funeral of the Anarchist Galli.* 1911. Oil, 6'6¼" × 8'6". Acquired through the Lillie P. Bliss Bequest, 1948. Carlo Carrà. Italian, born 1881. The Museum owns 1 oil and 2 prints by Carrà.

BOCCIONI. *The City Rises.* 1910. Oil, 6'6½" × 9'10½". Mrs. Simon Guggenheim Fund, 1951.

Boccioni had previously been painting in little spots like the French "divisionists"; but in *The City Rises*, with his enthusiasm for surging movement, he tore the divisionist veil of dots into ribbons of color somewhat as van Gogh, page 29, had done in 1889 with Seurat's Neo-Impressionist technique, page 25.

The vivid memory of a riot he had seen years earlier led Carrà not only to paint his most famous canvas but to pronounce the Futurist principle: "Painters have always shown us figures and objects arranged in front of us. *We are going to put the spectator in the center of the picture.*"

In the *Funeral* Carrà uses hot purples, oranges and ochres, broken silhouettes and flickering, fan-shaped patterns of flailing weapons to achieve his effect of commotion and emotion. Yet, fundamentally the painting is composed with the classic balances and counter-thrusts of the fifteenth-century battle pieces by Uccello which Carrà loved and was later to write about.

BOCCIONI. *Muscular Dynamism*. 1913. Charcoal, 34 × 23¼″. Purchase, 1949. Umberto Boccioni. Italian, 1882-1916. The Museum owns 2 sculptures, 1 oil, 6 drawings and 1 print by Boccioni.

"The world's splendor has been enriched by a new beauty, the beauty of speed . . . a roaring motor-car, hurtling like a machine gun, is more beautiful than the Winged Victory of Samothrace." So proclaimed the poet Marinetti in his *Manifesto of Futurism*, 1909. Yet, the great Futurist sculpture is not a speeding machine but a human figure; or perhaps Boccioni's *Unique Forms of Continuity in Space* is an evocation of both.

The *Continuity*, as the sculptor called it for short, was the climax of a long series of sculptures, paintings and drawings of the figure in violent motion—playing football, riding a bicycle or running. Among them is the superb charcoal study, *Muscular Dynamism*, reproduced at the left.

"Sculpture," Boccioni insisted, "should bring to life the object by making visible its prolongation into space. The confining of the enclosed statue should be abolished. The figure must be opened up and fused in space."[106]

Accepting his own challenge, Boccioni forces the muscles of the bronze *Continuity* into streamlined shapes as if under the distorting pressures of supersonic speed. A sense of gravity is further diminished by the flaming spiral of the figure, especially when seen from the front. Never before had organic velocity and energy been so emphatically expressed. *Continuity* is possibly the most important sculpture done in modern Italy.

In the *Manifesto of the Futurist Painters* the young artists had asked themselves ". . . can we remain insensitive to the frenzied activities of great capital cities?" Boccioni and Carrà shouted "no" in their huge canvases *The City Rises* and the riotous *Funeral of the Anarchist Galli*. The Paris member of the group, Severini, replied in his paintings of night clubs, for the *Manifesto* had explicitly declared Futurist enthusiasm for "the new psychology of night life, the hectic figures of the *viveur*, the *cocotte*, the *apache*" and (relapsing into Italian), the "*alcoölista*."

In his *Dynamic Hieroglyphic of the Bal Tabarin*, next page, Severini disintegrates the scene into a kaleidoscope of glittering movement, light, color and pasted-on sequins while the words POLKA, VALSE, and BOWLING float through the air.

BOCCIONI. *Unique Forms of Continuity in Space.* 1913. Bronze, 43½″ high. Acquired through the Lillie P. Bliss Bequest, 1948. (Photo Soichi Sunami.)

SEVERINI. *Dynamic Hieroglyphic of the Bal Tabarin.* 1912. Oil, with sequins, $63\frac{5}{8} \times 61\frac{1}{2}''$. Purchase, 1949. Gino Severini. Italian, born 1883; active chiefly in Paris. The Museum owns 1 oil and 1 drawing by Severini.

MORANDI. *Still Life*. 1916. Oil, $32\frac{1}{2} \times 22\frac{5}{8}''$. Acquired through the Lillie P. Bliss Bequest, 1949. Giorgio Morandi. Italian, born 1890. The Museum owns 2 oils and 6 prints by Morandi.

Only recently has Futurism begun to recover from the reaction against its own excessive publicity campaigns of before World War I. Today Boccioni takes rank, in creative energy at least, with de Chirico and Modigliani (pages 134-135, 104-105) among the great Italian artists of our time.

By contrast with Futurism, and indeed with the general hubbub of modern experiment, the art of Giorgio Morandi seems quietist. Yet no living Italian painter is more esteemed by his compatriots. Unlike all his more famous colleagues, Morandi has never been to Paris. In fact, for forty years now he has rarely left his native Bologna where he paints chiefly compositions selected from his great collection of old bottles. One of the earliest, subtlest and most elegant of these is the Museum's *Still Life*.

Right: MODIGLIANI. *Head.* Stone, 22¼″ high. Gift of Mrs. John D. Rockefeller, Jr. in memory of Mrs. Cornelius J. Sullivan, 1939. (Photo Soichi Sunami.)

Below: MODIGLIANI. *Caryatid.* c. 1914. Limestone, 36¼″ high. Mrs. Simon Guggenheim Fund, 1951. (Photo Soichi Sunami). Amedeo Modigliani. Italian, born 1884; worked in Paris where he died 1920. The Museum owns 3 oils, 2 sculptures and 5 drawings by Modigliani.

Almost all Modigliani's rare sculptures are architectural. The *Head* was intended to be used as a corbel in the jamb of a doorway; the *Caryatid,* had Modigliani's great talent as a sculptor not been ignored, might have supported a column, as do the kneeling figures of Italian Romanesque portals.

Modigliani's friend, Jacques Lipchitz, remembers that when the war broke out in 1914, Modigliani, who was too poor to buy his own materials, found a building stone on the Boulevard Montparnasse near a half-completed structure abandoned by the workmen who had been called up. From this stone Modigliani carved the *Caryatid,* one of his three life-size sculptures.

The sharp-edged, elongated lines of the *Head* were inspired by African Negro masks, but the *Caryatid* is as classic as the antique *Crouching Venus* of the Louvre. Its grandeur of line makes it one of Modigliani's strongest works in any medium. The back is especially beautiful.

"These are (let us be candid) erotic nudes for the most part, though dignified by conviction of style . . . Modigliani's women are not the grown-up cherubs of which the eighteenth century was fond. They are adult, sinuous, carnal and real, the final stage in the sequence leading from Giorgione's *Concert champêtre* to Manet's *Déjeuner sur l'herbe* and on to Lautrec and his contemporaries. Yet whereas a certain picturesqueness of evil attaches to Lautrec's works, and indeed to those of many modern artists from Rops to Pascin, Modigliani's sensuality is clear and delighted, like that of Ingres but less afraid. His nudes are an emphatic answer to his Futurist countrymen who, infatuated with the machine, considered the subject outworn and urged its suppression for a period of ten years."—James Thrall Soby[43]

Perhaps his last figure painting, the Museum's canvas was distinguished, apparently by the artist himself, with the title *Le grand nu*.

MODIGLIANI. *Reclining Nude (Le grand nu)*. c. 1919. Oil, $28\frac{1}{2} \times 45\frac{7}{8}$". Mrs. Simon Guggenheim Fund, 1950.

NADELMAN. *Man in the Open Air.* c. 1915. Bronze, 54½" high. Gift of William S. Paley, 1948. (Photo Soichi Sunami.) Elie Nadelman. American, born Poland 1882; Paris 1903-1914; New York 1914 until his death in 1946. The Museum owns 8 sculptures, 6 drawings and 3 prints by Nadelman.

FOUR SCULPTORS

Like Modigliani, other sculptors born in the 1880s skirted cubism and the influence of Negro or other exotic forms to find their mature styles within the broad tradition of European figure sculpture. Nadelman and Lachaise worked first in Paris, then in New York; Zorach, born in Russia, lives in America; Epstein, born in New York, is now Sir Jacob Epstein of London. Their work is highly personal, sometimes to the point of mannerism (in the best sense of that rehabilitated word).

Lincoln Kirstein writes that from 1914 on Nadelman was "preoccupied with the passing scene of fashion and high society. His drawings and freestanding figures in bronze and wood, clothed in simplifications of modern dress, would emerge as serious jokes, loving if ironic definitions of the mundane mask. They have important connections with the expressive profiles of Seurat . . ." (see page 24).

Shortly after his arrival in New York late in 1914, Nadelman exhibited at Alfred Stieglitz' pioneering gallery, "291." "Here, Nadelman showed his *Man in the Open Air*, recently completed in plaster, a figure in a bowler hat, supported by a tree-trunk whose slim branch quite simply grew up through his right arm. The single adornment of its elegant attenuation was a small bow-tie in free relief, casting echoing shadows on its broad shirt-front. At once comic, supple, and worldly, this was a culmination of a new development, a turn towards his full comment, as personal and precise as Guys, on *la vie moderne*. And yet the pose and its relationship to the supporting tree stump were a kind of whispered echo of the *Apollo Sauroktonos*, the *Boy with the Lizard*, of classical antiquity."[47]

William Zorach is the most distinguished among our older living sculptors who find the direct cutting of wood or stone a discipline with valuable esthetic consequences. In his *Christ*, the extreme hardness of the porphyry, its contrasting qualities when polished or left smooth, add greatly to its sculptural beauty. One need only imagine the piece cast in bronze to realize how superbly the sculptor has mastered his intractable material in hewing this exceptionally noble head.

EPSTEIN. *Portrait of Oriel Ross.* 1931. Bronze, 26¼" high. Gift of Edward M. M. Warburg, 1933. (Photo Soichi Sunami.) Jacob Epstein. British, born U.S.A. 1880. The Museum owns 3 sculptures by Epstein.

ZORACH. *Head of Christ.* 1940. Black porphyry, 14¼" high. Mrs. John D. Rockefeller, Jr. Purchase Fund, 1942. (Photo Herbert Matter.) William Zorach. American, born 1887. The Museum owns 3 sculptures, 2 watercolors and 1 drawing by Zorach.

Once we accept bronze as a surrogate for clay, Epstein's *Portrait of Oriel Ross* displays a mastery of material comparable to Zorach's in his stone head. Epstein makes no attempt to simulate exactly the texture of skin or hair. But by modeling the flesh with a slightly uneven surface and raking the hair with coarse, irregular striations he not only preserves the sense of his hands at work upon the plastic clay but gives the inert material an effect of intense vitality: not a facsimile of life but an equivalent.

The *Floating Figure* "was completed in plaster in 1927. At this time Lachaise had been much impressed by contemporary theories of space and time. He had been considering the almost unimaginable curve of the earth's ocean horizon line, straight to the physical eye, but progressing into an infinite curve; over and above this, even more incredible, the convolutions of the earth's curves enclosed in other more enormous orbits, of which our whole universe is possibly but a fragment. He had always felt the most sentient, universal subject of sculptural expression to be the human figure, and in his *Floating Woman* he attempted an embodiment of cosmic concepts.

"The heroic nude *Woman* is a culmination in this direction, the maturity of his maturity. Her strong legs seem almost forced deep in the ground, yet her large haunches exert little pressure. She exists in air as much as on the earth. She is a calmly savage figure, an idea of the feminine that has a serenity more dominating than tender. This figure is an uncompromising statement, not easy to regard with complacency . . .

"[Lachaise'] preferences in the art of the past illuminate his present activity. The past he loves best is remotest . . . mammoths and bison on the walls of stone caverns, beasts with shaggy mountainous bodies delicately balanced on small, careful hoofs. Or small paleolithic objects carved from ivory or stone, female bodies of refined grossness, with huge mounded breasts capable of suckling whole tribes . . . Next, he admires the clarity, precision and anonymity of the Egyptian stone carvers . . . Lastly he feels himself close to the Hindu sculptors of India and the Malay archipelagos" — Lincoln Kirstein[34]

LACHAISE. *Standing Woman*. 1932. Bronze, 7′4″ high. Mrs. Simon Guggenheim Fund, 1948. (Photo Eliot Elisofon.) Gaston Lachaise. American, born France 1882; died in New York 1935. The Museum owns 12 sculptures and 18 drawings by Lachaise.

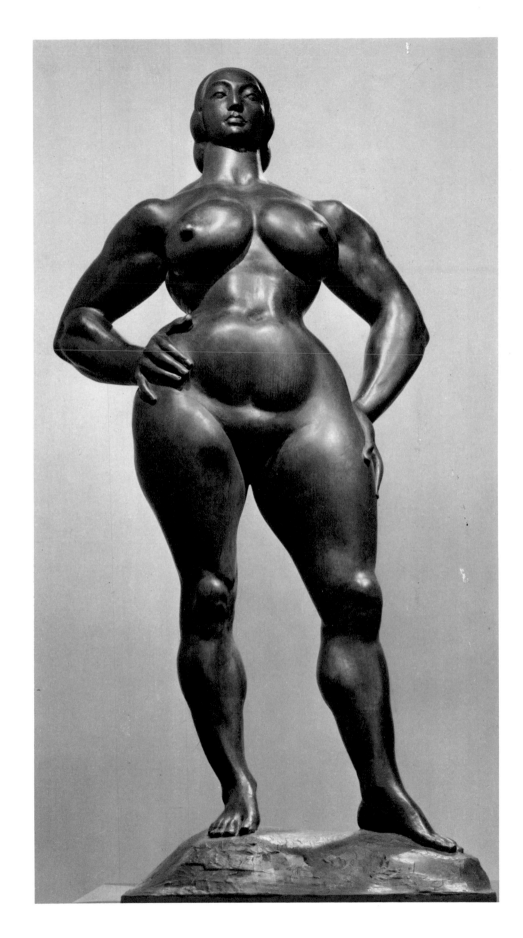

Opposite: LACHAISE. *Floating Figure*. 1927. Bronze, 53″ high. Given anonymously in memory of the artist, 1937. (Photo Soichi Sunami.)

SLOAN. *Roofs, Summer Night.* 1906. Etching, $5\frac{1}{4} \times 7''$. Gift of Mrs. John D. Rockefeller, Jr., 1940. John Sloan. American, 1871-1951. The Museum owns 120 prints by Sloan.

AMERICAN PAINTERS: THE OLDER GENERATION

Early in 1908 New York was scandalized by the exhibition of a group of painters called "The Eight." "Beauty" in the eyes of academic artists and their polite admirers had been betrayed by a "revolutionary black gang" who painted shabby street scenes, saloons, the interiors of cheap rooming houses, and rooftops cluttered with laundry. Not only their art but also, as so often happens to original artists, their morals and their politics were held suspect by those who preferred the nicely brushed still lifes, the snow scenes (with daring blue shadows!), fashionable portraits and genteel nudes which annually won prizes at the National Academy.

Of this "ashcan school" John Sloan was perhaps the most typical as well as the most belligerent. His best paintings and numerous etchings recall his early days as a newspaper illustrator. George Bellows was too young to belong to The Eight, but carried on in his best works the slice-of-life tradition of Sloan and Luks. Once, briefly, a professional baseball player, Bellows drew with an athlete's muscular vigor and sense of timing. One of the most dramatic moments in American ring history is recorded in his lithograph of Firpo knocking Dempsey through the ropes.

BELLOWS. *Dempsey and Firpo.* 1924. Lithograph, $18\frac{1}{8} \times 22\frac{1}{8}''$. Mrs. John D. Rockefeller, Jr. Purchase Fund, 1951. George Bellows. American, 1882-1925. The Museum owns 1 watercolor and 8 prints by Bellows.

HOPPER. *House by the Railroad.* 1925. Oil, 24 × 29″. Given anonymously, 1930. This was the first painting to enter the Museum's Collection. Edward Hopper. American, born 1882. The Museum owns 5 oils by Hopper, 2 watercolors and 10 prints.

Bellows died young and very famous in 1925. That was also the year Edward Hopper painted *The House by the Railroad.* He had been Bellows' fellow student, was even born the same year, but Hopper was still almost unknown. Even today he is as stubbornly unfashionable as he is greatly esteemed.

"My aim in painting," Hopper says, "has always been the most exact transcription possible of my most intimate impressions of nature."[27] When *The House by the Railroad* was first shown it was generally interpreted as satirical; more recently, nostalgic and romantic overtones have been discerned. Hopper denies both implications, reasserting his objectivity. Yet the quiet, haunting intensity of his best paintings induces feelings far deeper than the "facts" alone would warrant.

WEBER. *The Geranium*. 1911. Oil, $39\frac{7}{8} \times 32\frac{1}{4}''$. Acquired through the Lillie P. Bliss Bequest, 1944. Max Weber. American, born 1881. The Museum owns 5 oils by Weber, 15 gouaches, 1 drawing and 91 prints, including 11 in a book.

Opposite: FEININGER. *The Steamer "Odin," II*. 1927. Oil, $26\frac{1}{2} \times 39\frac{1}{2}''$. Acquired through the Lillie P. Bliss Bequest, 1943. Lyonel Feininger. American, born 1871; worked in Germany 1887-1936; U.S.A. since 1937. The Museum owns 2 oils by Feininger, 3 watercolors and 20 prints, including 10 in a portfolio.

Max Weber had studied with Matisse, known the Steins, Picasso, Delaunay, Apollinaire and Henri Rousseau, the last intimately. He returned to New York at the end of 1908, the year of the attacks on the "apostles of ugliness" such as John Sloan.

In 1911, the year he painted *The Geranium*, Weber's own works shown at Stieglitz' gallery were denounced as "travesties," "emanations" from a "lunatic asylum," "atrocities." As Holger Cahill remarked in 1930, "Max Weber has lived the history of modern art in America. Its search and tribulation, its rebellion against decadence, the natreds which it aroused, and its ultimate triumph are chapters in his life story."[120]

Like Whistler, Feininger made his great reputation in Europe as an expatriate generally ignored by his fellow Americans. In 1937 he returned to the United States. Just fifty years earlier, as a youth, he had sailed from New York to Hamburg in a small square-rigged steam brig such as he was often to paint later in a mood of nostalgia. The steamer *Odin* is a more modern craft, but she, too, and the sea and Baltic shore and those who watch have gone through what Feininger calls "the process of transformation and crystallization."

"I see great forces at work," Marin wrote Stieglitz, "the large buildings and the small buildings; the warring of the great and the small . . . each subject in some degree to the other's power. I can hear the sound of their strife and there is great music being played."

`Lower Manhattan` looks like an explosion—ominous simile—but the radiant nucleus (paper cut out and sewn on) was inspired by the gold leaf on the dome of the old World Building seen looking down from the top of the Woolworth Tower. From this dizzy height the eye plunges into the zigzag perspectives of buildings and car-dotted streets, grinding out to sea like a dynamited ice flow.

MARIN. *Lower Manhattan (Composing derived from top of Woolworth).* 1922. Watercolor, $21\frac{5}{8} \times 26\frac{7}{8}''$. Acquired through the Lillie P. Bliss Bequest, 1945. John Marin. American, 1870-1953. The Museum owns 3 watercolors and 11 etchings by Marin.

Left: DEMUTH. *Acrobats.* 1919. Watercolor, 13 × 7⅞″. Gift of Mrs. John D. Rockefeller, Jr., 1935. Charles Demuth. American, 1883-1935. The Museum owns 14 watercolors by Demuth.

Georgia O'Keeffe has produced few abstract paintings but they are among the most memorable in American art. Even in her paintings of objects—barns, mountains, trees, lakes, enormous flowers, clam shells, or white desert bones that fill the whole blue sky—she has the gift of isolating and intensifying the thing seen, or destroying its scale, until it loses its identity in an ambiguous but always precise beauty.

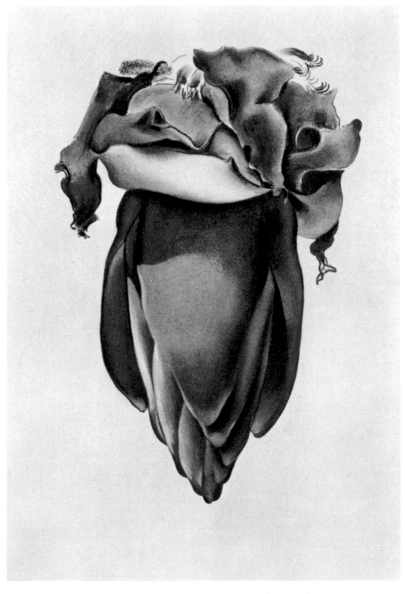

"In many of Demuth's figure pieces there is an emphasis on intricacy of balance, on those daring relationships of stance and muscular action which so delighted him in performances by acrobats and dancers. At times his art seems altogether Mannerist in its tensions and exaggerations of contour, and he was particularly fond of the 'C' curve formed by the figure of one acrobat arched outward from another, the whole framed by complementary arcs of color.

"In the *Acrobats* ... watercolor is applied film over film, with wonderful control of shading and transparency and a perfect mastery of the tonal resonance of black. The freer wash handling of the stage and backdrop provides a radiant foil to the figures ..."
—James Thrall Soby[76]

O'KEEFFE. *Banana Flower.* 1933. Charcoal, 21¼ × 14¼″. Given anonymously, 1936. Georgia O'Keeffe. American, born 1887. The Museum owns 1 oil and 4 drawings by O'Keeffe.

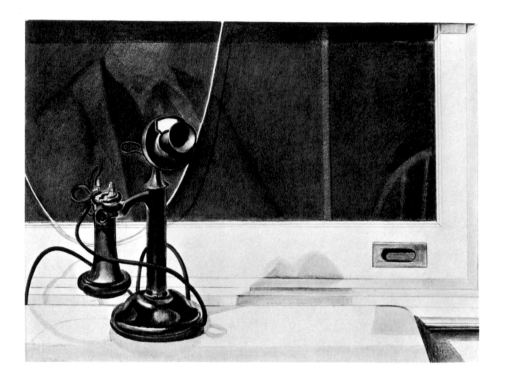

"Charles Sheeler gives us . . . a world of elements we can believe in, things for our associations long familiar or which we have always thought familiar . . .

"To discover and separate these things from the amorphous, the conglomerate normality with which they are surrounded and of which before the act of 'creation' each is a part, calls for an eye to draw out that detail which is in itself the thing, to clinch our insight, that is, our understanding, of it.

"It is this eye for the thing that most distinguishes Charles Sheeler."

— William Carlos Williams[62]

SHEELER. *Self Portrait.* 1923. Conté crayon, $19\frac{1}{4} \times 25\frac{1}{4}''$. Gift of Mrs. John D. Rockefeller, Jr., 1935. Charles Sheeler. American, born 1883. The Museum owns 2 oils, 6 drawings, 3 prints and 18 photographs by Sheeler.

Japan and the West combine successfully on a decorative level in the art of Tiffany, Bonnard and Guimard, page 215; in the early work of Yasuo Kuniyoshi they meet on the plane of humor, visual humor as sharp and precise and original as its most famous motif, the triangular cow. Later, Kuniyoshi was more completely absorbed in the general stream of American art in which he participated not only as a distinguished painter and craftsman but as a much loved and greatly honored leader.

KUNIYOSHI. *Fisherman.* 1924. Dry brush and India ink, $22 \times 28\frac{1}{8}''$. Given anonymously, 1936. Yasuo Kuniyoshi. American, born Japan 1893; to U.S.A. 1906; died in New York 1953. The Museum owns 2 oils, 3 drawings and 45 prints by Kuniyoshi.

DAVIS. *Visa*. 1951. Oil, 40 × 52″. Gift of Mrs. Gertrud A. Mellon, 1953. Stuart Davis. American, born 1894. The Museum owns 5 oils by Davis, 1 gouache, 1 watercolor, 2 drawings and a rug after his design.

"I very often use words in my pictures," Davis states, "because they are a part of urban subject matter."

In *Visa* the word CHAMPION, "clearly the subject matter of the painting," was derived from a matchbook cover. The word *else* answered the artist's need for a short word without associations. The phrase, *The amazing continuity*, besides "animating the area at the extreme right," refers to the experience of finding in paintings of very different subject matter and style the mysterious common factor, the "amazing continuity," which unites them as works of art. "The content of this phrase is real," Davis concludes, "as real as any shape of a face or a tree . . ."

HARTLEY. *Boots*. 1941. Oil on gesso panel, $28\frac{1}{8} \times 22\frac{1}{4}''$. Mrs. Simon Guggenheim Fund, 1942. Marsden Hartley. American, 1877-1943. The Museum owns 2 oils and 1 print by Hartley.

SPENCER. *City Walls*. 1921. Oil, $39\frac{1}{8} \times 28\frac{1}{4}''$. Given anonymously, 1936. Niles Spencer. American, 1893-1952. The Museum owns 4 oils and 1 print by Spencer.

"The term Realist, as it is applied to contemporary painting, has acquired a number of contradictory associations. These should be made clear if the aims of many present-day artists are to be understood.

"There is realism in the work of abstract artists. Picasso, for example, is always concerned with some basic reality . . . The deeper meanings of nature can only be captured in painting through disciplined form and design. The visual recognizability is actually irrelevant. It may be there or not."—Niles Spencer, 1941

The year Marsden Hartley painted *Boots* he wrote: "What do pictures mean anyhow—I have been trying to find out for at least half a lifetime . . . I have no interest in the subject matter of a picture, not the slightest. A picture has but one meaning—is it well done, or isn't it—and if it is, it is sure to be a good picture whether the spectator likes it or not . . . And I remember the old gag that we have heard so often, and is perhaps still being used: 'I don't know anything about art, I only know what I like,' and the only answer to that is—do you?"

Burchfield's watercolors were first assumed to be satirical—the back street of Main Street. When the artist denied this, romantic melancholy was proposed as a diagnosis. This was nearer the truth, especially if the word romantic be omitted. Of *Pippin House, East Liverpool, Ohio*, Burchfield writes simply that his "aim was to suggest a certain grimness pertaining to the winter season—a feeling of apprehension that exists on a dour day . . . with a storm in the offing."

In addition to his prophetic achievements as a painter, Arthur Dove was the most original American master of collage. *Grandmother*, as a representation, is more abstract than cubist collages such as Picasso's *Man with a Hat*, page 70, or Gris' *Breakfast*, page 76, yet Dove's materials are symbolically far richer and more complex. In the dada collages of Grosz and Ernst, pages 138, 139, subject is conceived with an air of irony or even malice; Dove's collage characterizations are on the contrary humorous or tender. The associations, the very textures of the materials laminated in the composition *Grandmother* are poetic in their intention, yet saved from a scrapbook sentimentality by a sure taste and sense of visual order.

BURCHFIELD. *Pippin House, East Liverpool, Ohio*. 1920. Watercolor, 26 × 19⅛". Gift of Mr. and Mrs. Alex L. Hillman, 1950. Charles Burchfield. American, born 1893. The Museum owns 9 watercolors by Burchfield.

DOVE. *Grandmother*. 1925. Collage of shingles, needlepoint, page from the Concordance, pressed flowers, 20 × 21¼". Gift of Philip L. Goodwin, 1939. Arthur G. Dove. American, 1880-1946. The Museum owns 1 oil and 1 collage by Dove.

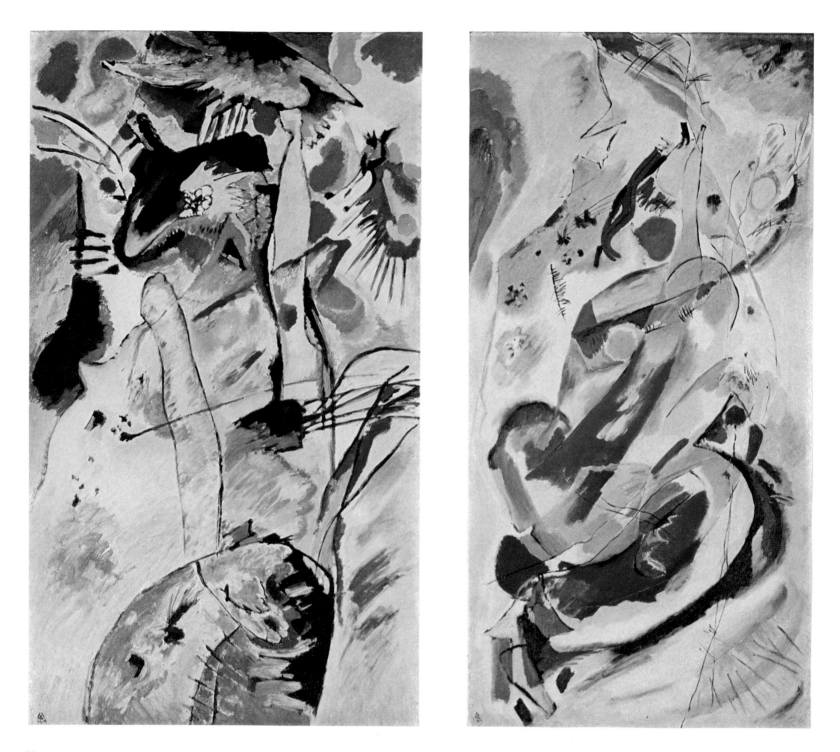

KANDINSKY. Two compositions, 1914, from a series of four. Oil on canvas. Left: $64 \times 36\frac{1}{4}''$; right: $64 \times 31\frac{1}{2}''$. Mrs. Simon Guggenheim, Fund, 1954. Wassily Kandinsky. Russian, born 1866, active in Munich, Moscow, Germany (the Bauhaus) and Paris where he died in 1944. The Museum owns 4 oils, 5 watercolors, 1 drawing **and 77 prints** by Kandinsky

PIONEERS OF ABSTRACT ART

In 1888 Gauguin asserted that "painting is an abstraction"; in 1908 Matisse announced that his goal was "above all, expression"; in 1910, in Munich, Kandinsky painted the first purely abstract expressionist picture. The two paintings reproduced opposite are somewhat later, but still in the artist's most significant period of abstract form and color projected with the maximum of spontaneous freedom. They are, to use Kandinsky's words, "a graphic representation of a mood and not a representation of objects."

Kandinsky's young countryman and future rival, Malevich, had been a cubist, analyzing, "geometrizing" nature but not yet losing sight of her. Then in 1913, perhaps inspired by a remark of Kandinsky, he showed "nothing more or less than a black square on a white background . . . It was not just a square I had exhibited . . ." he explained, "but rather the expression of non-objectivity." Five years later he showed *White on White*, the culminating demonstration of Suprematism "by which," he stated, "I mean the supremacy of pure feeling or perception in the pictorial arts." Thus Malevich countered Kandinsky's mysticism of color with his own mysticism of geometric purity.

Meanwhile in Holland, Mondrian (another ex-cubist) was also arriving at "geometric" abstraction, but gradually, after much trial and error, rather than by sudden intuition. His researches contributed greatly to the design vocabulary of *de Stijl*, page 217, the influential Dutch movement from which, however, he resigned in 1920.

MALEVICH. *Suprematist Composition: White on White.* 1918? Oil, $31\frac{1}{4} \times 31\frac{1}{4}''$. Extended loan. Kasimir Malevich. Russian, 1878-1935. The Museum owns 1 oil and 2 drawings by Malevich, and has in trust 6 oils and 4 drawings.

MONDRIAN. *Painting I*. 1926. Oil, $44\frac{1}{4} \times 44''$
(diagonals). Katherine S. Dreier Bequest, 1953.

Among Mondrian's mature compositions *Painting I* of 1926 is one of the most absolute. Four black lines, their lengths and widths varied with exquisite calculation, cut across the four corners of the diagonal canvas creating a subtly asymmetric equilibrium.

In New York fifteen years later, Mondrian, long a devotee of American jazz, found in boogie woogie a "dynamic rhythm" and a "destruction of melody which is the equivalent of the destruction of natural appearances."[80]

In its staccato, broken rhythms, *Broadway Boogie Woogie* looks back thirty years to Mondrian's emergence from cubism. His last completed painting, it offers a synthesis of his entire mature work.

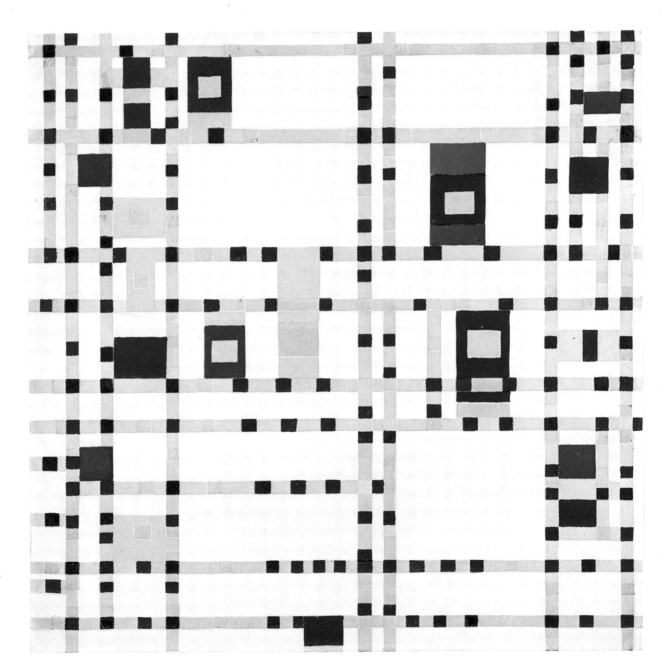

MONDRIAN. *Broadway Boogie Woogie.* 1942-43. Oil, 50 × 50". Given anonymously, 1943.

"For beauty three things are required. First, then, integrity of perfection: those things which are broken are bad for this very reason. And also a due proportion or harmony. And again, clarity: whence those things which have a shining color are called beautiful." —St. Thomas Aquinas: *Summa Theologiae*, circa 1270

"Simplicity is not an end in art, but one arrives at simplicity in spite of oneself, in approaching the real sense of things . . ."

"In sculpture the forms of naked human beings are no more beautiful than those of toads."

"High polish is a necessity which certain approximately absolute forms demand of some materials. It is not always appropriate, it is even very harmful for certain other forms."

"Direct cutting is the true road to sculpture, but also the most dangerous for those who don't know how to walk. And in the end, direct or indirect cutting means nothing, it is the complete thing that counts."

"When we are no longer children, we are already dead."

"Beauty is absolute equity." —Brancusi to Irène Codreane, in *This Quarter*, 1926

Brancusi is unique. And independent, though for a brief time he was associated with the Dutch *Stijl* movement. His art's ancestry: primarily the sculpture of West and Central Africa, and, by strong reaction, Rodin and, still earlier, his years of arduous study of human anatomy and morphology in the Bucharest Academy of Fine Arts. Those academic studies, though they may have led him to the above-quoted equation of toad with Venus, doubtless contributed to that implicit sense of organic life which informs even his most abstract sculpture.

The Museum's group of Brancusi's sculpture does not yet adequately represent the full range of his forms, nor does it fully demonstrate the sculptor's marvelous mastery of materials since pieces in wood are lamentably lacking.

However, the great grey marble *Fish* is one of Brancusi's capital works. It is the archetype of all fishes—subtly curved, delicately poised; the motionless swimmer, swift, powerful, tense and still.

Bought directly from Miss Pogany herself, her portrait is the original bronze of the earliest version of Brancusi's most celebrated head. The white marble *Maïastra* (the name of a mythical Rumanian bird) is the first in the long series of bird forms of which the shining *Bird in Space* is a later but not yet ultimate version.

The egg—that most perfect of organic forms—seems to be the unstated goal toward which Brancusi's sculpture tends, or an ideal from which it reluctantly departs. The *New-born*, appropriately, is egg-shaped, yet wrinkled brow and bawling mouth are not forgotten within the perfection of polished bronze.

BRANCUSI. *Left to right:*

Maïastra. 1912. Marble, 22″ high, on limestone base 70″ high. Katherine S. Dreier Bequest, 1953.

Bird in Space. 1919. Bronze, 54″ high. Given anonymously, 1934.

Fish. 1930. Marble, 71″ long. Acquired through the Lillie P. Bliss Bequest, 1949.

The New-born. 1920. Bronze after a marble of 1915, $8\frac{1}{4}″$ long, $5\frac{1}{4}″$ high. Acquired through the Lillie P. Bliss Bequest, 1943.

Mlle Pogany. 1913. Bronze, $17\frac{1}{4}″$ high. Acquired through the Lillie P. Bliss Bequest, 1953.

Constantin Brancusi. Rumanian, born 1876; in Paris since 1904. The Museum owns 5 sculptures by Brancusi. (Photo Herbert Matter.)

PEVSNER. *Torso.* 1924-26. Plastic and copper, 29½″ high. Katherine S. Dreier Bequest, 1953. (Photo Soichi Sunami.) Antoine Pevsner. French, born Russia 1886. The Museum owns 1 painting and 3 constructions by Pevsner.

Pevsner, formerly a painter who had known the work of the cubists in Paris, and his younger brother Gabo published their theory of constructivism in their *Realistic Manifesto*, Moscow, 1920, two years or so before the hostility of Soviet officials toward abstract art led to their leaving Russia. They stated, in part:

"One may watch with interest the experiments of the cubists. But these experiments are superficial, not fundamental; and the result is a rendering of volume and decorative surface as in traditional art . . .

"We deny volume as an expression of space. Space can no more be measured by volume than liquid by linear measure. Depth alone can express space. We reject mass as an element of sculpture . . .

"We shape our work as the engineer his bridge, the mathematician his formula of a planetary orbit . . ."

PEVSNER. *Developable Column.* 1942. Brass and oxidized bronze, 20¼″ high. Purchase, 1950. (Photo Herbert Matter.)

"I must affirm in the first place that the art represented — to keep to a specific example — by Gabo's 'Spiral Theme,' is the highest point ever reached by the aesthetic intuition of man. This form, hovering like a still but librating falcon between the visible and the invisible, the material and the immaterial, is the crystallization of the purest sensibility for harmonious relationships: and whereas, in constructivist art generally, this crystallization is a mere planning of static relationships, here an axial system crystallizes energy itself. Creation is a much abused word, applied loosely to imitations and logical constructions: it is justified only for that absolute lyricism we call 'pure poetry,' for music, for certain branches of mathematics, and for constructivism in the plastic arts (which includes architecture). But even within this absolute world there is an hierarchy, and at the summit I would place this spatial construction of Gabo's." —Herbert Read, in *Horizon*, 1942

GABO. *Spiral Theme*. 1941. Plastic, $7\frac{1}{2}''$ high; base $24 \times 24''$. Advisory Committee Fund, 1947. (Photo Soichi Sunami.) Naum Gabo. American, born Russia 1890. The Museum owns 6 constructions by Gabo, 4 of them small models.

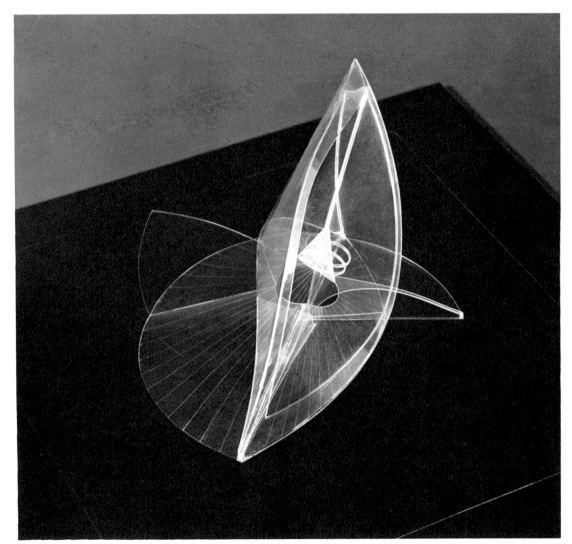

THREE FANTASTS

The intense interest in the esthetic values of form and design which so stimulated the synthetists, page 31, the fauves, pages 46-47, the cubists, pages 67-79, the futurists, pages 98-102 and the various abstractionists, pages 77, 120-121, cumulatively produced after World War I several kinds and degrees of reaction: neo-classicism, for instance, page 81; romantic or objective realism, pages 116, 152, 160, or art with deliberate social or political content, pages 153-157.

But possibly the most important and surely the most original reaction against formal values was the fantastic and anti-rational art of the dadaists, pages 137-139, and the surrealists, pages 140-145. They were anticipated to some extent by late medieval masters such as Bosch, and by Goya and Blake, Ensor and Redon, pages 34-35, but their immediate predecessors were Klee, Chagall and de Chirico. None of these three however took an active part in dada or surrealism, and all three insisted upon the importance of form in their art; Chagall and Klee in fact adapted some of the devices of the cubists.

"Never have I illustrated a literary motif. I have made plastic form, and only afterwards have I taken pleasure when a poetic and a plastic idea 'accidentally' coincide." —Klee, in his diary, 1906

"No one, of course, can deny the importance of the title, *Twittering Machine*, for the Klee here reproduced. The image is laughable to begin with, but to enjoy it fully we must know what manner of machine is shown. Yet once the subject is identified, visual expression takes over completely, and what is portrayed is not a literary idea but an auditory experience, as often happens in Klee's art. And note with what extraordinary subtlety the sound of the image is conveyed. The bird with an exclamation point in its mouth represents the twitter's full volume; the one with an arrow in its beak symbolizes an accompanying shrillness—a horizontal thrust of piercing song. Since a characteristic of chirping birds is that their racket resumes as soon as it seems to be ending, the bird in the center droops with lolling tongue, while another begins to falter in song; both birds will come up again full blast as soon as the machine's crank is turned. The aural impression of thin, persistent sound is heightened by Klee's wiry drawing, and his color plays a contributory part, forming an atmospheric amphitheatre which sustains and amplifies the monotonous twitter."

—James Thrall Soby[76]

KLEE. *Senile Phoenix*. 1905. Etching, $10\frac{1}{8} \times 7\frac{1}{2}''$. Purchase, 1951.

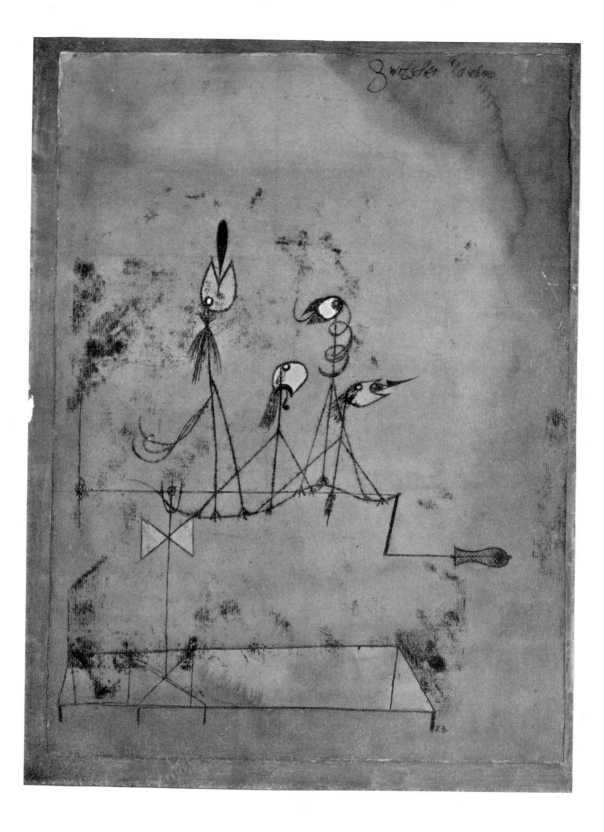

KLEE. *Twittering Machine (Zwitscher-Maschine).* 1922. Water-color and ink, 16¼ × 12″. Purchase, 1939.

"There is a laughter which is to be put on the same dignified level as higher lyrical emotions, and which is as distant as heaven from the convulsions of the vulgar clown!" — Nicolai Gogol, quoted by Klee in his diary, 1904

KLEE. *Little World (Kleinwelt).* 1914. Etching, $5\frac{5}{8} \times 3\frac{3}{4}''$. Purchase, 1951.

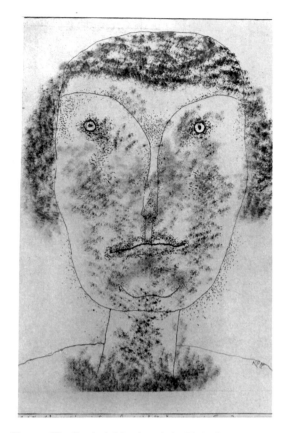

KLEE. *The Crooked Mouth and the Light Green Eyes of Mrs. B. (Der schiefe Mund und die hellgrünen Augen der Frau B.).* 1925. India ink, $6\frac{1}{2} \times 4\frac{1}{4}''$. A. Conger Goodyear Fund, 1950.

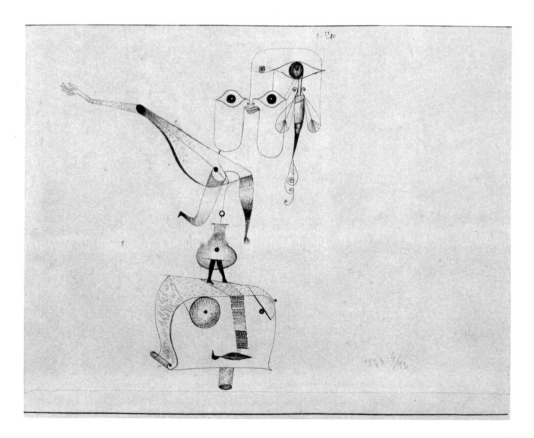

KLEE. *A Balance-Capriccio (Ein Gleichgewicht-Capriccio).* 1923. India ink, $9 \times 12\frac{1}{8}''$. A Conger Goodyear Fund, 1950. Paul Klee. Swiss, 1879-1940; lived in Germany, 1906-1933. The Museum owns 5 oils by Klee, 15 watercolors, and gouaches, 7 drawings, and 75 prints, including 10 in an illustrated book.

KLEE. *Equals Infinity (Gleich Unendlich)*. 1932. Oil, 20¼ × 26⅞″. Acquired through the Lillie P. Bliss Bequest, 1950.

"The release of the graphic elements, their grouping into complex subdivisions, the dissection of the object into different sides and its reconstruction into a whole, the pictorial polyphony, the achievement of balance through an equilibrium of movement—all these are advanced problems of form, decisive for formal knowledge, but not yet art in the highest sense. In the highest sense, an ultimate mystery lies behind the ambiguity which the light of the intellect fails miserably to penetrate."—Klee, 1919

"Art plays an unwitting game with ultimate things, yet achieves them nevertheless . . ."
—Klee, 1919

". . . everything vanishes round me and good works rise from me of their own accord. My hand is entirely the implement of a distant sphere. It is not my head that functions but something else, something higher, something somewhere remote. I must have great friends there, dark as well as bright . . . They are all very kind to me." —Klee, 1918

The cubists had broken up, superimposed and rearranged the objects they painted. Influenced by them, Chagall went further. In *I and the Village* he juggles the remembered images of his native Vitebsk, ignoring natural color, relative size, even the laws of gravity!

On his birthday, a couple of weeks before their marriage, Chagall's fiancée brought him a bouquet. In her autobiography she recalls their rapture: "Soon I forget the flowers. You work with your brushes . . . Your canvas quivers . . . You pour on color . . . Suddenly . . . you jump into the air . . . You float among the rafters. You turn your head and you twist mine too . . . and both together we rise over the clean little room . . ."

"'How do you like my picture?' you ask . . . You wait and are afraid of what I may tell you. 'It's very good . . . you float away so beautifully. We'll call it the Birthday.'"

Opposite: CHAGALL. *I and the Village.* 1911. Oil, $75\frac{5}{8} \times 59\frac{5}{8}''$. Mrs. Simon Guggenheim Fund, 1945.

CHAGALL. *Birthday (L'Anniversaire).* 1915. Oil on cardboard, $31\frac{3}{4} \times 39\frac{1}{4}''$. Acquired through the Lillie P. Bliss Bequest, 1949. Marc Chagall. Born Russia, 1889; has worked in Paris, Moscow, New York, Vence. The Museum owns 5 oils by Chagall, 2 watercolors, 1 pastel, 67 ballet designs, and 278 prints, including 239 in 4 illustrated books.

DE CHIRICO. *Nostalgia of the Infinite.* 1913-14? (dated 1911 on the painting).
Oil, $53\frac{1}{4} \times 25\frac{1}{2}''$. Purchase Fund, 1936.

"The beautiful appearance of the dream world, in the production of which every man is a perfect artist, is the prerequisite of all plastic art."—Nietzsche, *The Birth of Tragedy,* 1872

". . . Thought must so far detach itself from everything which is called logic and sense, it must draw so far away from human fetters, that things may appear to it under a new aspect, as though illuminated by a constellation now appearing for the first time." —de Chirico, 1913

"The last clause in the above quotation gives us another clue to the nature of de Chirico's . . . theories. While the cubists and their disciples wished to tear the visible world to pieces in order to rebuild it from what they considered to be sounder materials, de Chirico wanted to *relight* the painter's world, to restore a sense of the uncanny in suggesting scenes and objects, to give art the bright and disturbing clarity 'of the dream and of the child mind.' In this aim he was, of course, a vital forerunner of the entire surrealist movement."[11]

"The towers series reaches its climax with the *Nostalgia of the Infinite* . . . The composition . . . includes a number of the most effective properties of de Chirico's strange world of reverie—a foreground box or abandoned van, a portico sidling into view, a shadow cast by an unseen presence, two tiny figures dwarfed by their vast setting, empty windows in the tower whose pennants blow vigorously amid an atmosphere otherwise totally inert. The image is especially piercing and memorable in that its thin pigment is astonishingly luminous, almost incandescent, as though lighted from beneath the canvas.

"If the *Nostalgia* evokes an extraordinarily dreamlike illusion of infinite space and quiet, we must not disregard the skillful plastic formality through which the illusion has been achieved. Because de Chirico was intent on restoring to painting a sense of poetic mood (and this in an era when most advanced artists were bitterly repenting romanticism's ecstasies and tears), his early art is often judged solely by lyric as opposed to classical standards, a fact about which he himself protested at the time of his first one-man show, held in Rome in 1919: 'The word *metaphysics* with which I have christened my painting ever since the time I worked in Paris during the subtle and fertile pre-war years, caused annoyance, bad humor and misunderstandings of considerable proportions among the quasi-intellectuals on the banks of the Seine. The customary sarcasm, which soon degenerated into a hackneyed phrase, was: *c'est de la littérature.*'

"It is true, of course, that nearly all de Chirico's early paintings are dominated by their oneirocritical content and in this sense might conceivably be thought 'literary' on casual glance. But the hushed spatial serenity of the *Nostalgia* is achieved through a quite abstract handling of form, testifying to the atavistic impetus of the artist's Renaissance heritage. The image is one of the most concentrated in all de Chirico's early art. It is as well an eloquent illustration of Nietzsche's theory, proposed in *The Will to Power*—'The phenomenal world is the adjusted world which we believe to be real.'"—James Thrall Soby[11]

In 1913 de Chirico (a devout reader of Nietzsche) expanded the curiously "adjusted" phenomena of his paintings to include still life. Then, not long afterwards, he added ominous figures of manikins such as those in the drawing, *The Mathematicians*.

"One of the strangest feelings left to us by prehistory is the sensation of omen. It will always exist. It is like an eternal proof of the non sequitur of the universe. The first man must have seen omens everywhere, he must have shuddered at each step." —de Chirico

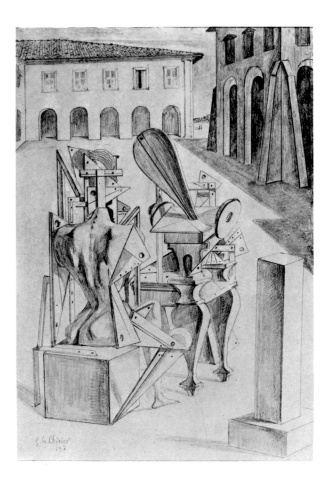

DE CHIRICO. *The Mathematicians.* 1917. Pencil, $12\frac{1}{4} \times 8\frac{5}{8}''$. Gift of Mrs. Stanley Resor, 1935. Giorgio de Chirico. Italian, born 1888. The Museum owns 5 oils by de Chirico, 1 drawing and 17 prints, including 16 in 2 portfolios.

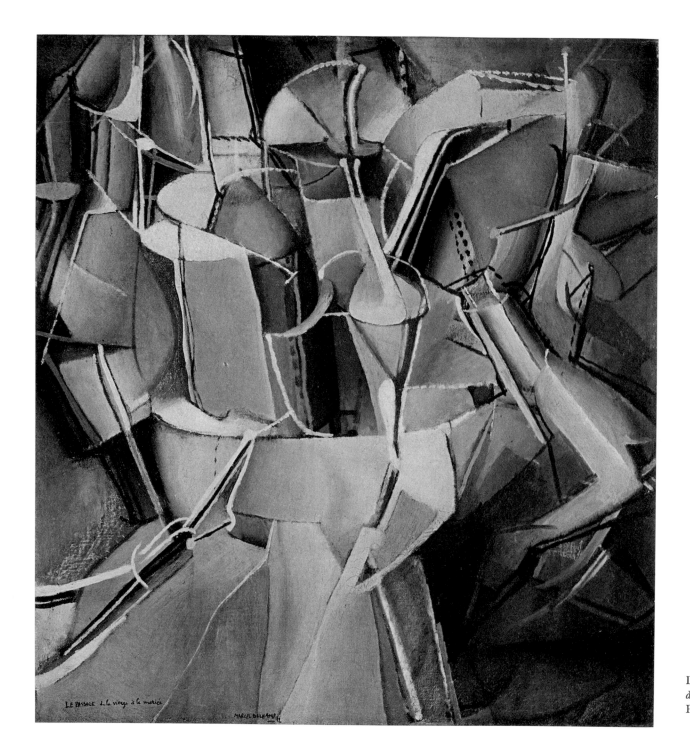

LE PASSAGE à la vierge à la mariée

MARCEL DUCHAMP 12

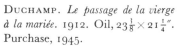

Duchamp. *Le passage de la vierge à la mariée.* 1912. Oil, $23\frac{1}{8} \times 21\frac{1}{4}''$. Purchase, 1945.

A year before it was exhibited in the New York "Armory Show" of 1913, Duchamp's *Nude Descending a Staircase* had aroused controversy in Paris. Duchamp's fellow cubists objected to its "literary" title; whereupon Duchamp, sniffing orthodoxy, withdrew it from their exhibition. *Le passage de la vierge à la mariée*, of the same year, also moves beyond cubism in its ambiguous fusion of mechanical and organic, its arresting title and cryptic sentiment.

DADA AND SURREALISM

The *Passage* was one of Duchamp's last easel pictures. Thus, by the spring of 1913 when the Armory Show made him a famous painter he was to paint very few more canvases. This was three years before dadaism assumed a name.

"Dada," Duchamp later remarked to James Sweeney, "was a metaphysical attitude . . . a sort of nihilism . . . a way to get out of a state of mind—to avoid being influenced by one's immediate environment, or by the past: to get away from clichés—to get free."[80]

No artist has ever guarded his freedom with a more scrupulous conscience: "I have forced myself to contradict myself in order to avoid conforming to my own taste."

3 stoppages étalon was a radical gesture against painting, against "café and studio platitudes," and against the conventional certitudes of science. With laconic precision Duchamp described this "anti-artistic" experiment: *Un mètre de fil droit, horizontal, tombé d'un mètre de haut* (A meter of taut thread, horizontal, dropped from a meter's height). Thrice repeated, the experiment was then recorded by fixing the three threads to glass panels and finally by using their accidental contours as templets for three wooden "yardsticks." Thus was the meter mocked and the *étalon* (standard) traduced by the laws of chance.

Though imitated by abstract painters, Duchamp's "small glass" (at the right) is thoroughly dada in its title and its elaborate mockery of a scientific or mathematical demonstration.

DUCHAMP. *To be looked at with one eye, close to, for almost an hour.* 1918. Oil, collage, etc. on glass, $20\frac{1}{8}$" high × $16\frac{1}{8}$" wide × $1\frac{3}{8}$" deep. Katherine S. Dreier Bequest, 1953.

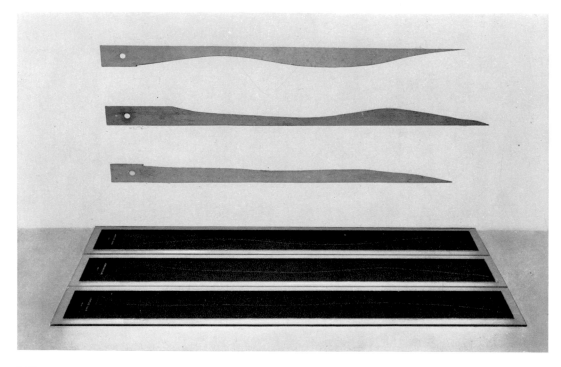

DUCHAMP. *3 stoppages étalon.* 1913-14. Three threads glued on three glass panels $49\frac{1}{2} \times 7\frac{1}{4}$" each; three flat wooden strips repeating the curves of the threads, averaging $44\frac{1}{4}$" in length. Katherine S. Dreier Bequest, 1953. Marcel Duchamp. American, born in France, 1887. The Museum owns 2 oils, 4 dada objects and constructions, 1 collage, designs for chessmen and 1 film (page 211) by Duchamp.

137

Right: MAN RAY. *Admiration of the Orchestrelle for the Cinematograph.* 1919. Airbrush, 26 × 21½". Gift of A. Conger Goodyear, 1937. Man Ray. American, born 1890; lives in Paris. The Museum owns 1 painting, 121 photographs, 36 "rayographs" (see page 189), 3 films and a chess set (page 227) by Ray.

Below: ERNST. *The Little Tear Gland That Says Tic Tac (La petite fistule lacrimale qui dit tic tac).* 1920. Gouache on wallpaper, 14¼ × 10".Purchase, 1935. Max Ernst. American, born Germany 1891; France 1922-1941, then U.S.A. The Museum owns 8 oils by Ernst, 2 gouaches, 10 collages, etc., 1 sculpture and 44 prints, including 8 in a portfolio, 23 in 4 books, and 1 poster (page 229).

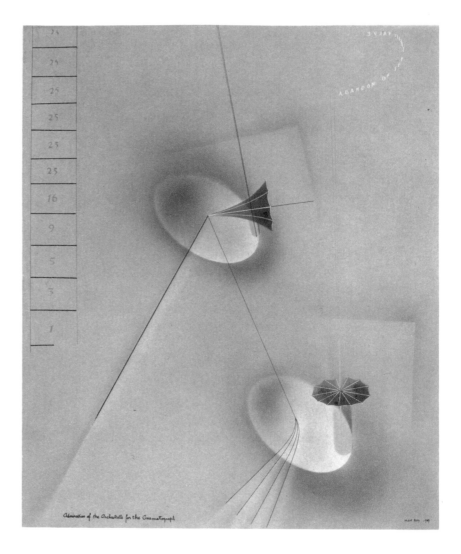

Dada was named in Zurich in 1916 but it began independently a year or so earlier in New York. Duchamp was its leader, Man Ray among his chief abettors, Stieglitz' gallery at 291 Fifth Avenue its headquarters, and the magazine "291" its chief organ.

Machine fantasies preoccupied the dadaists wherever they were. In Man Ray's airbrushed "aerograph" the "orchestrelle" (an invented word for a mechanical orchestra) is symbolized by the phonograph horn which, flattened out below, suggests a merry-go-round. Above, like a pennant, waves the slogan ABANDON THE SAFETY VALVE. The admired cinematograph is represented by a film strip with each frame numbered to indicate acceleration until a constant projection speed is reached.

After the armistice of 1918 dada groups sprang up in Paris and in revolutionary Germany. Max Ernst, aided for a time by Hans Arp, led the movement in Cologne. His dada machine-joke, like Man Ray's, involves time, sound and movement. In addition, anatomy, physiology, mechanics and an absurd pathos are mingled in subtle visual nonsense.

Dada in Berlin was bitter and violent and politically involved as George Grosz' anti-military drawing on page 153 suggests. That exclamation of fury was drawn two years before Grosz pasted a machine-heart upon a criminalized portrait of his close friend John Heartfield, a fellow dadaist and an expert master of photomontage.

In Hannover, Kurt Schwitters was active as a one-man dada movement in poetry, prose and architecture as well as painting and sculpture and, more often, collage. His collages are composed with exquisite taste of jetsam salvaged from the

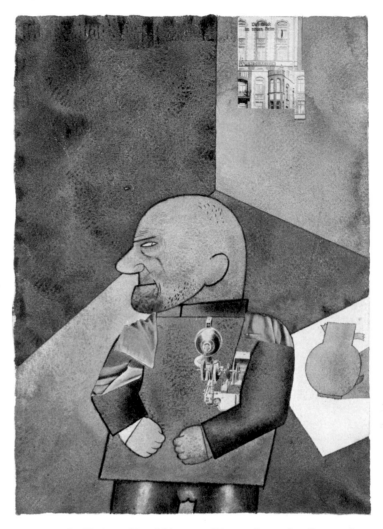

GROSZ. *The Engineer Heartfield*. 1920. Watercolor and collage, 16 × 11¼". Gift of General A. Conger Goodyear, 1952.

SCHWITTERS. *Merz 83: Drawing F (Zeichnung F)*. 1920. Collage of cut paper wrappers, announcements, tickets, 5¼ × 4½". Katherine S. Dreier Bequest, 1953. Kurt Schwitters. German, 1887-1948. The Museum owns 23 collages and 15 prints by Schwitters.

streets. Schwitters identified his work in all media by a single word of his own invention: *Merz*. "*Merz*," he explained, "stands for freedom from all fetters . . . Freedom is not lack of restraint, but the product of strict artistic discipline."

Though dadaists such as Schwitters and Duchamp demonstrated their genuine passion for both freedom and discipline in their work, these commendable ideals do not explain dada. Outraged by the stupidity and folly of World War I and its aftermaths, the dadaists declared war against the conventions, tastes and standards of respectable society, even against reason itself. Yet because some of them were men of great talent they produced from their anarchic anger and ennui works of art of originality and lasting interest. Furthermore they abruptly broadened the horizons of art, preparing the way for new developments, among them surrealism.

"Art is a fruit which grows out of a man like fruit out of a plant like a child out of a mother. While the fruit of a plant has its own form quite unlike that of a balloon or a president in a cutaway the artistic fruit of man shows a ridiculous tendency to imitate the appearance of other things . . . I love nature but not its substitutes." In these often-quoted words from his "dada diary," Hans (later Jean) Arp, the leading artist among the Zurich dadaists, declared art's independence and at last provided Maurice Denis' famous "battle horse" of 1890 (page 79) with a rider—no less than a "president in a cutaway." Obviously, since the French kindergarten word for hobbyhorse is *dada*.

Birds in an Aquarium is characteristic of Arp's jigsawn dada reliefs both in title and in form. Its soft, asymmetric, curving contours seem related to clouds, lakes and amoebas. *Human Concretion*, fifteen years later, is the epitome of organic abstraction—or more correctly "concretion," the term preferred by Arp and his mentor, Kandinsky. "I remember," Arp writes, "a discussion with Mondrian in which he distinguished between art and nature, saying that art is artificial and nature natural. I do not share his opinion. I believe that nature is not in opposition to art. Art is of natural origin . . . spiritualized through man's sublimation."

ARP. *Birds in an Aquarium.* c. 1920. Painted wood relief, $9\frac{7}{8} \times 8''$. Purchase, 1937. (Photo Soichi Sunami.)

ARP. *Human Concretion.* 1935. Cast stone, $19\frac{1}{2}''$ high. Gift of the Advisory Committee, 1937. (Photo Herbert Matter.) Jean (Hans) Arp. French, born Alsace, 1888. The Museum owns 1 oil by Arp, 1 collage, 7 painted wood or string reliefs, 67 prints and a rug after his design.

"The Surrealists drew from darkest abysses of their instincts those forces which had been ignored by tacit consent, and gave form to the painful, disquieting, exciting metamorphoses of the subconscious. Like the German Romanticists, they did not shrink from hailing the night as 'liberator,' and gave to dreams and hallucinations an honored place in their poems, their pictures and even their lives. Reasonableness they stigmatized as a hoax which hides love and poetry from us with a veil of hypocrisy."—André Masson at the Baltimore Museum of Art, 1941

Masson's *Battle of Fishes* may well have been drawn and painted in a quasi-automatic technique "without any esthetic or moral preoccupation"; and its sadistic creatures lacerating each other among patches of underwater sand and blood do anticipate the injunction of the surrealist pontiff, André Breton: "Beauty will be convulsive or will not be." Yet, with all its Freudian savagery, the subject seems sublimated by the art of one of the best French painters of his generation.

In contrast to the passionate, feverish line of Masson, Max Ernst's surrealism is meditative, ingenious, exploratory, even humorous. His poetry is less violent, more complex, and his forms range from the abstract to an expert magic realism which anticipates Dali. In *Birds above the Forest*, by striating the paint with a comb, he unites in a mysterious community of texture the forms of flying creatures and the forest out of which they soar into nocturnal blackness.

ERNST. *Birds above the Forest.* 1929 Oil, 31¼ × 25¼″. Katherine S. Dreier Bequest, 1953.

MASSON. *Battle of Fishes.* 1927. Oil, sand, pencil, 14¼ × 28¼″. Purchase, 1937. André Masson. French, born 1896; in U.S.A. 1941-46. The Museum owns 3 oils, 2 pastels, 1 collage, 3 drawings by Masson, and 44 prints including 17 in 4 books and 12 in a portfolio.

About the time he painted *Catalan Landscape*, Miro was nearly starving. He recalls that he used in his compositions "drawings into which I put the hallucinations provoked by my hunger." He also saw much of the surrealist poets. Under their influence he concluded that in painting "one must go beyond form to achieve poetry."[42]

The *Catalan Landscape* is indeed a poem as well as a composition of form and color. Its similes and metonymies are far-fetched but explicable. The letters SARD refer to the *sardana*, a Catalan dance, and from a top-shaped ship at sea flies the Spanish naval flag. The picture's subtitle, *The Hunter*, identifies the principal human figure who stands mustached and bearded, a pipe in his mouth, a heart palpitating in his breast; his right hand holds his leashed dog, his left a flaming gun; a trail winds before him. Across the foreground races a rabbit with frightened eye and triangular tail. In the distance is a round tree with a leaf and beyond that the hunter's eye or perhaps the sun, the "eye of day," as Shakespeare put it.

A decade later, in 1933, Miro produced a magnificent series of large paintings, among them the Museum's *Composition*. Against a softly atmospheric background are suspended silhouetted or outlined forms which suggest a pastoral with a seated dog and horned cattle. The composition is remarkable in Miro's art for its serenity and elegance.

MIRO. *Catalan Landscape (The Hunter)*. 1923-24. Oil, $25\frac{1}{2} \times 39\frac{1}{2}''$. Purchase, 1936.

MIRO. *Composition.* 1933. Oil, $68\frac{1}{2} \times 77\frac{1}{4}''$. Gift of the Advisory Committee, 1937. Joan Miro. Spanish, born 1893; worked in Paris. The Museum owns 9 oils by Miro, 1 gouache, 1 drawing, 139 prints, including 94 in 2 books and 15 in a portfolio, 1 relief, and a rug after his design.

TANGUY. *Mama, Papa Is Wounded!* 1927. Oil, $36\frac{1}{4} \times 28\frac{1}{4}''$. Purchase, 1936. Yves Tanguy. American, born France, 1900. The Museum owns 3 oils, 1 gouache, 2 drawings, 20 prints and a copper plate by Tanguy.

DALI. *The Persistence of Memory.* 1931. Oil, $9\frac{1}{2} \times 13''$. Given anonymously, 1934. Salvador Dali. Spanish, born 1904; in U.S.A. since 1940. The Museum owns 3 oils by Dali, 1 drawing and 47 prints including 44 in 2 books.

OPPENHEIM. *Fur-covered Cup, Saucer and Spoon.* 1936. Purchase, 1946. Study Collection. Meret Oppenheim. Swiss, born 1913.

Tanguy, and later Dali, in their pursuit of the marvelous, follow de Chirico into a vivid hallucinatory world "where anything can happen." All achieve an emphatic illusion of depth but Tanguy alone fills his "realistic" space exclusively with invented, unrealistic forms. Thus he foregoes the complex associations of familiar images, creating instead ultralunar landscapes with their own unique flora and fauna.

Tanguy paints slowly and speaks reluctantly about his art. Not so, Dali: "Be persuaded that Salvador Dali's famous limp watches are nothing else than the tender, extravagant and arbitrary paranoiac-critical camembert of time and space . . ."

Of all the surrealist "objects of concrete irrationality" Meret Oppenheim's *Fur-covered Cup, Saucer and Spoon* is the most renowned. It has exerted a disquieting fascination comparable to that of Dali's limp watches. Cornell's object-poem, *Taglioni's Jewel Casket,* in spite of its glass ice-cubes, is perhaps more neo-romantic than surrealist.

CORNELL. *Taglioni's Jewel Casket.* 1940. Jewelry, glass, etc. in a wooden box, $11\frac{7}{8}''$ long. Labeled: "On a moonlight night in the winter of 1835 the carriage of Marie Taglioni was halted by a Russian highwayman, and that enchanting creature commanded to dance for this audience of one upon a panther's skin spread over the snow beneath the stars. From this actuality arose the legend that to keep alive the memory of this adventure so precious to her, Taglioni formed the habit of placing a piece of artificial ice in her jewel casket or dressing table where, melting among the sparkling stones, there was evoked a hint of the atmosphere of the starlit heavens over the ice-covered landscape." Gift of James Thrall Soby, 1953. Joseph Cornell. American, born 1903. The Museum owns 3 object-poems by Cornell.

SCULPTORS AND CONSTRUCTORS: THE MIDDLE GENERATION

Of the sculptors and constructors born about the year 1900 three stand out: the American, Alexander Calder, the Englishman, Henry Moore and the Swiss, Alberto Giacometti. All three were affected by the kind of near-abstract art closely associated with surrealism. And all three, it is worth noting, share one great distinction: each is the first native sculptor in the history of his country's art to have won a great international reputation.

Early in 1932, just before they were first exhibited, Calder asked Marcel Duchamp what he should call his new moving constructions.[7] Duchamp (pages 136-137) immediately answered "mobiles." A year earlier, Jean Arp (page 140) had named Calder's first static constructions "stabiles." The nomenclature of Calder's art could scarcely have had more distinguished sponsors, though Mondrian was a greater inspiration to Calder, and Miro had greater influence upon his art.

Of his mobiles Calder said in 1951: "I think that . . . the underlying sense of form in my work has been the system of the Universe, or part thereof . . . a rather large model to work from.

"What I mean is that the idea of detached bodies floating in space, of different sizes and densities, perhaps of different colors and temperatures . . . and some at rest, while others move in peculiar manners, seems to me the ideal source of form . . . I would have them deployed, some nearer together and some at immense distances . . . And great disparity among all the qualities of these bodies, and their motions as well.

"Then there is the idea of an object floating —not supported. The use of a very long thread . . . seems to best approximate this freedom from the earth.

"Thus what I produce is not precisely what I have in mind—but a sort of sketch, a man-made approximation.

"That others grasp what I have in mind seems unessential, at least as long as they have something else in theirs."[109]

CALDER. *Whale.* 1937. Stabile, sheet steel, 6′6″ high. Gift of the artist, 1950. (Photo Soichi Sunami.) Alexander Calder. American, born 1898. The Museum owns 1 sculpture by Calder, 3 "wire drawings," 3 mobiles, 1 stabile, 1 constellation, 1 print and a necklace.

CALDER. *Lobster Trap and Fish Tail*. 1939. Mobile, steel wire and sheet aluminum, about $8\frac{1}{2}'$ high, about $9\frac{1}{2}'$ diameter. Commissioned by the Advisory Committee for the Museum stair well, 1939. (Photo Frank Lerner.)

MOORE. *The Bride*. 1940. Cast lead and copper wire, 9⅛″ high. Acquired through the Lillie P. Bliss Bequest, 1947. (Photo Soichi Sunami.) Henry Moore. British, born 1898. The Museum owns 6 sculptures, 4 drawings and 12 prints by Moore.

Henry Moore has been a student of medieval and primitive sculpture and generously acknowledges his debt to such older contemporaries as Brancusi, Picasso and Arp. Particularly during the late 1930s, Moore was preoccupied with the synthesis of abstract form and surrealist psychological researches. In 1937, a few years after he had done *Two Forms*, Moore wrote: "The meaning and significance of form itself probably depends on the countless associations of man's history. For example, rounded forms convey an idea of fruitfulness, maturity, probably because the earth, women's breasts, and most fruits are rounded, and these shapes are important because they have this background in our habits of perception. I think the humanist organic element will always be for me of fundamental importance in sculpture, giving sculpture its vitality."

Moore's countrymen, recognizing that they have in their midst a great sculptor, have given him during the past decade a number of monumental commissions, among them a *Madonna and Child* for a church at Northampton and the *Family Group* for the grounds of a school in Hertfordshire. (Recently he completed an important American commission, four huge abstract figures for the *Time-Life* building in London.)

The *Family Group* was studied and restudied over a period of five years in scores of drawings and clay sketches. The final large version of which the Museum owns a cast is one of Moore's most complex compositions.

MOORE. *Two Forms*. 1934. Pynkado wood, 11″ high. Gift of Sir Michael Sadler, 1937. (Photo Soichi Sunami.)

MOORE. *Family Group*. 1945-49. Bronze, 59¼" high. A. Conger Goodyear Fund, 1951. *Family Group* was commissioned for the Barclay School at Stevenage, Hertfordshire. The Museum's cast is the second. (Photo Soichi Sunami.)

GIACOMETTI. *The Palace at 4 A.M.* 1932-33. Construction in wood, glass, wire, string, 25″ high. Purchase, 1936. (Photo Herbert Matter.)

In 1933, at the height of his surrealist activity, Giacometti published in *Minotaure* some notes about *The Palace at 4 A.M.*, now perhaps his best-known work:

"For years now I have made only sculptures which have already appeared complete in my mind's eye. My function has been to reproduce them in three dimensions without changing the slightest detail and without asking myself at the moment what their meaning could be . . . Once the piece has been constructed, I tend to remember images, impressions, events which have moved me deeply though often unconsciously . . .

"For example, take the sculpture representing a palace. This object took shape little by little in the late summer of 1932. By autumn it was so precise an image that to execute it took me no more than a day. It is related without any doubt to a period in my life which had come to an end a year earlier, when six whole months, hour by hour, were passed in the company of a woman who, concentrating all life in herself, magically transformed my every moment . . . In the night we used to construct a fantastic palace out of matchsticks. At the least mistaken movement, the whole miniature construction would collapse: and always we would start it over again.

"I do not know why it came to be inhabited by a backbone in a cage—the backbone the woman sold me . . . on one of the first nights I met her in the street—and by one of the skeleton birds which she saw the very night before our life together came to an end—the skeleton birds which were hovering high up . . . in the great unroofed hall among exclamations of astonishment at four o'clock in the morning.

"In the middle rose the scaffolding of a tower, its top perhaps unfinished, perhaps fallen in ruin. On the other side there appeared the statue of a woman in which I recognized my mother, just as she impressed me in my earliest memories. The mystery of her long black dress touching the floor troubled me: apparently a part of her body, it frightened and confused me . . . This figure stands against the same curtain thrice repeated, the very curtain I saw when I opened my eyes for the first time. Fascinated, I fixed my gaze upon this brown curtain beneath which, along the polished floor, filtered a narrow gleam of light . . .

"I can say nothing of the object in front of the board . . . I identify it with myself."

Of the recent *Chariot*, that image of delicately balanced instability, Giacometti wrote Pierre Matisse in words which are both circumstantial and baffling:

"In 1938, at the Bachet Hospital I was astonished by a clinking wagon which was being wheeled around the room. In 1947 I saw the sculpture as clearly as if it already existed before my eyes, and in 1950 it was already situated in the past; but this is not the only motive that impelled me to do this sculpture.

"The *Chariot* was done because of the necessity of having the figure in empty space in order to see it better and to situate it at a precise distance from the floor."

GIACOMETTI. *Chariot*. 1950. Bronze, 57″ high. Purchase, 1951. (Photo Eliot Elisofon). Alberto Giacometti. Swiss, born 1901; works in France. The Museum owns 4 sculptures, 1 painting and 8 prints by Giacometti.

PORTRAITS

Portraiture, once a major branch of painting, has largely sunk into the hands of fashionable specialists. Nevertheless, as in the past, the best portraits are painted by artists of broader achievement whose chief concerns are other than a flattering rendering of likeness.

BÉRARD. *Portrait of Jean Cocteau.* 1928. Oil, $25\frac{5}{8} \times 21\frac{1}{4}''$. Mrs. John D. Rockefeller, Jr. Purchase Fund, 1940. Christian Bérard. French, 1902-49. The Museum owns 2 oils and 1 theatre design by Bérard.

Some of the most distinguished portraits done in Paris during the last quarter century are by the neo-romantic painter and theatre designer "Bébé" Bérard. Many of these are of the artist's friends such as the poet, Jean Cocteau, page 13. And so are several portraits by Balthus who throughout the 1930s stubbornly maintained the realist tradition of Courbet, in that decade less prevalent in Paris than it was in the 1920s or is now. His beautifully painted portrait of Miro and his young daughter is affectionate yet unflinchingly direct and honest.

BALTHUS. *Joan Miro and His Daughter Dolores.* 1937-38. Oil, $51\frac{1}{4} \times 35''$. Mrs. John D. Rockefeller, Jr. Purchase Fund, 1938. Balthus (Balthasar Klossowsky). French, born 1908. The Museum owns 2 oils by Balthus.

PROTEST AND SATIRE

In the social, political and military turmoil of the twentieth century, artists have been embroiled along with their fellow citizens. Under the Fascist and Soviet dictatorships, indeed wherever politicians impose their ignorant and vulgar prejudices upon the artist and his supporters, very little art of quality has been forthcoming. By far the best art of social significance, even by communists, has been produced in the unregimented Western democracies where artists along with workers, business men, and farmers continue to share the benefits and disappointments of a comparatively free culture.

Powerful graphic artists assaulted the *status quo* in Germany at the end of World War I, though Käthe Kollwitz had several years before been persecuted by the Kaiser. George Grosz is unsurpassed in the savage humor of his attacks on militarism and bourgeois complacency; but Otto Dix's war etchings are completely humorless: he had fought four years on the Western Front.

GROSZ. *Fit for Active Service*. 1918. Pen, brush and India ink, $14\frac{5}{8} \times 13\frac{1}{8}''$. Purchase, 1947. George Grosz. American, born Germany 1893; to U.S.A. 1932. The Museum owns 2 oils by Grosz, 2 watercolors, 1 collage, 5 drawings and 33 prints, including 19 in 2 portfolios.

DIX. *Meeting a Madman at Night*. From the portfolio *Der Krieg*. 1924. Etching, aquatint and drypoint, $10\frac{1}{4} \times 7\frac{5}{8}''$. Gift of Mrs. John D. Rockefeller, Jr., 1934. Otto Dix. German, born 1891. The Museum owns 2 oils by Dix, 1 watercolor, 1 drawing and 64 prints, including 59 in 2 portfolios.

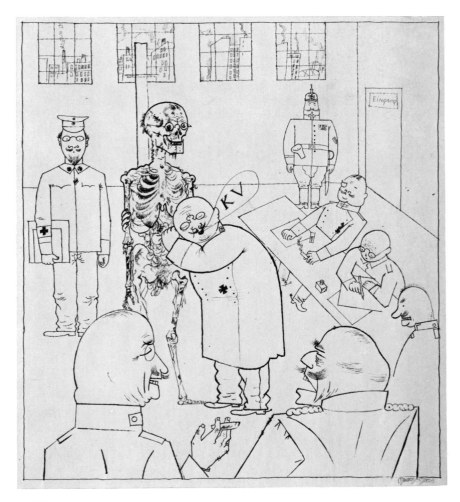

RIVERA. *Agrarian Leader Zapata*. 1931. Fresco, 7'9¼" × 6'2". Commissioned by Mrs. John D. Rockefeller, Jr. for the Rivera exhibition at the Museum, 1931. Purchase, 1940. Diego Rivera. Mexican, born 1886. The Museum owns 1 fresco, 2 oils, 1 watercolor, a sketchbook of 45 watercolors, 7 drawings, 24 ballet designs and 9 prints by Rivera.

In Mexican mural painting twentieth-century social comment is raised to an heroic scale. Its most famous master, Diego Rivera, painted his frescoes in Mexico and the United States (the U.S.S.R. snubbed him) during the period 1925-1935. His *Agrarian Leader Zapata* may be compared with Orozco's dynamic *Zapatistas* (next page).

Orozco painted *Dive Bomber and Tank* in the Museum before the eyes of the public during the last days of June, 1940 while the world was still reeling from the fall of France. Asked to explain his sinister grey allegory Orozco replied: "The public refuses to SEE painting. They want to HEAR painting . . . they prefer to LISTEN to the barker . . . Free lectures every hour for the blind, around the Museum. This way, please . . ."

OROZCO. *Dive Bomber and Tank*. 1940. Fresco, 9′ × 18′, on six panels 9′ × 3′ each. Commissioned through the Mrs. John D. Rockefeller, Jr. Purchase Fund, 1940. Orozco is seen at the right of the photograph finishing the mural.

"A painting is a poem," Orozco continued, "and nothing else. A poem made of relationships between forms as other kinds of poems are made of the relationships between words, sounds or ideas."[48]

Such "anti-humanist" contempt for the puzzled public and such a "formalist" definition of painting might well have been assailed by his communist rivals. But Orozco's great spirit was anarchic and angrily anti-totalitarian, politically, socially and religiously. The epic heroism of his frescoes of the peons' rebellion is recalled in his most famous easel painting, *Zapatistas*.

Siqueiros, the third of the great Mexican muralists, is also a master of pictorial fury. Though politically an orthodox communist, the surrealist shock of his imagery, his symbolic use of color, and the brutal violence of his drawing have nothing in common with pedestrian Socialist Realism.

Opposite: OROZCO. *Zapatistas.* 1931. Oil, 45 × 55″. Given anonymously, 1937. José Clemente Orozco. Mexican, 1883-1949. The Museum owns 1 six-section fresco, 5 oils, 1 tempera, 4 drawings and 14 prints by Orozco.

SIQUEIROS. *Echo of a Scream.* 1937. Duco on wood, 48 × 36″. Gift of Edward M. M. Warburg, 1939. David Alfaro Siqueiros. Mexican, born 1898. The Museum owns 6 duco paintings and 4 prints by Alfaro Siqueiros.

157

Cândido Portinari of Brazil, the best known painter of South America, is concerned less with the revolutionary violence which moves the Mexicans than with the understanding portrayal of the poor at work on coffee plantations or fishing or dancing on St. John's Day. *Fishermen* demonstrates his brilliance as a draftsman, his sympathy as a man.

The municipal triumvirate who grace Jack Levine's *The Feast of Pure Reason* illustrate some remarks of his written in 1938: "... It is my privilege to put these gentlemen on trial, to give them every ingratiating characteristic they might normally have, and then paint them, smiles, benevolence and all, in my own terms ...

"The artist must sit in judgment and intelligently evaluate the case for any aspect of the world he deals with. The validity of his work will rest on the humanity of his decision." [73]

Above: PORTINARI. *Fishermen.* 1940. Brushing in oil, $25\frac{1}{4} \times 19\frac{5}{8}''$. Purchase, 1941. Cândido Portinari. Brazilian, born 1903. The Museum owns 1 mural, 2 oils, 2 drawings and 9 prints by Portinari.

LEVINE. *The Feast of Pure Reason.* 1937. Oil, $42 \times 48''$. Extended loan, from the U.S. WPA Art Program. Jack Levine. American, born 1915. The Museum owns 1 oil by Levine and has 2 on extended loan.

While on view at the Tate Gallery, London, Butler's prize-winning model for a monument to the Unknown Political Prisoner was destroyed by a refugee artist who denounced it as anti-humanistic rubbish. Newspapers and academic sculptors attacked it as "futuristic" and "abstract."

Unlike the Washington Monument in Washington, or the Cenotaph in London—and contrary to hasty and prejudiced press accounts—Butler's design is not at all abstract. To many thoughtful and receptive observers, it is a movingly dramatic and human conception.

The construction is ambiguous but relevant in that it suggests a cage, a gibbet or a guard's watch tower. The artist did not wish to tie the imagination to a literal setting. For the same reason he preferred to suggest the prisoner's invisible presence at the scene of his sufferings rather than to show his physical body.

In the highest sense the design seems humanistic without being banal or sentimental. The three great bronze women who stand in watchful meditation beneath the empty scaffold-cage give it meaning, pathos and dignity and recall the women beneath the cross or at the empty tomb of another "political prisoner" of two thousand years ago.

Vespigniani's sensitive drawing of a hanged partisan prisoner is more explicit. The artist was himself for a brief time a political prisoner.

BUTLER. *The Unknown Political Prisoner (Project for a monument)*. 1952. Bronze with stone base, 17⅞" high. Mrs. Saidie A. May Fund, 1953. Replica substituted for the original model which was damaged during the exhibition of the international competition at the Tate Gallery, London, 1953. It had won the first prize. The design calls for three bronze figures 8 feet high. (Photo Soichi Sunami.) Reg Butler. British, born 1913. The Museum owns 3 sculptures, 1 drawing and 1 print by Butler.

VESPIGNANI. *Hanged Man.* 1949. Ink, 15⅞ × 7¼". Purchase, 1950. Renzo Vespignani. Italian, born 1924. The Museum has 4 drawings and 2 prints by Vespignani.

ALBRIGHT. *Woman.* 1928. Oil, 33 × 22″. Given anonymously, 1948. Ivan Le Lorraine Albright. American, born 1897. The Museum owns 1 oil, 1 sculpture and 2 prints by Albright.

AMERICAN SHARP-FOCUS PAINTING

Picturesque dilapidation in a painting, whether of a woman or of great Rome herself, need not spring from a romantic love of ruins, even when every wrinkle, every tumbled brick is rendered.

Albright writes[72] of his exacting art with unromantic irony: "I have painted herrings that changed from purple to an orange oxide, women whose torrid flesh folds resembled corrugated mush, lemons and artificial fur . . . But all things, whether a bluebottle fly or red flying hair, have had their points and counterpoints and . . . I will amuse myself looking . . . through my ill-ground bifocal glasses that make an aberration next to the object I am looking at."

Peter Blume's painting of a city, opposite, suggests perspectives of time, centuries of cumulative construction and disintegration, immeasurable complexities of human vulgarity, courage, misery, corruption, and hope.

Loren MacIver's city is simply a two-by-three-foot stretch of macadam. It shows no ruts worn by chariot wheels but its graffito might have been chalked in Rome, for children's games change little.

"Quite simple things lead to discovery . . ." MacIver writes,[86] "This is what I would like to do with painting: starting with simple things, to lead the eye by various manipulations of colors, objects and tensions toward a transformation and a reward . . . My wish is to make something permanent out of the transitory, by means at once dramatic and colloquial . . . "

MacIver. *Hopscotch.* 1940. Oil, 27 × 35⅞″. Purchase, 1940. Loren MacIver. American, born 1909. The Museum owns 3 oils by MacIver.

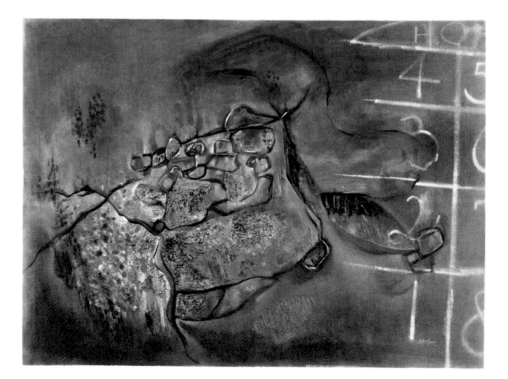

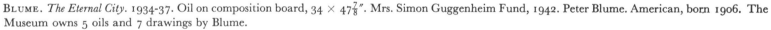

BLUME. *The Eternal City*. 1934-37. Oil on composition board, 34 × 47⅞″. Mrs. Simon Guggenheim Fund, 1942. Peter Blume. American, born 1906. The Museum owns 5 oils and 7 drawings by Blume.

In 1932 Peter Blume visited Italy on a Guggenheim Fellowship. After a six months' stay he came back determined to put what he had seen and felt and thought into one picture. Five years later, after arduous effort, *The Eternal City* was finished.

Over a fantastically elaborate vision of violence, beauty and decay scowls the head of Mussolini, inspired, the artist writes, by a papier-maché, jack-in-the-box-like statue of the dictator seen in Rome. "I made the head strident, like nothing else in the picture: antithesis, dissonance. It hurt me aesthetically to paint the head but . . . the question of harmony was superseded by other considerations."

The Eternal City may be compared with Boccioni's ebullient allegory, *The City Rises*, page 99. Rome and Milan differ significantly but so do the paintings' dates: 1935 and 1910.

SHAHN. *Handball.* 1939. Tempera on paper, $22\frac{1}{4} \times 31\frac{1}{4}''$. Mrs. John D. Rockefeller, Jr. Purchase Fund, 1940. Ben Shahn. American, born 1898. The Museum owns 9 paintings, 1 drawing and 13 prints by Shahn; also posters and book illustrations.

"The artist, perhaps more than the grocer or the ice-man, is natively inclined to try to peer into the truth of things. In a way, it might be said that he has a vested interest in truth. It is his business to present to the world new aspects of reality. Thus, in developing his own outlook, in clarifying his beliefs, in creating his own style of work, his significant imagery, he must constantly seek wider understanding. He has to know what he thinks in order to communicate to others . . .

"Of our fine art there are the two main streams, one humanistic, necessarily asking the question, 'to what end?' greatly concerned with the implications of man's way of life; the other, the abstract and non-objective . . .

"It is the mission of art to remind man from time to time that he is human, and the time is ripe, just now, today, for such a reminder."

—Ben Shahn, at the University of Buffalo, 1951

"My aim is to escape from the medium with which I work. To leave no residue of technical mannerisms to stand between my expression and the observer. To seek freedom through significant form and design rather than through the diversion of so-called free and accidental brush handling . . . Not to exhibit craft, but rather to submerge it, and make it rightfully the handmaiden of beauty, power and emotional content." —Wyeth, 1943 [72]

Christina, Wyeth writes, is his neighbor. "Her physical limitations are appalling. The challenge to me was to do justice to her extraordinary conquest of a life which most people would consider hopeless. Christina's world is outwardly limited—but in this painting I tried to convey how unlimited it really is."

WYETH. *Christina's World*. 1948. Tempera on gesso panel, $32\frac{1}{4} \times 47\frac{1}{4}''$. Purchase, 1949. Andrew Wyeth. American, born 1917.

RECENT ROMANTIC AND SURREALIST PAINTING

"I paint to rest from the phenomena of the external world . . . and to make notations of its essences with which to verify the inner eye." —Morris Graves[73]

"I've never been too much affected by birds . . . but when I first saw Morris Graves' *Blind Bird* I felt as if a new dimension had been added to me personally. This was a great work of the spirit . . ." —Ben Shahn to Selden Rodman[119]

GRAVES. *Blind Bird.* 1940. Gouache, $30\frac{1}{8} \times 27''$. Purchase, 1942.
Morris Graves. American, born 1910. The Museum owns 13 gouaches and watercolors and 4 drawings by Graves, and has 4 wax paintings on extended loan.

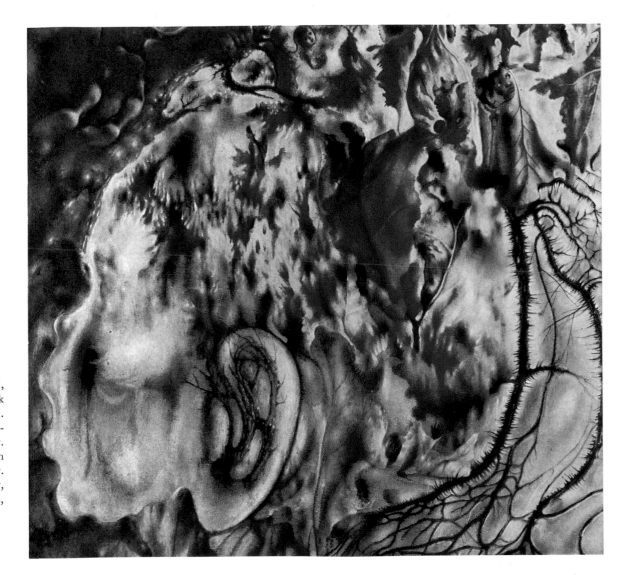

TCHELITCHEW. Head of Winter. Detail, about 27×29″, to the right of the tree trunk in *Hide-and-Seek (Cache-cache)*. 1940-42. Oil, 6′6½″ × 7′¼″. Mrs. Simon Guggenheim Fund, 1942. Pavel Tchelitchew. American, born Russia, 1898; worked in Berlin, Paris, England, U.S.A., Italy. The Museum owns 1 oil by Tchelitchew, 7 gouaches and watercolors, 10 drawings, and 90 ballet designs.

In Sussex in 1934 Tchelitchew sketched an ancient gnarled oak. "It took eight years," he wrote later, "for this tree to grow and become *Hide-and-Seek*." In 1938, after the image had lain fallow in his mind for a long time, he first drew the tree as two hands, and then, in the drawing at the left, with finger-branches reaching up from a foot which presses its toe-roots into the earth. The contours of the tree suggested the profiles of children. Other children were added until the seeker may find scores of them hiding among the leaves.

Hide-and-Seek—"which grew as a plant, animal or child grows—not forced"—is a very large and intricate composition of multiple metamorphic images, forms within forms, sprung from the artist's mind, he believes, by free association, though some traditional symbols are suggested. Mysterious ardors and anxieties of childhood seem fused with benign or violent forces of nature. The tree of life becomes the clock of the seasons; its greens and fiery reds and wintry blues celebrate the annual cycle of death and rebirth.

TCHELITCHEW. *Tree into Hand and Foot* (study for *Hide-and-Seek*). 1939. Watercolor and ink, 14 × 9¼″. Mrs. Simon Guggenheim Fund, 1942.

165

Lam of Cuba and Matta of Chile, internationally by far the best-known painters of their respective countries, both emerged "in the light of surrealism" in Paris during the late 1930s. Matta has remained expatriate; his chief return to Latin America was his visit to Mexico in 1941 when he painted the volcanic *Listen to Living*.

Originally a protegé of Picasso, then of Breton, Lam lives much of the time in Cuba. Himself part Negro, he often embodies Afro-Cuban symbolism and magic in his painting.

MATTA. *Listen to Living (Ecoutez vivre)*. 1941. Oil, $29\frac{1}{2} \times 37\frac{1}{8}''$. Inter-American Fund, 1942. Sebastian Antonio Matta Echaurren. Chilean, born 1912. The Museum owns 3 oils, 2 drawings, and 3 prints by Matta.

LAM. *The Jungle*. 1943. Gouache, $94\frac{1}{4} \times 90\frac{1}{2}''$. Inter-American Fund, 1945. Wifredo Lam. Cuban, born 1902. The Museum owns 3 gouaches, and 2 prints by Lam.

Having lived much abroad where he has won great admiration especially as a colorist, Tamayo is regarded with suspicion by his politically or nationalistically-minded country-men. Yet his work is essentially Mexican: *Animals* for instance, is a savage metamorphosis of those engaging terra-cotta images of little dogs fattened for fondling and eating by the Tarascans a thousand years ago.

Francis Bacon's brilliantly painted and profoundly disturbing hallucination is strictly twentieth century. Surrounded by butchered sides of beef, this human carnivore stands on a chromium-plated rostrum equipped with multiple microphones. The lower part of his head with its vermilion stubble glistens in the spotlight but an umbrella shades the upper part—if any.

TAMAYO. *Animals.* 1941. Oil, $30\frac{1}{8} \times 40''$. Inter-American Fund, 1942. Rufino Tamayo. Mexican, born 1899. The Museum owns 3 oils and 2 prints by Tamayo, and has 1 watercolor on extended loan.

BACON. *Painting*. 1946. Oil and tempera, $77\frac{7}{8} \times 52''$. Purchase Fund, 1948. Francis Bacon. British, born 1910. The Museum owns 2 oils by Bacon.

DUBUFFET. *Snack for Two (Casse-croûte à deux)*. 1944.
Oil, $28\frac{1}{4} \times 23\frac{1}{4}''$. Gift of Mrs. Saidie A. May, 1949.
Jean Dubuffet. French, born 1901. The Museum owns
3 paintings by Dubuffet and 34 prints in a book.

YOUNGER ARTISTS OF POST-WAR EUROPE

During the decade following World War II abstract traditions have generally
prevailed in the painting and sculpture of the Western World. This is quite
contrary to the general trend toward realism or neo-classicism which followed
World War I. Abstract art is also, of course, directly in opposition to the banal
Socialist Realism imposed upon artists by the Communist Party in the U.S.S.R.
and elsewhere, too, wherever the Party succeeds in dominating the artist.

Though it flourishes in Germany, Switzerland, Italy and even Spain, European
abstract painting is probably to be found at its best in Paris where, for the first
time, it seems predominant. Hans Hartung, German by birth and training, is
perhaps the best master of calligraphic abstraction. His sweeping, rather dry,
line is supported by transparent color of exceptional freshness. Nicolas de Staël
by contrast has built thick slabs of paint into a composition of sober dignity.

Possibly the most original painter to have emerged in Paris since the war is
not abstract in his art. A man of exceptional intelligence and maturity, Jean
Dubuffet combines a childlike style with bold innovations in surface handling
and a grotesque sense of humor. Bernard Buffet, the most striking talent among
the youngest French artists, was just twenty when he painted his big self portrait.
Emaciated in drawing, meagre in color, sparse in composition, its style is perhaps
more convincing than its sentiment.

HARTUNG. *Painting.* 1948. Oil, $38\frac{1}{4}$
$\times 57\frac{1}{2}''$. Gift of John L. Senior, Jr.,
1952. Hans Hartung. French, born
Germany 1904; to Paris 1935. The
Museum owns 1 oil and 2 prints by
Hartung.

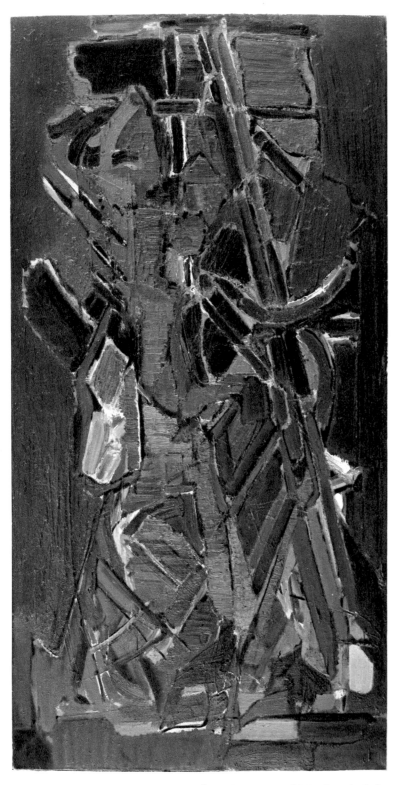

STAËL. *Painting.* 1947. Oil, 77 × 38⅛″. Gift of Mr. and Mrs. Lee A. Ault, 1951. Nicolas de Staël. French, born Russia, 1914. The Museum owns 2 paintings by Staël.

BUFFET. *Self Portrait.* 1948. Oil, 82¼ × 40⅝″. Purchase, 1951. Bernard Buffet. French, born 1928. The Museum owns 2 paintings and 1 drawing by Buffet.

MARINI. *Horse and Rider.* 1947-48. Bronze, 38¼″ high. Acquired through the Lillie P. Bliss Bequest, 1948. (Photo Soichi Sunami.) Marino Marini. Italian, born 1901. The Museum owns 2 sculptures, 1 drawing and 3 prints by Marini.

FAZZINI. *The Sibyl.* 1947. Bronze, 37¼″ high. Gift of Mr. and Mrs. John de Menil, 1952. (Photo Soichi Sunami.) Pericle Fazzini. Italian born 1913.

Since the War the British and the Italians seem to have taken the lead in European sculpture.

Marino Marini already had a considerable national reputation during the 1930s. Today he is one of the foremost European sculptor working with traditional forms. "I do not," he said recently, "make any distinction between abstract and figurative sculpture, providing it is real sculpture in either case. What matters above all is the quality of a work of art. As for myself, since I am a Mediterranean, I can express myself freely only through the human."

Marini's *Horse and Rider* was inspired by the haunting memory of peasant refugees riding their farm horses while they watched the skies for raiding planes.

Fazzini is the most prominent of the Roman sculptors. Naturalistic and informal in his small figures, he achieves a brilliant if somewhat mannered elegance in major works such as the Museum's *Sibyl*.

RENAISSANCE OF AMERICAN PRINTMAKING

Any survey of contemporary printmaking must consider the British engraver Stanley William Hayter. In 1939 he moved his studio, *Atelier 17*, from Paris, where he had been associated with the surrealists, to New York. His technical ingenuity and insistence on direct use of the burin changed the direction of the intaglio print in America, and artists such as Gabor Peterdi and Mauricio Lasansky continue Hayter's tradition of teacher and engraver.

More recently there has been a considerable revival of interest in the woodcut, particularly the large woodcut in color, stimulated by the pioneers Louis Schanker and Adja Yunkers.

Both the copper plate and the wood block for the two prints reproduced below exploit actual textures such as cloth and wire mesh to increase the pictorial effect of the image when printed. The prints also suggest the international scope of printmaking in America. Of the older generation no innovator has surpassed Hayter. Among the younger artists Antonio Frasconi, a Uruguayan, has worked in many parts of the United States since 1945. These two examples cannot indicate the important achievement of other printmakers. They do, however, demonstrate three characteristics of American printmaking today: use of color and textures, emphasis on large scale prints, and, less immediately apparent, experimentation followed by technical innovations. —W. S. L.

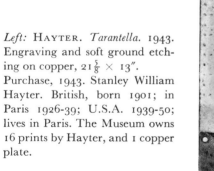

Left: HAYTER. *Tarantella.* 1943. Engraving and soft ground etching on copper, $21\frac{5}{8} \times 13''$. Purchase, 1943. Stanley William Hayter. British, born 1901; in Paris 1926-39; U.S.A. 1939-50; lives in Paris. The Museum owns 16 prints by Hayter, and 1 copper plate.

Right: FRASCONI. *The Storm Is Coming.* 1950. Color woodcut, 22 $\times$ $15\frac{1}{2}''$. Inter-American Fund, 1952. Antonio Frasconi. Uruguayan, born 1919; in U.S.A. since 1945. The Museum owns 6 prints by Frasconi.

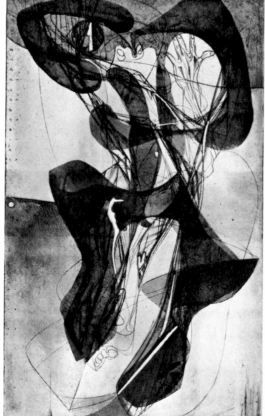

173

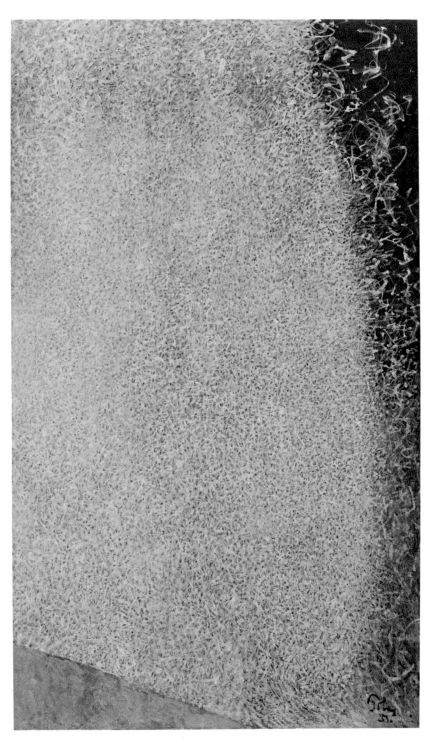

TOBEY. *Edge of August.* 1953. Casein on composition board, 48 × 28″. Purchase, 1954. Mark Tobey. American, born 1890. The Museum owns 1 casein and 2 tempera paintings by Tobey.

RECENT AMERICAN ABSTRACT ART

Abstract art has been particularly strong in the United States in recent years. The between-wars reputation of Alexander Calder, pages 146-147, has increased until he is now the best-known and most admired American artist throughout the world. And Jackson Pollock, among younger painters, is beginning to win a similar position.

Abstract expressionism—the tradition anticipated in various ways by van Gogh, Monet, Redon and Matisse but firmly established by Kandinsky about 1912—has for a decade involved more talented artists in America than has the quasi-geometric tradition of Piet Mondrian, page 123, or Gabo and Pevsner, pages 126-127. Many of the works of the American abstract expressionists are, moreover, saturated with emotion which continually threatens to burst through the surface tension of the cryptogram into recognizable images, and sometimes explodes as in de Kooning's *Woman*, page 177. De Kooning and Pollock and a number of the best younger abstract expressionists are in no sense committed to abstraction as a program or dogma.

"Our ground today," Mark Tobey wrote in 1947, "is not so much the national or the regional as it is the understanding of this single earth . . . America more than any other country is placed geographically to lead in this understanding, and if from past habits of behavior she has constantly looked toward Europe, today she must assume her position, Janus-faced, toward Asia, for in not too long a time the waves of the Orient shall wash heavily upon her shores."[86]

Mark Tobey is much older than Pollock or de Kooning but, like them, he first won general recognition after World War II. He has studied Chinese art and, living on the West Coast, looks across the Pacific to a tradition of abstract calligraphy more subtle and ancient than Kandinsky's mysticism of "spiritual harmony" through color.

GORKY. *Agony.* 1947. Oil, 40 × 50½″. A. Conger Goodyear Fund, 1950. Arshile Gorky. American, born Russia 1904; died 1948. The Museum owns 4 oils, 1 drawing and 1 print by Gorky.

Though preliminary drawings indicate a room with furniture, Gorky's *Agony* seems abstract or, at least, cryptic. We know that the artist had already entered into that dark period of personal misfortune, anxiety and physical pain which was to culminate in his suicide, but if his suffering and foreboding are expressed in *Agony* they are in no way detailed. Instead the artist's passion is distilled into a painting of pulsating ominous beauty.

ROSZAK. *Spectre of Kitty Hawk*. 1946-47. Welded and hammered steel, brazed with bronze and brass, $40\frac{1}{4}''$ high. Purchase, 1950. (Photo Soichi Sunami.) Theodore J. Roszak, American, born 1907.

Of the *Spectre of Kitty Hawk* the sculptor writes: "In the same way that the forms of a sculpture try to reconcile the ambiguities that are within it and that produce it . . . the subject metaphorically tries to relate at once several things in remote periods of history. The *Spectre* is the pterodactyl, an early denizen of the air both savage and destructive. Present day aircraft has come to resemble this beast of prey, hence the re-incarnation of the pterodactyl at Kitty Hawk . . . I think it is interesting and relevant that Orville Wright in the last days of his life mused about his brainchild with apprehension and misgivings. He died a disillusioned man, and the Myth of Icarus completes another circle, tangent to pragmatic America."

After years of comparative obscurity, de Kooning won great esteem as an abstract expressionist whose forms were rarely recognizable. Yet by 1950, he had begun a long-drawn-out and apparently desperate striving with the image of a seated woman. This obsessive figure struggles to be born in a dozen canvases which culminate in the large, formidable and highly disturbing *Woman* of 1952, opposite. In a public statement[109] made at the Museum in 1951 de Kooning had expressed his impatience and described his predicament: "The argument often used . . . that painting could be like music and, for this reason, that you cannot paint a man leaning against a lamppost, is utterly ridiculous . . . Art never seems to make me peaceful or pure. I always seem to be wrapped in the melodrama of vulgarity. I do not think . . . of art in general as a situation of comfort." In any case de Kooning's *Woman* is the most controversial American painting of recent years and one of the most admired by young artists.

DE KOONING. *Woman, I.* 1952.
Oil, 76 ×̦ 58″. Purchase, 1953.
Willem de Kooning. American,
born The Netherlands 1904; to
U.S.A. 1926. The Museum owns
2 oils by de Kooning.

177

In *Number 1* of 1948, Pollock used no brush but, laying his canvas on the floor, trickled the fluid paint on it from above, his hand weaving the thick stream of color back and forth and around until he created a rhythmic, variegated, transparent labyrinth.

Number 1 presents an extraordinary adventure for the eye—an adventure which involves excitement and discovery, pitfalls, fireworks, irritations and delights. As your eye wanders, a mysterious sense of depth and internal light develops in the whirling dynamo of lines. Then, when your eye escapes again to the edge of the vortex, you find that the artist has vividly restored the flat reality of his huge canvas by slapping it with his own paint-covered hands.

POLLOCK. *Number I.* 1948. Oil, 68 × 104″. Purchase, 1950. Jackson Pollock. American, born 1912. The Museum owns 3 paintings by Pollock.

His fellow painter, Alfonso Ossorio,[83] finds other and profounder values in Pollock's art: "... His painting confronts us with a visual concept organically evolved from a belief in the unity that underlies the phenomena among which we live ... An ocean's tides and a personal nightmare, the bursting of a bubble and the communal clamor for a victim are as inextricably meshed in the coruscation and darkness of his work as they are in actuality. His forms and textures germinate, climax and decline, coalesce and dissolve across the canvas. The picture surface, with no depth of recognizable space or sequence of known time, gives us the never ending present. We are presented with a visualization of that remorseless consolation—in the end is the beginning."

The vehement expressionism of Pollock, Gorky, de Kooning and Roszak on the previous pages is possibly more prevalent in American art of the early 1950s but a more static contemplative abstraction also flourishes.

Those who know the Buddhist art of the Far East will understand from Lassaw's own words that the tranquillity of his *Kwannon* is intentional: "While the work was in progress, I was particularly concerned with different aspects of Kwannon, the Japanese name of the Lord of Compassion and Pity ... Although I never try to depict or narrate or communicate, I feel that something of Kwannon entered this piece of sculpture ...

"I'll know more about this work in a few years. The artist, almost like the spectator, knows little (in a profound way) of his work when it is new."

LASSAW. *Kwannon.* 1952. Welded bronze with silver, 6' high. Katharine Cornell Fund, 1952. (Photo Soichi Sunami.) Ibram Lassaw. American, born 1913.

TOMLIN. *Number 20.* 1949. Oil, 7′2″ × 6′8¼″. Gift of Philip C. Johnson, 1952. Bradley Walker Tomlin. American, 1899-1953.

Though associated until his untimely death with the recent American renascence of abstract painting, Tomlin had already worked in the cubist tradition during the 1930s. His abstract style still seems cubist, or, better, Mondrianist (page 123) in its deliberation and sense of perfect control. *Number 20* of 1949, possibly his most important work, demonstrates his mastery of pictorial counterpoint—hooked, light-toned, ribbon-like calligraphy moving against a background of disturbed rectangles. Decorative elegance is given depth by an aristocratic sobriety of spirit.

Lippold's tense, delicately calculated art stands at a pole opposite that of the impulsive and compulsive gestures of expressionism. "The fragile snowflake," Lippold writes, "appears in more variations of form than any kind of 'permanent' sculpture. The spider's web is both a jewel for the branch and a noose for the fly . . . My preference in material is Space, captured by the most seductive other materials I can arrange."[83]

Of his *Variation Number 7: Full Moon* Lippold observes: "We can hope—even prove—that our wisdom is stronger than our weapons. This construction is such proof. The firmer the tensions within it are established, the more placid is its effect. Patience and love are the elements which gave it life, and patience and love must be used in all dealings with it; its hanging and its seeing."

LIPPOLD. *Variation Number 7: Full Moon.* 1949-50. Brass rods, nickel-chromium and stainless steel wire, 10' high. Mrs. Simon Guggenheim Fund, 1950. (Photo Soichi Sunami.) Richard Lippold. American, born 1915.

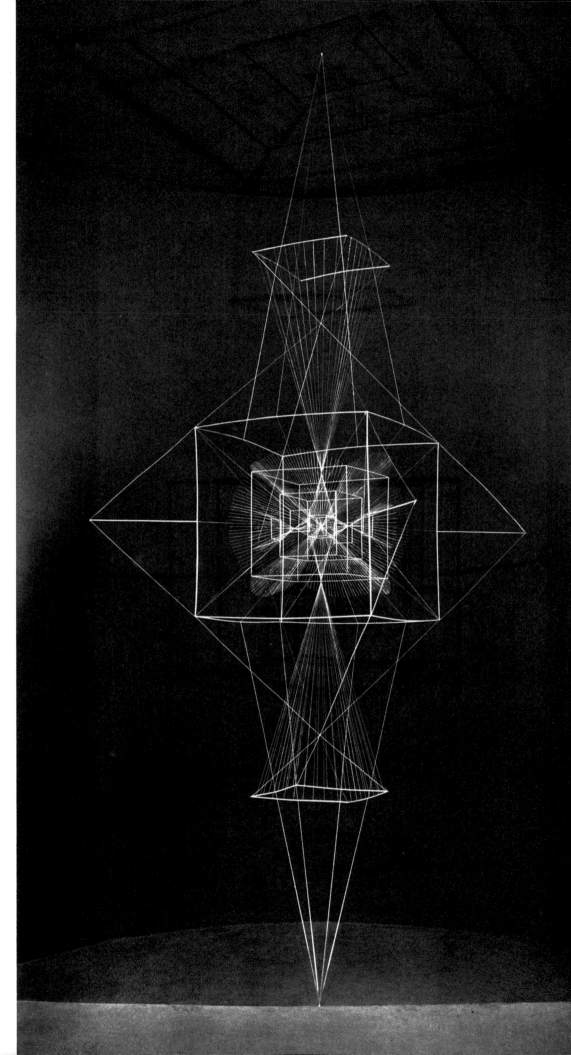

DESIGNS FOR THE THEATRE

Never before our century have so many of the greatest painters given their talents to designing for the theatre. Serge Diaghilev, of the Russian ballet, was the most brilliant impresario to enlist their collaboration, first in St. Petersburg, then in Paris; his example has been followed, though with somewhat less éclat, during the quarter century or more since his death.

The Museum's collection of dance and theatre design, originally the Dance Archives, was founded by Lincoln Kirstein in 1939. Together with books, photographs and other documentation are many original designs for costumes and settings, some of a high artistic quality quite independent of their theatrical purpose. From time to time other drawings and watercolors have been added to the original gift so that the collection now includes a considerable body of work, particularly for Russian and American ballet companies. Among the better-known artists are Eugene Berman, Marc Chagall, Diego Rivera, Pavel Tchelitchew, Franklin Watkins, all represented by suites of designs; and Christian Bérard, Paul Cadmus, Horacio Butler, Nathalie Gontcharova, Michael Larionov, Fernand Léger and many others by one or more drawings each.

Top: GONTCHAROVA. *Le Coq d'Or:* design for scenery for the ballet produced by the Ballets Russes, Paris, 1914. Gouache, $18\frac{1}{8} \times 24\frac{1}{4}''$. Acquired through the Lillie P. Bliss Bequest, 1947. Theatre Arts Collection. Nathalie Gontcharova. Russian, born 1881; lives in Paris. The Museum also owns 1 oil by Gontcharova.

Center: CHAGALL. *Aleko:* design for scenery for the ballet produced by the Ballet Theatre, Mexico City and New York, 1942. Gouache, $15\frac{1}{4} \times 22\frac{1}{2}''$. Acquired through the Lillie P. Bliss Bequest, 1945. Theatre Arts Collection.

Bottom: BERMAN. *Devil's Holiday:* design for scenery for the ballet produced by the Ballet Russe de Monte Carlo, New York, 1939. Gouache, $11\frac{7}{8} \times 15\frac{7}{8}''$. Gift of Paul Magriel, 1942. Theatre Arts Collection. Eugene Berman. American, born Russia 1899; worked in Paris; U.S.A. since 1936. The Museum owns 3 oils by Berman, 22 ballet designs, 55 prints including 53 in 2 portfolios, and 1 model for scenery.

PHOTOGRAPHY

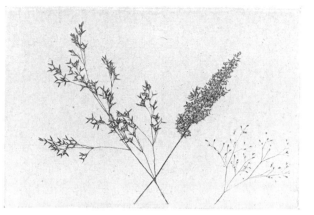

Photography has become an indispensable tool in nearly all fields of human activity. As a witness of places, times and events, it records with an exactness beyond the scope of any other visual means. Because of the magnitude and variety of these functions, its esthetic potentialities are sometimes overlooked. When practised by the artist, photography becomes a medium capable of giving form to ideas and incisive expression to emotions.

The photographer is served by a technique differing completely from that practised by the painter, who begins with blank surface and then by more or less complicated procedures, always under complete control, is able gradually to achieve a growth and realization of his concept. The photographer begins with a completed image; and compared with the painter, the controls available to him are hardly worth the mention. By the same token there are no primitive or archaic phases in photography. The process itself was born as a completed achievement and most of the earliest photography suffers little by comparison with that of today.

The Museum of Modern Art was the first museum to make the art of photography an important part of its program; and the inclusion of the following pages in this book again demonstrates that this Museum is unique among art museums in the extent of its recognition of photography.

While the Museum possesses outstanding examples of some of the earliest photography, its collection is predominantly of twentieth-century prints. It contains the work of widely recognized photographers as well as experimental and exploratory work by newer talents— work marking a continuing effort to penetrate the surface appearance of reality or seeking to translate into pattern and design the magic detail of a fragment of growth or of deterioration. In the collection, there are prints that give evidence of man's passionate search for truth, rendered with technical precision and mental precision, separately or on occasion together. The swift freezing of a exact instant; the gamut of feeling written on the human face in its contrasts of joy, serenity or despair; the beauty of the earth that man has inherited and the wealth and the confusion that man has created within this inheritance— all these are rendered with a sense of timelessness and exactitude. The art of photography as it is used on the printed page or in exhibitions, as well as in films and television, is moving swiftly toward wider and wider horizons.

EDWARD STEICHEN
Director, Department of Photography

Above: TALBOT. *Wheat.* c. 1853. Gift of M. T. Talbot. William Henry Fox Talbot. English, 1800-1877.

CAMERON. *Sir John F. W. Herschel.* 1867. Gift of Edward Steichen. Mrs. Julia Margaret Cameron. English, born Calcutta, 1815-1879. Mrs. Cameron introduced the photography "close-up." Her portraits go beyond the obvious appearances of the human mask.

Below: BRADY. *Ruins of Richmond.* 1865. Purchase Fund. Matthew B. Brady. American, 1823-1896. Brady's Civil War photographs comment as well as record.

STIEGLITZ. *The Terminal*. 1892. Photogravure. Given anonymously. Alfred Stieglitz. American, 1864-1946. Stieglitz translated the everyday snapshot of an exact instant into warm human equations.

Below: MUYBRIDGE. Plate 494 from series *Animal Locomotion*. 1887. Gift of Mrs. Jane K. Murray. Eadweard Muybridge. English, 1830-1904. This analysis of motion foreshadowed the cinema and the sequence story in photo-journalism.

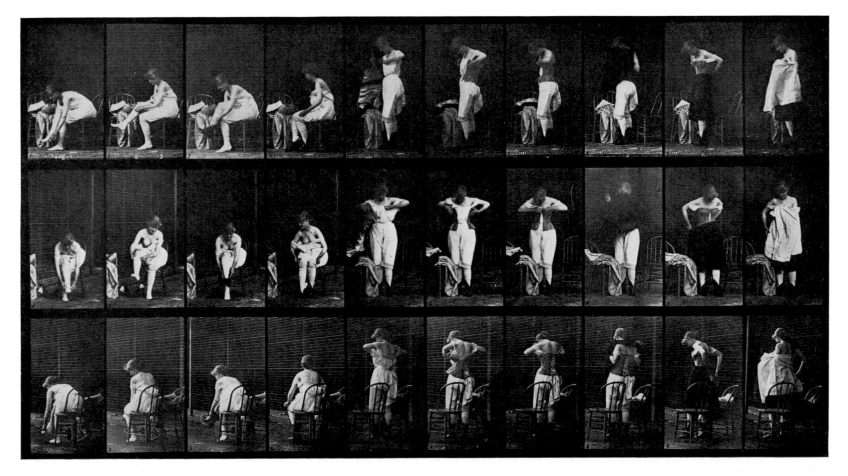

STEICHEN. *Rodin—The Thinker*. 1902. Photogravure. Gift of the photographer. Edward Steichen. American, born 1879.

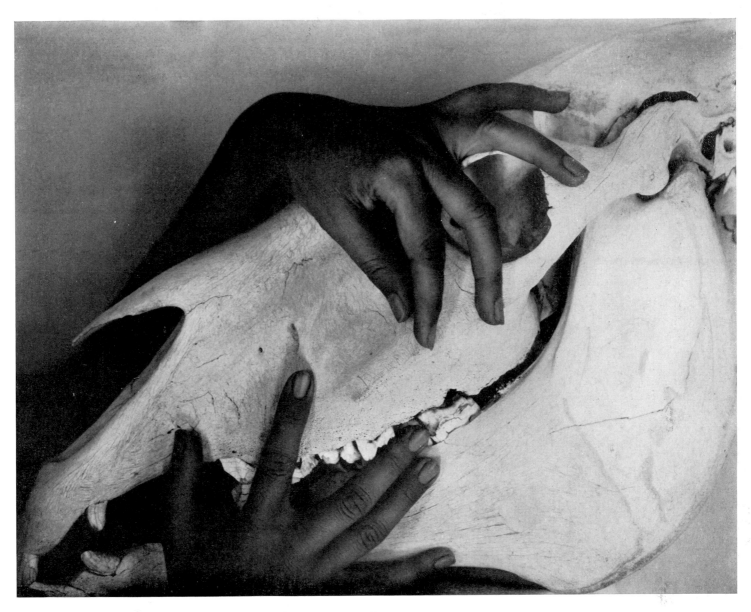

STIEGLITZ. *O'Keeffe's Hands and Horse's Skull*. 1930. Given anonymously.

ATGET. Photograph. Given anonymously. Eugene Atget. French, 1856-1927.

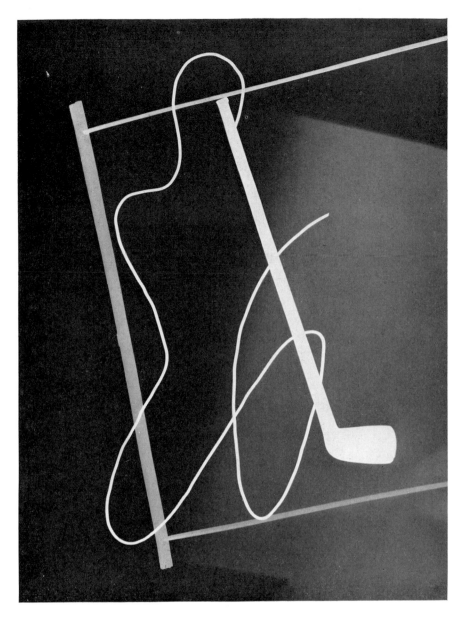

RAY. *Rayograph*. 1928. Gift of James Thrall Soby. Man Ray. American, born 1890. A group of objects serves in establishing a composition directly on photographic paper without the use of a camera.

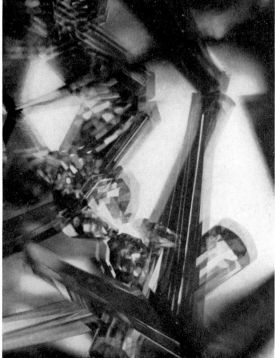

COBURN. *Vortograph # 1*. About 1917. Gift of the photographer. Alvin Langdon Coburn. American, 1882. This pattern photographed through a kaleidoscope is the earliest known example of abstract photography.

SHEELER. *White Barn, Bucks County, Pennsylvania.* 1915. Purchase Fund. Charles Sheeler. American, born 1883. Sunlight, and the pattern and texture on the flat surface of an old barn are organized with the simple dignity of a hymn.

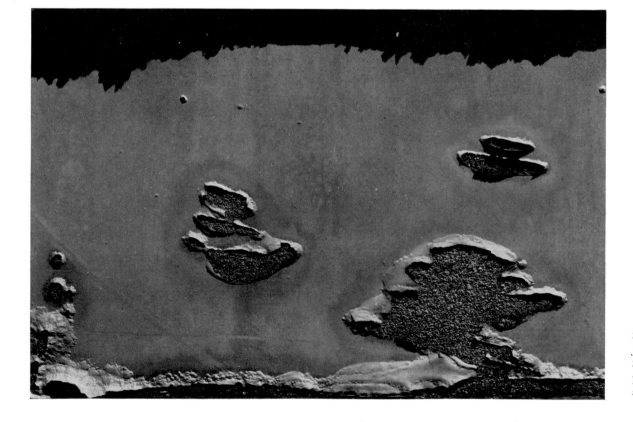

SISKIND. Photograph. Mrs. Charles J. Liebman Purchase Fund. Aaron Siskind. American, born 1903. The pattern of erosion on a small section of a wall becomes an abstract design.

EVANS. *A Graveyard and Steel Mill in Bethlehem, Pennsylvania*. 1935. Farm Security Administration photograph. Walker Evans. American, born 1903.

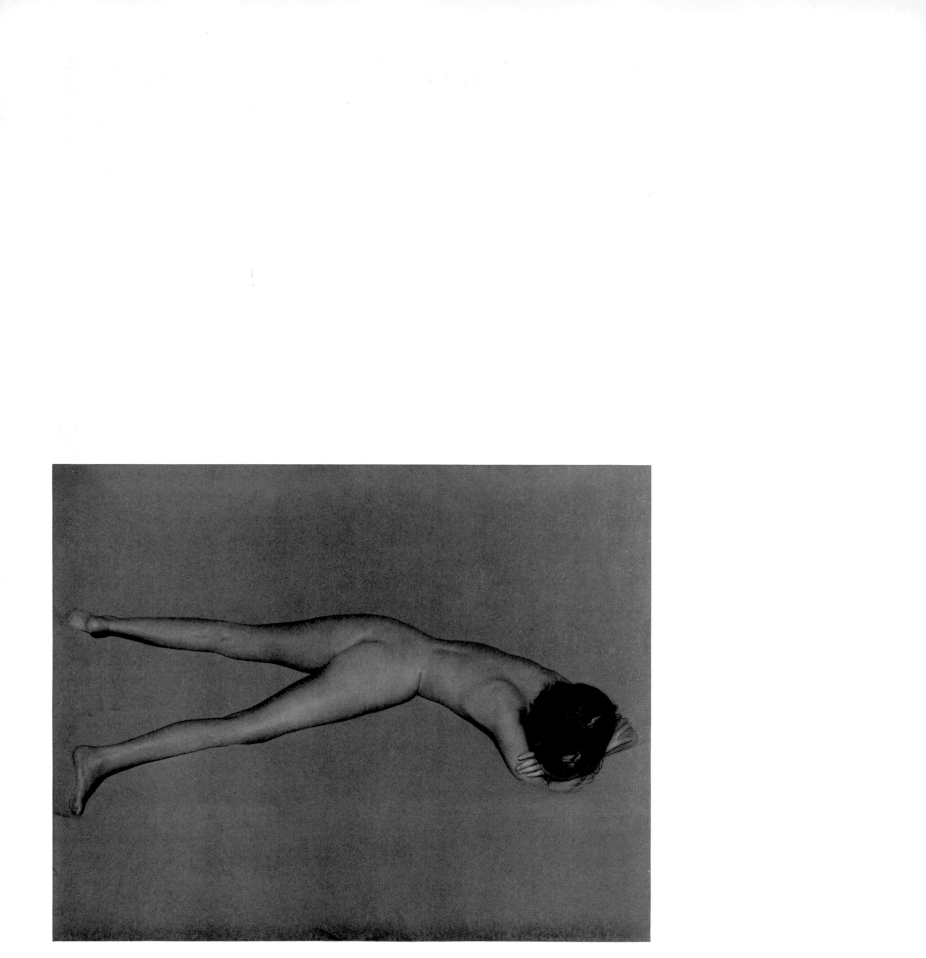

WESTON. *Nude on Sand.* 1936. Gift of Edward Steichen. Edward Weston. American, born 1886.

ADAMS. *Moonrise, New Mexico*. 1941. Gift of the photographer. Ansel Adams. American, born 1902.

CARTIER-BRESSON. *Madrid, Spain.* 1933. Given anonymously. Henri Cartier-Bresson. French, born 1908.

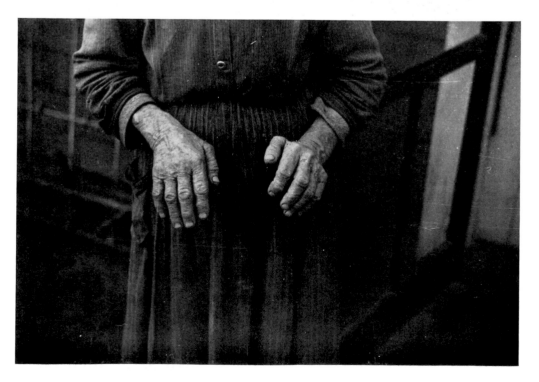

LEE. *Hands of Old Homesteader, Iowa.* 1936. Farm Security Administration photograph. Russell Lee. American, born 1903.

LANGE. *A Depression Breadline, San Francisco*. 1933. Gift of Albert M. Bender. Dorothea Lange. American, born 1895. The bitter poignant story of the Depression is concentrated in this single document.

BRASSAÏ. *Un Fort des Halles (A Strong Man of the Paris Markets)*. Given anonymously. Brassaï (Gyala Halász). French, born Transylvania 1899.

MATSUMOTO. Photograph. Nelson A. Rockefeller Purchase Fund. Tosh Matsumoto. American, born 1920.

LEVITT. *Children.* 1940. Given anonymously. Helen Levitt. American, born 1913.

SOMMER. *Max Ernst*. 1946. Nelson A. Rockefeller Purchase Fund. Frederick Sommer. American, born Italy 1906. The superimposing of two images appropriately intensifies the portrait of a surrealist.

Below: NEWMAN. *Igor Stravinsky*. Gift of the photographer. Arnold Newman. American, born 1918. A decorative unity is established by a stylized disciplined juxtaposition of the composer and a piano.

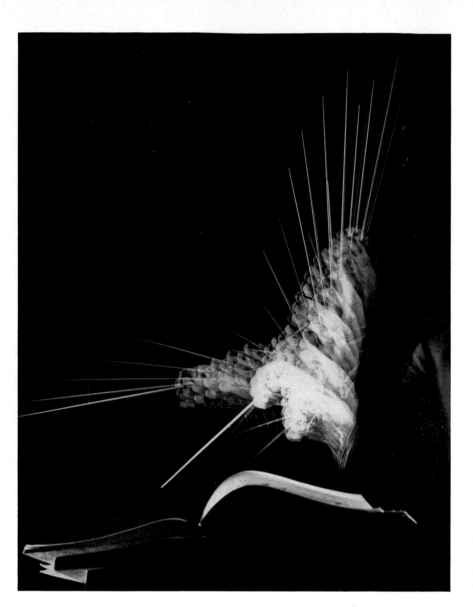

MILI. *Conductor Conducting in $\frac{3}{4}$ Time*. Given anonymously. Gjon Miii. American, born Albania 1904. Photography has been enlivened by Mili's use of Edgerton's stroboscopic technique for the esthetic rendering of form in motion.

CALLAHAN. Photograph. Mrs. Charles J. Liebman Purchase Fund. Harry Callahan. American, born 1913. A sensitive statement of a simple fact about nature creates a sophisticated calligraphy.

THE FILM LIBRARY

"Stills," such as are reproduced here, cannot represent the artistic quality or character of a motion picture. Reproductions of paintings, however inadequate, can at least attempt to present the whole object, but a film exists in time, and a still shot from it can no more suggest the whole than a single bar from a piece of music can render the structure of the entire composition. Even the purely narrative elements of a film are hard to elicit from a single still; what spectator who has not very recently seen the film would deduce unaided that the scene from *La Grande Illusion*, reproduced on page 210, intends to suggest Pierre Fresnay's aristocratic disgust at being searched by a German guard? An *assemblage* of stills can give some hint of the style of one film-maker—the quality of his light, the character of his camerawork. But films themselves exist on the screen, and nowhere else.

Yet, if stills do less than justice to individual films, they can indicate something of the scope of a film collection, in this case the greatest film collection in the world, that of the Museum of Modern Art Film Library, assembled by Iris Barry during fifteen years from a dozen countries. Reviewing these stills can help us judge to what extent the Film Library has fulfilled its mandate to collect, preserve and show the artistically and historically significant films produced throughout the world over the past sixty years—with due regard to the fact that the United States remains the major source, as it was the principal pioneer, of film production.

The gaps are obvious. An important Japanese film is represented in its French version, *Les Volontaires de la Mort*, but no Hindu, Moslem, Chinese, or South African films are in the collection, and the Latin American and Australian films so far secured are negligible. Moreover, though many hundred European films are in the Film Library's possession, the scale is heavily weighted on the side of the major film-producing countries, France, Germany, the U.S.S.R., Sweden, Great Britain, and Denmark. The Museum possesses no Spanish, Balkan, or Finnish films, and Italy, Holland, Belgium, and Central Europe are most inadequately represented. To remedy this lack will be the work of the next five years, beginning in 1954 when the Museum will acquire and present a retrospect of the Italian film.

Yet, if the Film Library's collection is not so complete geographically as would be desirable, such diverse films as *Song of Ceylon, October, Moana, Triumph of the Will, Prelude to War*, demonstrate how far the motion picture has traveled in its brief fifty years, how deeply it has penetrated into human affairs, how many purposes, good and bad, it has dynamically served, beyond its usual purpose of providing effortless entertainment. It will doubtless astonish many to learn that there are more documentary, instructional, and propagandist films in the collection than fiction or entertainment films.

Equally surprising may be the fact that the number of titles in the collection from the period 1896-1912 is far greater than that of films of later date. But when the Film Library was founded in 1935, it was clearly its first obligation to rescue the primitives of the art before they were forever lost through neglect and chemical deterioration. Only by a miracle, only just in time, were these ancient and then-forgotten films saved. By 1940 the Film Library had rescued much of the work of Georges Méliès and his lively contemporaries, Zecca, Cohl, and Durand; the entire surviving Biograph and Edison production of the years 1900-1912 had been acquired; many of the works of D. W. Griffith, some of those of Thomas H. Ince, and all of those of Douglas Fairbanks were presented to the Museum by the artists themselves or their heirs: the foundations of the great collection had been firmly laid. Since then, the scope of the collection has extended in every direction, thanks to the cooperation of American and European producers, other film archives, and individual film enthusiasts, until it is now the most widely representative, as well as largest, aggregation of films in institutional hands.

Films are greatly loved by all sorts and conditions of men, and it was tempting to try to satisfy human curiosity and nostalgia in the selection of stills reproduced here. Space however is so limited that it is impossible to include many well-remembered, though perhaps inaccurately remembered, popular movies, or those others like Sarah Bernhardt's *Queen Elizabeth* or Noel Coward's *Cavalcade*, which helped confer respectability upon the screen if they added nothing else to it. The stills which follow represent principally masterworks from the collection, and among them chiefly those films which owe least to the traditional arts and most to the unique and still unfolding powers of a medium which is the lineal descendant of the magic carpet and the ancestor, perhaps, of the time machine.

RICHARD GRIFFITH
Curator, Museum of Modern Art Film Library

MÉLIÈS, *A Trip to the Moon*, 1902.

PORTER, *The Life of an American Fireman*, 1902.

PORTER, *The Great Train Robbery*, 1903.

200

GRIFFITH, *The Lonely Villa*, 1909:
Mary Pickford, Marion
Leonard.

GRIFFITH, *The Lonedale Operator*,
1911: Blanche Sweet.

GRIFFITH, *The New York Hat*,
1912: Mary Pickford, Lionel
Barrymore.

GRIFFITH, *The Musketeers of Pig
Alley*, 1912.

THE DEVELOPMENT OF NARRATIVE: BEGINNINGS

Beginning in 1897 the Frenchman, Georges Méliès, introduced a theatrical form of story-telling to the screen by shooting successive scenes from a fixed camera position. As in *A Trip to the Moon*, opposite, he designed every scene for each of his films on paper before beginning production.

In America, Edwin S. Porter, a cameraman-director for the Edison Company, began the invention of cinematic narrative with *The Life of an American Fireman*, opposite. This simple film, nine-hundred feet long, shows a fire chief day-dreaming of his wife and child; an alarm is sent in and the firemen rush to a burning house where one of them rescues a woman and child. The story is told much after the manner of Méliès' "artificially arranged scenes," though more fluently, but the introduction in the second scene of a close-up of a hand opening a fire-alarm box was revolutionary. It disregarded fixed theatrical conventions and pointed toward the development of a new form of narrative peculiar to the screen.

It was Porter who, the following year, directed *The Great Train Robbery*, opposite, most famous of primitive films and ancestor of all subsequent gangster and Western movies.

THE DEVELOPMENT OF NARRATIVE: D.W. GRIFFITH

Between 1908 and 1916, D. W. Griffith made the greatest individual contribution to the development of narrative. Gradually freeing the screen from stage conventions, finding the way to compose his material artfully by cutting and editing, establishing a new type of acting, he laid down the basis of film form and revealed the film's capacity to provoke ideas and feelings by hitherto unknown means.

In the extremely remarkable series of short films which Griffith made for the American Biograph and Mutoscope Company between 1908 and 1912, the art of the motion picture can be seen in process of invention. In *The Lonely Villa*, "stage conventions are abandoned, the action broken into shorter scenes, movement is much freer, parallel action is developed through cross-cutting . . ." In *The Lonedale Operator*, there is "greater variety of set-ups and camera angles, long and close shots; the scenes are edited tersely and no longer begin with the entrance of the characters." In *The New York Hat*, "Griffith set the camera close to his material if he wished for intimate detail and withdrew it for broad effects; he then *composed* his film out of selected lengths of these close shots and long shots." In *The Musketeers of Pig Alley*, "the camera placements and the free movement of the action in unlimited space are especially notable, the acting is relaxed and natural, the camera seems to reach out for what is significant, and, at the same time, almost to be recording everyday life."*

* These and most following quotations are from *Film Notes*, bibl. 85.

Left:
PASTRONE and GUAZZONI,
Cabiria, 1914.

Right:
GRIFFITH, *The Birth of a Nation,*
1915.

By the time Griffith left Biograph in 1913, the foundations of modern technique had been laid.

The arrival in the United States of the Italian feature-length spectacles *Quo Vadis* and *Cabiria* astounded American audiences and spurred American film-makers to enlarge their conceptions. In particular they determined Griffith to surpass the Italian "miracles" with an indigenous theme, *The Birth of a Nation.* This most celebrated of all films, revived the passions of the Civil War, created more controversy than any film before or since, and probably earned more money. It established David Wark Griffith as the master of the motion picture, and nearly everyone connected with its making went on to greater fame. It still remains the yardstick by which other films are measured, for grandeur of scale, for sweeping emotion, for success.

Aside from these historic values, this film remains one of the most esthetically satisfying yet made. Says Gilbert Seldes: "It has structure, proportion, coherence, and integrity. It can be separated into a dozen different themes or stories, but it obstinately remains one film, into which all the parts are woven . . . In *The Birth of a Nation,* the spectacle and the melodrama and the private dramas interplay, in proper balance; a dominant tone is given to the entire picture, and the subsidiary episodes are played in related keys. The cutting is perfectly done, so that interest is always kept in an episode for itself, then dispersed or concentrated elsewhere, to return to the first episode for its relation to all the others; it is cinematic counterpoint. The rhythms are delicately felt; the whole picture has space and sweep.

"... The highest point of emotion in the film was done without a close-up; it was in fact made profound and universal because the face of the principal player was not shown and the emotion was conveyed not by the registering of emotion but by movement, as is proper to the moving picture. That was the moment of the Southern soldier's return to his wrecked home . . . From behind the door, as the soldier enters, comes the arm of his mother drawing in her son with an immemorial gesture, taking to her breast his sorrows and the sorrows still to come."

GRIFFITH, *The Birth of a Nation.*

Left:
GRIFFITH, *Intolerance*, 1916:
St. Bartholomew's morn.

Right:
GRIFFITH, *Intolerance:* the walls
of Babylon.

GRIFFITH, *Intolerance:*
Mae Marsh.

GRIFFITH, *Intolerance:* Miriam
Cooper, Walter Long.

GRIFFITH, *Intolerance,* Robert
Harron.

Intolerance, the formal masterpiece of the movies, consists of four stories told simultaneously—of ancient Babylon, the Crucifixion, St. Bartholomew's Eve, and the modern slums. All four stories weave in and out of one another, until at the climax they merge and "history itself seems to pour like a cataract across the screen." As such, it is, in Terry Ramsay's words, "the only film fugue," and, also as such, it entirely failed of public popularity.

In *Intolerance* Griffith demonstrated, more profoundly than anyone has before or since, the film's capacity to build a universe out of atoms of space and time, but it seemed then that he had ranged too far. As Pudovkin, the Russian director, said: "the abundance of matter forces the director to work the theme out quite generally ... and consequently there is a strong discrepancy between the depth of the motif and the superficiality of its form." [116]

It is possible that Pudovkin's criticism, echoed by so many, may not have applied to the original version of the film, four hours long, which Lillian Gish states to have been as intimate, detailed, and emotionally convincing as the released version is generalized. But no one believed in 1916 that human beings could survive four hours of projection, and Griffith was persuaded to reduce his negative to thirteen reels.

No one has ever imitated the formal idea upon which *Intolerance* is based, and the film remains a ruined Colosseum—a quarry from which later builders have taken only what they best could use. Its compositional structure served as the model upon which the Soviet theories of film-making have been based; its spectacle "has been in the back of every film-maker's mind ever since"; and its parallelisms between epochs have irresistibly drawn all serious directors. What remains to be successfully imitated is this film's use of the human countenance, figure, gesture, and gait to mirror unconscious passions. "The handling of the actors in intimate scenes has never been equaled either for depth or for humanity, particularly in the modern sequence. This searching realism, this pulsing life, comes not only from Griffith's power to mould his players but, in equal measure, from his editorial skill."

WIENE, *The Cabinet of Dr. Caligari*, 1919: Conrad Veidt.

MURNAU, *The Last Laugh*, 1924: Emil Jannings.

LANG, *Metropolis*, 1926: Brigitte Helm.

THE FILM IN GERMANY

About 1919, the major impetus to film experiment passed to Germany with the production of *The Cabinet of Dr. Caligari*, a work of several hands, the main contributors to which were writers Carl Mayer and Hans Janowitz, directors Robert Wiene and Fritz Lang, producer Erich Pommer, and designers Hermann Warm, Walter Reimann, and Walter Rohrig. Although it remains the most famous of all experimental films, actually the experimental element in *Caligari* consisted in an attempt to transfer bodily the methods and symbols of expressionist painting and the expressionist theatre to the screen, and it was on this that its contemporary reputation was based. "*Caligari* was recognized as having something to do with art, and so it had, though at this distance it is possible to question whether it had, basically, much to do with the art of the cinema. It was for its settings that *Caligari* was first acclaimed and has remained famous. They are not particularly cinematic, and, indeed, hardly anything takes place in the film that could not have been presented identically on a stage." *Caligari*'s constricted use of the camera in stage-like sets places it outside the historical succession of cinematography, and it has had no real descendants, but its influence has been far-reaching in that it "suggested that the motion picture had as yet no more than scratched the surface of its potentialities." Beyond that, this film which utilized so tiny a segment of the total area of cinematic means still managed, within that segment, to create a living and self-consistent world. "Even today, these settings of painted canvas and hangings and shadows retain their power to suggest the atmosphere of menace and of madness which they were intended to express."

Experiment continued in the German studios through the middle of the silent era and, after a decline, sharply revived with the coming of the talkies. The symbology of psychoanalysis played a part in many films, notably *Warning Shadows*, a neglected but much more mature picture than *Caligari*, and vestiges of expressionism persisted until the middle years of the decade, when it was succeeded as an esthetic influence by what we now call "science-fiction" as in *Metropolis* and by *die neue Sachlichkeit* (the new objectivity); the latter impulse produced a series of films which, merely naturalistic on the surface, had socialist tendencies or implications. These films, and especially those of Pabst (*The Joyless Street*, *The Love of Jeanne Ney*) abandoned the fluid, continuous, camera movement which had been the principal feature of German film style since 1924 (*The Last Laugh*) and introduced a disjunct cutting technique, based

PABST, *The Joyless Street*, 1925.

STERNBERG, *The Blue Angel*, 1929: Emil Jannings.

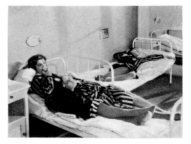

WINSLOE, *Mädchen in Uniform*, 1931.

LANG, *M*, 1931: Peter Lorre.

EISENSTEIN, *Armored Cruiser Potemkin*, 1925: Three motifs from the Odessa steps sequence.

on multiple camera set-ups, like that of American and Soviet films. With the coming of sound, Josef von Sternberg's *The Blue Angel* revived the moving camera but married it to the naturalistic tradition, as did many other films in the brief period before Hitler's rise to power, such as *Mädchen in Uniform* and *M*. After 1933, such experiment as was permitted to exist was harnessed to propaganda.

THE SOVIET FILM

Since 1919 the film in Russia under state control has been used consciously as an instrument of propaganda and instruction. Directors were at first encouraged to make experiments likely to result in more effective films, and the group around Lev Kuleshov, which included Eisenstein and Pudovkin, deliberately set out to derive a theory of composition and structure from the films of D. W. Griffith and the American film in general. The first fruit of this Aristotelian approach to the new art was *Armored Cruiser Potemkin*.

"The importance of cutting and editing is the most widely recognized revelation of *Armored Cruiser Potemkin*. The sensations of fear, panic, and machine-like murder in the Odessa steps sequence could only have been communicated by this revolutionary cutting method. What must be remembered is that the total construction and frame-compositions of *Potemkin* were gauged and carried out with these particular juxtapositions in mind. The shots taken on the steps were filmed looking forward to the cutting table as much as were the famous shots at the end of the fourth reel—three marble lions which become one single rearing lion in the editor's hands and the audience's eyes. Heretofore, the movement of a film had depended largely on the action

EISENSTEIN, *Ten Days that Shook the World*, 1927.

ROOM, *Bed and Sofa*, 1926.

PUDOVKIN, *Storm Over Asia*, 1929.

within the sequence of shots. Eisenstein now created a new film rhythm by adding to the content the sharply varying lengths and free associations of the shots, a technique growing directly from his interest in psychological research. Besides the behavioristic stimulation made possible by this method, a new range of rhythmic patterns and visual dynamics was opened by *Potemkin*. This new process is usually distinguished from the usual process of putting a film together by calling it 'montage,' the French-Russian term, which is not to be confused with montage-effects as currently employed in Hollywood."

Of the twelve recurrent motifs which compose the mosaic of the Odessa steps sequence, three are reproduced on page 205.

Despite the extremes to which it has been carried, and the neglect into which it has recently fallen, montage remains the theoretic basis of film art. As a compositional method, it proved flexible enough in the years immediately following *Potemkin* to accommodate such varied themes as the development of a "class character" (*Mother*), the reconstruction of a historic event from a propagandist viewpoint (*Ten Days that Shook the World*), anti-colonialist propaganda (*Storm Over Asia*), psychological-social analysis (*Fragment of an Empire*) and what can only be called film poetry (*Arsenal*). In a famous manifesto of 1928 Eisenstein and Pudovkin extended the montage theory to the sound film even before they had had opportunity to work in the new medium.

Their theories were never to be realized. The same expediencies which had prompted the state to grant them freedom to create a "revolutionary art" now caused the withdrawal of that freedom. The "intellectual" films of Eisenstein, Pudovkin, and their colleagues were insufficiently popular with the masses whose lives and deeds they celebrated; all were censured for their "formalist" esthetics and a new era of "socialist realism" was proclaimed to have been ushered in with the production of *Chapayev*. What this has meant in practice has been the nearly total abandonment of the montage theory and methods in the Soviet Union, and a wholesale return to theatre tradition. The pioneer Soviet directors conformed as best they could; in *Alexander Nevsky* Eisenstein threw himself into another kind of formalism, more acceptable to the state and not unrelated to the methods and effects of one of his political opposite numbers, Cecil B. DeMille.

ERMLER, *The Fragment of an Empire*, 1929.

DOVZHENKO, *Arsenal*, 1929.

EKK, *The Road to Life*, 1931.

VASILYEV, *Chapayev*, 1934: Boris Babochkin, Boris Blinov.

EISENSTEIN, *Alexander Nevsky*, 1938.

CHAPLIN, *The Kid*, 1920:
Chaplin, Jackie Coogan.

HILLYER, *The Toll Gate*, 1920:
William S. Hart.

STROHEIM, *Greed*, 1924: Jean
Hersholt, Zasu Pitts, Gibson
Gowland.

THE AMERICAN FILM

After the burst of creative activity which had its climax in 1916, American film-makers devoted themselves to refining the narrative technique of which they were pre-eminently the inventors, and to the production of large numbers of films geared to the tastes of a mass market which was regarded as having expanded to its limits. Experiment continued in the commercial studios, but only in concert with, and by the leave of, the policy just described. Charles Chaplin, "the greatest creative figure ever associated with the screen," is almost the sole exception; since 1918 he has produced his films with his own finance and very much as he pleased. A partial exception was Erich von Stroheim, who, though working in the big studios, made his films without regard for the preferences of his employers or of the public. Unable to come to terms with boxofficialdom or to resolve the structural problems of his films, he was seldom able to send a picture to the screen as he originally conceived it, or even as he shot and edited it. His work is unequal, opulent, florid, and instinct with a searing realism which owes as much to the artist's knowledge of human passions as to his profound understanding of the pitiless power of the camera's eye. Even the fragment of his literal version of Frank Norris' novel *McTeague*, released as *Greed*, remains one of the greatest examples of cinematography extant.

Under the conditions described above, the most fertile vein which the American film has worked has been that of comedy, especially what had hitherto been called "low" comedy. This is close to the tastes of the mass audiences on whom the movies depend for existence and has a decided affinity for a visual medium. Among the several brilliant comedians who, like Chaplin, graduated from the school of Mack Sennett to stardom in the '20s and '30s, Buster Keaton developed slapstick into wry and sometimes metaphysical comment. His odd and significant hero is "without friends and relatives and he is generally incapable of associating with his fellow-

NIBLO, *The Three Musketeers*,
1921: Douglas Fairbanks.

KEATON and CRISP, *The
Navigator*, 1924: Keaton.

LUBITSCH, *So This Is Paris*, 1926:
Lilyan Tashman, Monte Blue.

SEASTROM, *The Wind*, 1928:
Lillian Gish.

VIDOR, *Hallelujah*, 1929: Harry
Gray, Fannie Belle de Knight.

beings on a human basis, but mechanical devices, though inimical to him, are the only 'beings' which can 'understand' him. . . He always wins in the end; not, like Chaplin, by romantically escaping from the world of machinery and the police into a realm of human freedom, but, on the contrary, by fatalistically throwing his humanity into the whirlpool of mechanical forces. He is a hero by the grace of un-reason and un-feelingness, and in this respect a very modern hero indeed."

Amongst actor-producers who rose to fame by reason of some trait of personality or physique, William S. Hart's "severe yet impassioned figure" dominated a series of admirable films, while Douglas Fairbanks became a world favorite because, "like most great entertainers, he did one thing superbly and all the time. It consisted in a range of gestures of the whole body, exquisitely coordinated. The sight of this in motion, whatever the plot was saying, is a kind of spiritual grace."

Of European directors imported to the United States, Ernst Lubitsch, the German, and Victor Seastrom, the Swede, best adapted themselves to Hollywood conditions, Lubitsch by virtue of his discreetly Americanized version of "Continental sophistica-tion." The sincere and hard-working Seastrom found an ally in Lillian Gish and between them they produced one of the most eloquent of the last silent films, *The Wind*: "every use is made of the film's ability to speak volumes by small things. The scene in which the wife dismembers the beef carcass while the girl irons her unsuitable dress contains the maximum of suggestion: the life of the whole house with its com-plex emotional stresses is fully rendered."

The coming of sound brought all development to a halt, as the camera and microphone were chained to the sound "stage," and to stage methods. King Vidor freed both at one stroke in the second year of the talkies with his *Hallelujah!* a film which faced all the esthetic problems raised by sound as few films have since, and which achieved in its dialogue an authenticity of human speech as no other film has. The next year, Lewis Milestone's *All Quiet on the Western Front* and Josef von Stern-berg's *Morocco* continued to explore the new compound medium, reducing dialogue to a subsidiary narrative function and once more, as in silent films, expressing both plot and theme through action, camera, and editing. Thereafter, the rapidly develop-ing sound medium resumed such traditions as slapstick (*Million Dollar Legs*), satire (*Bombshell, Duck Soup, Destry Rides Again*), camera trickwork (*The Invisible Man*), and the super-production (*Mutiny on the Bounty*). More typical, perhaps, were films like

CUKOR, *Camille*, 1936: Greta
Garbo.

208

FLEMING, *Bombshell*, 1933: Lee Tracy, Jean Harlow.

STERNBERG, *Morocco*, 1930: Adolph Menjou, Marlene Dietrich.

MILESTONE, *All Quiet on the Western Front*, 1930: Lew Ayres, Raymond Griffith.

CLINE, *Million Dollar Legs,* 1932: Ben Turpin.

Camille, The Thin Man, and *Mr. Deeds Goes to Town* which, through more credible charactcrizations and more natural (if still theatrical) dialogue, sought to adjust and refine the uneasy compromise between film and theatre on which most sound films rested, and still rest. More recently another form of narrative has appeared, this time under the influence of the novel, in which the story is told by an invisible narrator who bridges continuity gaps which would be hard to realize visually, and who, in the interests of suspense, unfolds the plot little by little in the form of flashbacks (*The Lost Weekend*). That this method, too, is a compromise has not deprived it of the approval and support of a public which cares little about esthetic *hubris* if it does not unduly impede the space, movement, and vitality on which the appeal of the movies depends.

LLOYD, *Mutiny on the Bounty,* 1935: Clark Gable, Charles Laughton.

WHALE, *The Invisible Man*, 1933: William Harrigan, Claude Rains.

VAN DYKE, *The Thin Man*, 1934: William Powell, Myrna Loy.

BRACKETT and WILDER, *The Lost Weekend,* 1945: Ray Milland.

CAPRA, *Mr. Deeds Goes to Town,* 1936: Gary Cooper.

CLAIR, *The Crazy Ray*, 1923: Albert Prejean.

CLAIR, *The Italian Straw Hat*, 1927: Olga Tschechova, Vital Geymond, Albert Prejean.

CLAIR, *Le Million*, 1930: René Lefevre.

THE FRENCH FILM AND THE SCANDINAVIAN FILM

"... The cinema is not in our blood. There are few nations which nurture all the arts ... I prophesy—we shall see in the future if I am right—that France has no more aptitude for the cinema than she has for music." When Louis Delluc wrote these words, France had already made her greatest contribution to the screen: for in France, Méliès, and after him Linder and Zecca and Durand, had invented film comedy and laid down all its basic principles. What Delluc was attacking by implication was a French tendency which persists to this day—a preoccupation with a form of film which stands in relation to the main line of cinematographic development as opera stands to music or the theatre. Even such remarkable French achievements as *La Grande Illusion* and *Carnival in Flanders* owe more to mature writing, and to the skills of the corps of great French actors, than to the more specifically cinematic arts—the arts of the camera and the cutting bench. In the best of them, we sense "something brilliant, but foreign to the medium."

But René Clair's comedies owe nothing to any older artistic tradition—nothing to anyone but his own cinematic predecessors, Méliès and Sennett and Chaplin. No films express themselves more fully through the unique powers of the film medium than *The Crazy Ray* and *The Italian Straw Hat* and *Le Million*. They create a new world which obeys laws of its own, yet this magic world has been composed out of the materials of everyday life in France. They are understood everywhere, and in France only too well. Yet Clair's films are no rebuke to Delluc; they rebuke instead a characteristic of our time by no means confined to French film-makers and audiences —an artistic admiration for the artistically unsuitable.

Paradoxically, France has also always nurtured the experimental film and it was to France, as the native home of the avant garde, that the Dane Carl-Theodor Dreyer came to make the greatest experiment of all, his masterpiece *La Passion de Jeanne d'Arc*. In Scandinavia, between 1914 and 1923, the Swedish and Danish directors

CLAIR, *A Nous la Liberté*, 1931: Raymond Cordy.

FEYDER, *Carnival in Flanders*, 1936: Louis Jouvet, Françoise Rosay.

RENOIR, *La Grande Illusion*, 1937: Pierre Fresnay.

SEASTROM, *The Phantom Chariot*, 1921: Seastrom.

STILLER, *Gösta Berling's Saga:*
Lars Hanson, Greta Garbo.

DREYER, *The Passion of Joan of Arc*, 1928: Falconetti.

CLAIR, *Entr'acte*, 1924.

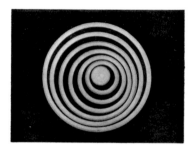

DUCHAMP, *Anaemic Cinema*, 1926.

KIRSANOV, *Menilmontant*, 1925.

WATSON, *The Fall of the House of
Usher*, 1928.

DALI and BUNUEL, *Le Chien
Andalou*, 1929.

LÉGER and MURPHY, *Ballet
Mécanique*, 1929.

developed in isolation a film style peculiar to themselves, a blend of legend and naturalism which deeply impresssed American and other European film-makers in famous films like *The Phantom Chariot* and *Gösta Berling*. But the Scandinavian home market was inadequate to support home industries when production costs soared, and its artists dispersed elsewhere in search of work—Dreyer to France, Asta Nielson to Germany, Stiller and Seastrom and Christianson to the United States. Now, many of them have returned, and Scandinavian film production has resumed in a new field, that of documentary.

AVANT GARDE

Although the French commercial cinema has long been dominated by the theatrical tradition, paradoxically it is in the field of experiment that, next to comedy, France has excelled. A cinematic "School of Paris" grew up during the 1920s which exerted influence and was emulated throughout the world. Here, influences from the American film, from literature, and especially from painting at first prevailed. The same Louis Delluc whose pessimism has been quoted above carried on the tradition of Griffith and Ince in *Fièvre* and *Eldorado*; *Ballet Mécanique* introduced machine-cubism to the screen; *Entr'acte* was Dada to the bone; and *Emak Bakia* and *Le Chien Andalou* were *consciously* surrealist films. The persistent interest of French intellectuals in the unknown powers of the new medium has kept alive in Paris a spirit of inquiry which has existed nowhere else to the same extent, and which has borne significant fruits for the cinema. The avant garde has served as a training-ground for many young talents; it gave us Clair and Renoir; and its post-war revival, in America as well as France, reminds us at every turn how little we still know about an art so many times pronounced a completed thing, or a dead one.

WRIGHT, *Song of Ceylon*, 1934.

RIEFENSTAHL, *Olympia*, 1936.

LORENTZ, *The River*, 1937.

THE FILM OF FACT AND OPINION

It was as an instrument of instruction and persuasion that the motion picture was first admired—and feared. Its vividness and its power to arouse emotion were among the first incentives to censorship, and not only its relative unpopularity but also a certain caution contributed to the tardiness of the fact film's development. It was indeed in war time, rather than in peace, that the fact film has, in Grierson's phrase, "met a felt want"; it took the urgent need for mass-indoctrination in a hurry to overcome the indifference or timidity of governments, institutions, and commercial producers (except of course in Nazi Germany and Soviet Russia where the powers of the medium were studied intensely in peace as in war). It was only in World War II that the film's ability to "emotionalize facts and rationalize emotions" was fully developed in Frank Capra's "Why We Fight" series of Army films. Before that, none of the democracies except Britain had made an organized attempt to discover what part the "film of life" could play in democratic processes. In Britain, John Grierson drew together into "the British documentary film movement" a group of educators, journalists, poets, artists, and film-makers who attempted, with historic success, to create a new form of dramatic instruction for use, primarily, in adult education outside the classroom—education in the fundamentals of modern life, including economics, sociology and psychology. British documentary was emulated in the America of the New Deal by Pare Lorentz, Ralph Steiner, Willard Van Dyke, and other new talents. The techniques and technicians of British and American peace time documentary were absorbed by the war effort.

All these attempts to manipulate facts in order to manipulate opinions drew inspiration from the work of a man whose chief interest was in the unmanipulated fact itself. Robert Flaherty was "the first film director to understand that the eye

CAPRA, *Prelude to War*, 1942.

FLAHERTY, *Nanook of the North*, 1922.

FLAHERTY, *Moana*, 1926.

MATTER, *Works of Calder*, 1949.

McCay, *Gertie the Dinosaur*, 1909.

Disney, *Skeleton Dance*, 1929.

of the camera does not behave like the human eye, which selects from a field of vision only what interests its owner. The camera's eye unselectively records everything before it." Flaherty wanted "what the camera's eye could show him that his own eye could not see"—and, if audiences found in his films a unique spirit of enquiry, of integrity, and of humanity, these qualities derived from his approach to the camera, the fundamental instrument of film-making.

ANIMATION

Survage, *Design for an Abstract Animated Film*, 1913.

After 1933, most animated films were produced in color. Since it is still impossible to reduce Technicolor films to 16mm, the collection is poor in works of animation of the sound period (and this fact also accounts for its poverty in color films of any kind). However, the program, "A Short History of Animation," provides a complete outline of the development of animation from the early work of Winsor McCay through the period 1915-1926, which saw the production of many animated series based on comic strip characters like Mutt and Jeff and Felix the Cat, to the early sound era, which brought the advent of Walt Disney, whose first Silly Symphony, *Skeleton Dance*, remains a masterwork of its kind. The Museum has also recently become the custodian of the work of the pioneer abstract animators Hans Richter and Oskar Fischinger, and it has long possessed Leopold Survage's designs for an abstract animated film, conceived in 1913.

Richter, *Rhythmus 21*, 1922.

Fischinger, *Motion Painting 1*, 1947.

ARCHITECTURE AND DESIGN

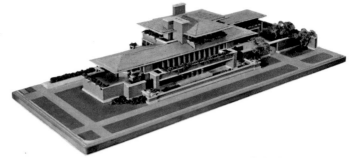

Frank Lloyd Wright: Robie
House, Chicago. 1909. Model

When the Museum was founded it was proposed that standards be defined and history written for architecture and design as well as for painting and sculpture. The Museum, through its Department of Architecture and Design, is indeed the principal institution in the world concerned with the qualitative selection and collection of modern architectural, industrial and graphic design.

The Department's first show at the Museum, held in 1932, was an international exhibition of modern architecture. Through photographs and models it showed the extraordinary revolution that had occurred in architecture, especially during the previous decade, but there was, of course, no way to "collect" the buildings themselves. The Department therefore established a photographic file which formed at that time the most comprehensive documentation of modern architecture. Scale models provided another means of representing buildings, and have been an important part of the Department's collection since its beginning. Of greater intrinsic and esthetic value is a group of drawings by architects.

Since it was founded, the Department has held exhibitions devoted to the work of individual architects, as well as a series of exhibitions concerned with the qualitative selection of contemporary American architecture. Two, called "Built in U.S.A.," covered respectively the periods 1932-1944 and 1946-1952. The second of these exhibitions included presentation of buildings by means of three-dimensional color slides, which have since been incorporated into the Department's collection of architectural photographs.

In the past twenty-two years single buildings of technical or esthetic importance have been shown in models and photographs, such as Frederick Kiesler's Endless House, Buckminster Fuller's Geodesic Dome, Paul Nelson's Suspended House, Frank Lloyd Wright's Loeb House and Johnson Wax Company office buildings, Mies van der Rohe's Chicago apartment houses, and Konrad Wachsman's steel airplane hangar. Many other exhibitions have been devoted to aspects of modern architecture as diversified as buildings commissioned by the U.S. Department of State, and two complete houses—the first by Marcel Breuer and the second by Gregory Ain—built in successive years in the Museum's garden to provide a full-scale demonstration of some of the planning features and furnishings characteristic of modern American architecture.

The plans of the Department had from the beginning (although it was called at first simply the "Department of Architecture") involved the related arts which in scale extend all the way from teaspoons to town planning. Furniture design in the twentieth century has been particularly influenced by architecture, much of the most beautiful modern furniture having been, in fact, designed by architects. The Department has formed a highly selective collection of furniture, including examples of the Art Nouveau of about 1900, important as the first style to break completely with historical revivalism. Unfortu-

continued on page 216

214

Posters—Jacques Villon: *Le Grillon*, 1899. Lithograph. Purchase. Henri de Toulouse-Lautrec: *Jane Avril*, 1899. Lithograph. Gift of Mrs. John D. Rockefeller, Jr., 1946. (Both from Print Room)

Screen—Pierre Bonnard. 1897. Lithograph. Mrs. John D. Rockefeller, Jr. Purchase Fund, 1949. (Print Room)

Furniture designed by Hector Guimard: *wood picture frame*, c. 1900 (with photograph and sketch of Paris Métro entrance designed by Guimard); *desk with removable top*, c. 1905; *bronze picture frame*, c. 1909; *desk chair*, c. 1905; *bronze umbrella stand*, c. 1902; *side table*, c. 1908. Gifts of Mme Guimard, 1949

Wallpaper sample—Maurice Denis. c. 1900. Lithograph. Purchase, 1952. (Print Room)

Vases L. C. Tiffany: *four favrile glass vases*, c. 1900. Edgar Kaufmann, Jr. Purchase Fund, 1947-53

Jewel Casket—Charles Knox for Liberty & Co., London (William Craythorne, craftsman): silver with mother-of-pearl, enamel and turquoise, 1900. Gift of the family of Mrs. John D. Rockefeller, Jr., 1949

Art Nouveau or Jugendstil or "Style 1900" was the first decorative style to break with historical revivalism. Influenced by the curvilinear patterns of Japanese Ukiyo-e prints, it embraced everything from poster design to architecture with forms often reminiscent of plants and flowers. Straight lines were avoided, even in picture frames, and the sinuous whiplash curve became Art Nouveau's typical contour in a vocabulary of shapes that was international in character.

nately, this part of the collection is lacking in works by the best designers of the period, such as Mackintosh and Gaudi, who stood outside the strict Art Nouveau style.

The next phase in the historical development of modern design represented in the collection is De Stijl, a Dutch movement of the early 1920s whose esthetic has had such a pronounced influence. The collection includes some one hundred and eighty examples of furniture, ranging from an 1860 Thonet bentwood chair to the recent series of chairs by the American designer Charles Eames. In several instances objects in the collection, most notably the Eames chairs, are in themselves a direct or indirect result of competitions held by the Museum.

There are many small objects in the collection: Tiffany glass, typewriters, calculators, lamps, sewing machines, kitchen utensils, fabrics, pottery and glassware. Of central importance to the Department's collection—as they are to concepts of form peculiar to twentieth-century art—are those objects first shown in 1934 and since that time character- ized as Machine Art. Geometric, precise, machine-finished, often integral parts of ma- chines themselves, like propeller blades and steel springs, these objects represent an attitude towards design so basic and powerful that even the twentieth-century handcrafts- man has come under its spell.

In general the collection has been formed from material exhibited in the Museum; examples of Lobmeyr glass, Art Nouveau and Thonet chairs were all first shown in the Museum and then acquired by the Department. One of the important sources for the collection is the annual exhibition of objects available in America, called "Good Design," under the direction of Edgar Kaufmann, Jr. This project is an outgrowth of the "Useful Objects Under $5.00" exhibitions initiated by John McAndrew in 1938. But the col- lection has intentional limits. Although there have been two automobile exhibitions the Department does not collect automobiles, which are inconvenient to store, nor does it collect objects too much under the influence of fashion and, therefore, of ephemeral value.

Bentwood rocking chair. 1860 design. Thonet Industries, Inc. Gift of Café Nicholson

Within the field covered by the Department's work is graphic design: posters, signs, letterheads, and other combinations of word and image. As with furniture, the poster collection begins with work of the 1890s, specifically that of Toulouse-Lautrec and Steinlen, and continues through to the 1952 *New York Times* series. The highlights of the collection are the great poster developments of the 1920s and the 1930s starting with the Russian Suprematists, the German Bauhaus and, later, the French movement headed by Cassandre and Carlu, and the London Underground series by McKnight Kauffer. The post-war period is covered in greater detail and includes almost every country. The collection boasts certain key groups of graphic design, among them being the unique Tschichold collection of De Stijl, Bauhaus and Dada material. Nevertheless there are gaps in the historical sequence which the Department hopes to fill. Meanwhile, material is constantly being added individually and through gifts of large privately owned collections.

PHILIP C. JOHNSON
Director, Department of Architecture and Design

Paintings (left to right)—Theo van Doesburg: *Rhythm of a Russian Dance*, 1918 (oil. Acquired through the Lillie P. Bliss Bequest). Van Doesburg: *Composition (The Cow)*, 1916-17 (oil. Purchase). Van Doesburg and van Eesteren: *Color Construction*, 1922 (gouache. Edgar Kaufmann, Jr. Fund). Piet Mondrian: *Composition C*, 1920 (oil. Purchase)

Furniture—Gerrit Rietveld: *Armchair*, 1917 (painted wood. Gift of Philip C. Johnson). *Table lamp*, 1924 (metal. Gift of the designer)

Typography—Frederick Kiesler: *Catalog cover and one page*, 1924 (Gift of the designer). Van Doesburg: *De Stijl magazine cover*, 1921 (Purchase)

De Stijl, 1917-1928, was initiated by Dutch painters during World War I, and like Art Nouveau developed a unifying concept affecting all the arts. But where Art Nouveau was richly curvilinear and dependent on organic forms, De Stijl reduced the elements of composition to rectangular forms independently articulated, asymmetrically grouped, and painted in clear, flat colors.

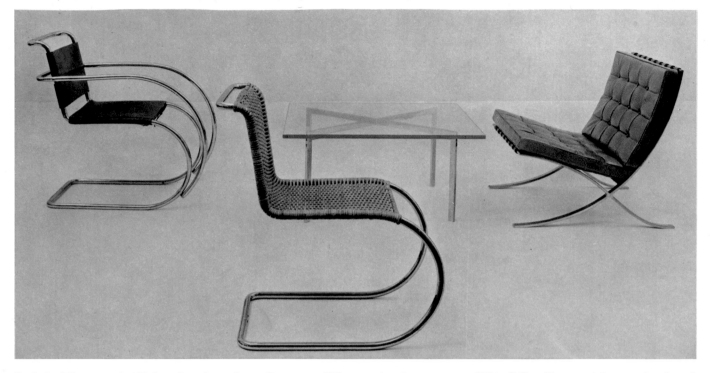

Ludwig Mies van der Rohe. American, born Germany 1886. LEFT TO RIGHT: *Armchair*, 1926 (chrome-plated steel and leather. Gift of Edgar Kaufmann, Jr.). *Side chair*, 1926 (chrome-plated steel and woven cane. Gift). *Coffee table*, 1930 (chrome-plated steel and plate glass. Gift of Knoll Associates). *"Barcelona" chair*, 1929 (chrome-plated steel and leather. Gift of Knoll Associates)

Walter Gropius, Le Corbusier and Ludwig Mies van der Rohe were the leaders of modern architecture in the generation following Frank Lloyd Wright. Mies succeeded Gropius as Director of the Bauhaus, and since 1938 has been Director of the Illinois Institute of Technology's Department of Architecture. Mies is perhaps most famous for his German Pavilion at the Barcelona Exposition of 1929, and for two entirely glass-walled steel skyscrapers built in Chicago in 1951. His architecture is characterized by the logic and clarity of its structure, and by the use of space as a fluid, almost tangible medium modulated by planes and surfaces of fine materials: onyx, travertine, colored glass, bronze and polished steel. The furniture Mies has designed reveals, like his architecture, a classic serenity of line and an unparalleled elegance. The Museum's collection includes fifty drawings by Mies van der Rohe of his own buildings.

Mies van der Rohe: Tugendhat House, Brno, Czechoslovakia. 1930. Model

Le Corbusier, the great theorist and pioneer of twentieth-century design, has had perhaps the most decisive effect on the course of architecture in our time. In the 1920s, with Amédée Ozenfant, he published and wrote for the magazine *L'Esprit Nouveau* and developed a semi-cubist style of painting called Purism. In softly colored abstractions of bottles, pitchers, and glasses he often anticipated the floor plans and elevations of his revolutionary buildings. Characteristic of his architecture are seemingly weightless multi-colored volumes, raised free of the ground, and wall surfaces arranged so that the spaces they contain are presented in strict, measured sequence. The most famous of his buildings are the Villa Savoye (1930), and the apartment house in Marseilles (1951). Le Corbusier's furniture, like his painting, sculpture, architecture and city planning, reveals a mastery of plastic form and calculated proportion, and a structural logic informed with taste and wit.

Le Corbusier (Charles-Eduard Jeanneret). French, born Switzerland 1888. TOP TO BOTTOM: *Still Life*, 1920 (oil on canvas. Van Gogh Purchase Fund). In collaboration with Pierre Jeanneret and Charlotte Perriand, gifts of Thonet Industries, Inc.: *Armchair*, 1929 (chrome-plated steel and canvas). *Ajdustable reclining chair*, 1927 (chrome-plated steel, canvas and leather). Model: *Villa Savoye (Les Heures Claires)*, Poissy-sur-Seine, France. 1930 (Purchase)

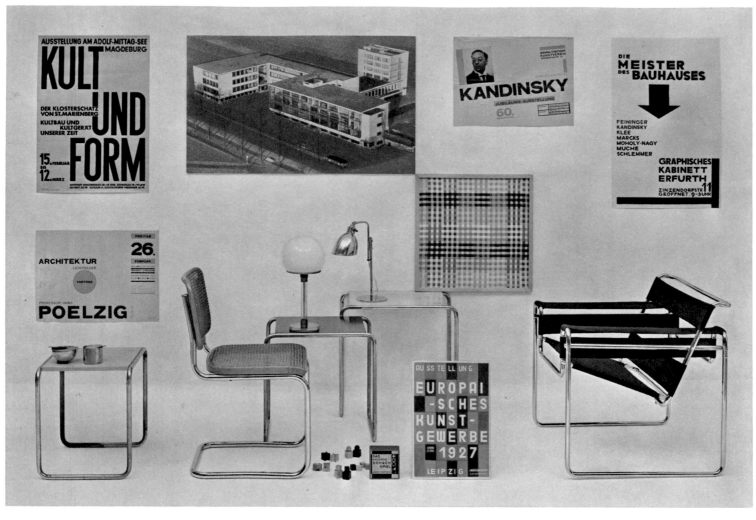

Bauhaus Building, Dessau, by Walter Gropius, 1925-26. Photograph. Purchase. (The model, on tour in Europe, was not available for inclusion in the photograph.)

Posters—George Dexel: *Kult und Form*. Unknown designer: *Meister des Bauhauses*. Other 3 posters by Herbert Bayer, 1926-27. Gifts of Philip C. Johnson

Table Cloth (framed) — Anni Albers: woven cotton, c. 1926. Purchase.

Chess Set — J. Hartwig: wood, 1924. Given anonymously

Furniture (chromed tubular steel framing)—Marcel Breuer: *3 end tables*, 1926, gift of Dr. Anny Baumann; *side chair*, 1928, purchase; *armchair*, 1925, gift of Herbert Bayer

Ash Trays — Marianne Brandt: *chromed steel and brass ash trays*, c. 1924-26. Gift of John McAndrew

Lamps—K. Jucker and W. Wagenfeld: *glass and metal lamp*, c. 1924. Gift of Philip C. Johnson. Christian Dell: *chromed metal lamp*, 1926. Gift of Mrs. Stanley Resor

The Bauhaus school, from 1919 to 1933, was the focal point in the integration of design with the machine age. Bauhaus designers of many nationalities approached all problems with a rational simplicity, employing straight lines and inventive use of materials (as in chairs of chrome-plated steel tubes). Bauhaus became a household word in Germany for the advanced design of the period. The school's main building at Dessau, designed by Walter Gropius, its founder and first director, is itself one of the great works of the 1920s. Many former members of the Bauhaus now live in the United States, Gropius himself having served as Chairman of Harvard's School of Architecture for fifteen years.

In this century of adventurous engineering, models of buildings serve as three-dimensional records of structural systems or spatial concepts which, in the absence of a suitable client, may never be realized. In Paul Nelson's *Suspended House*, for example, individual rooms are hung in mid-air from great steel trusses, and connected to each other by ramps and stairs. A completely different concept of architecture is suggested by Frederick Kiesler's model for a house whose interior space is contained by a shell forming floor, walls, and roof in one continuous surface. Buckminster Fuller's model of a dome, without engineering precedent, serves as a study for the many experimental versions of it that have actually been built.

Paul Nelson. American, lives in France. Model for a *Suspended House*, 1938. Metal. Gift of the Advisory Committee

Frederick Kiesler. American, born Austria. Model for the *Endless House*, 1951. Terra cotta. Purchase

Skidmore, Owings & Merrill. Gordon Bunshaft, Chief Designer. American. Model for *Lever House* (built, New York 1952). Gift of Lever Brothers

R. Buckminster Fuller. American. Model for a *Geodesic Dome*, 1952. Metal. Gift of the architect

The precise geometric shapes of seemingly undesigned machines and hand tools, became, in the 1920s, a matter of conscious esthetic choice influencing even the hand craftsman as well as painters, sculptors, and architects. To describe what therefore constitutes the chief design characteristic of our age the Museum invented the phrase "Machine Art," in 1934, when all the objects in these photographs were first exhibited.

All objects are gifts, 1934, of the American manufacturers unless otherwise noted. TOP, LEFT TO RIGHT: *Crucibles and evaporating dish* (Coors Porcelain Co. Purchase). *3 vases* (Walter Dorwin Teague for Corning Glass Works, Steuben Division). *Boiling flasks* (Pyrex. Corning Glass Works). *3 beakers* (Coors Porclain Co.). *2 flasks* (German glass. Eimer & Amend). *2 vases*, 1908 (porcelain. Frank G. Holmes for Lenox, Inc.). *Evaporating dishes* (Pyrex. Corning Glass Works)

BOTTOM, LEFT TO RIGHT: *Tray, flower bowl, and plate*, 1928 (copper and chromium. Walter von Nessen for Chase Brass & Copper Co., Inc.). *Baker's bowl* (steel. Lalance & Grosjean Mfg. Co.). *Outboard propeller* (Aluminum Co. of America). *Boat propeller* (bronze. Electric Boat Co.). *Coil of strip stainless steel* (American Steel & Wire Co.). *2 plumb bobs* (brass. Eugene Dietzgen Co., Inc.). *Serving tray*, 1928 (Nessen for Chase Brass & Copper Co., Inc.). *Bevel protractor and 3 outside calipers* (steel. Brown & Sharpe of New York, Inc.). *Bearing spring, spring and 2 spring sections* (steel. American Steel & Wire Co.). *Automobile piston* (Aluminum Co. of America). *Circular saw* (steel. Henry Disston & Sons, Inc.). *4 hotel sauté pans* (Aluminum Cooking Utensil Co.). *Yale lock* (steel. Yale & Towne Mfg. Co.). *Flush valve* (chromed brass. Scovill Mfg. Co.). *Self-aligning ball bearing* (steel. SKF Industries, Inc.). *Hotel sauce pan* (steel. Lalance & Grosjean Mfg. Co.)

The basic response to form evident in machine art has evolved towards a freer acceptance of compound curves and sculpturally modulated surfaces. Most of the objects in these photographs were designed *after* 1934, the date of the Museum's first Machine Art exhibition.

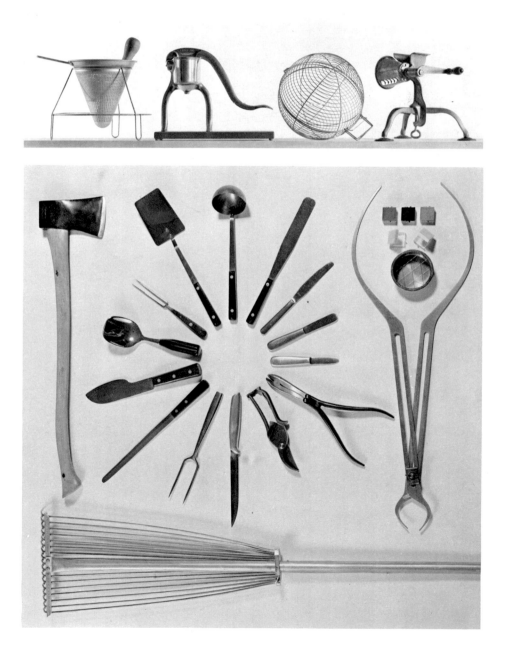

TOP, LEFT TO RIGHT: *2 tumblers*, c. 1943 (plastic. U.S. Navy messware. Watertown Mfg. Co.). *Cookie cutters* (tin. Purchase). *Tapping die* (steel. Anchor Tool Co.). *Table-top tripod* (Waltham Screw Co. Gift of Willoughby Camera Stores, Inc.). *Water tumbler and bowl*, 1945 (plastic. Earl S. Tupper for Tupper Corp.). *Tumbler*, c. 1947 (stainless steel. Vollrath Co.). *Wastepaper basket* (plastic. Plas-Tex Corp.,). *Pitcher*, 1940 (stainless steel. Rex A. Stevens for Carrollton Mfg. Co. Gift of Bloomingdale Brothers Inc.;). *Electric iron* (Landers, Frary & Clark,). *Bowl*, 1951 (enameled metal. Edward Stone for N.S. Gustin Co.). *Cocktail shaker*, c. 1939 (chromed steel. W. Archibald Welden for Revere Copper & Brass, Inc.). *U.S. Navy messware* (plastic. Watertown Mfg. Co.). *Cigarette box* (chromed metal. Cravell Inc. Purchase,). *Powder jar* (plastic, Italian. Gift of Greta Daniel)

MIDDLE, LEFT TO RIGHT: *Food strainer*, 1932 (aluminum. The Aluminum Cooking Utensil Co. Gift of Lewis & Conger). *Fruit press* (aluminum. Gift of Hammacher Schlemmer & Co., Inc.). *Salad washer*, c. 1946 (metal wire. M. Schimmel for Raymar Industries, Inc. Purchase). *Food grinder*, 1922 (aluminum. J. H. Lickert for Griscer Industries. Gift of R. H. Macy & Co.)

BOTTOM, LEFT TO RIGHT: *Axe* (steel. Collins Tools. Gift of Abercrombie & Fitch Co.). *Garden rake*, 1945 (aluminum. Vernon P. Steele for Kenco Products Corp. Purchase). *Meat fork*, c. 1950 (German, stainless steel. Gift of Philip C. Johnson). *Ice cream spade* (chromed metal. G. T. Williams Mfg. Co. Gift of Lewis & Conger). *Kitchen tool* (chromed metal. Ontario Knife Co. Gift of Lewis & Conger). *Meat slicer* (stainless steel. Ekco Products Co.). *Carving fork and knife*, 1946 (stainless steel and aluminum. Dean Pollock for Gerber Legendary Blades. Purchase and gift of Abercrombie & Fitch Co.). *Pruning shears*, 1951 (Rudolf Moethe for J. A. Henckels. Gift of Edgar Kaufmann, Jr.). *Shoemaker's tool*, 1916 (Sargent & Co. Gift of Philip C. Johnson). *Clam and oyster knives*, 1940 (K. Murphy Co. Gift of Lewis & Conger). *Dinner knife*, 1937 (stainless steel. International Silver Co. Gift of Greta Daniel). *Spatula, soup ladle and cake turner*, 1944-46 (stainless and vanadium steel. Gifts of Ekco Products Co.). *Caliper*, 1946 (Alex J. Ettl. Sculpture House). *5 pill boxes* (plastic. Gift of Greta Daniel). *Ashtray* (aluminum. Burchard, Inc.)

TOP, LEFT TO RIGHT: Eero Saarinen and Charles Eames, Americans: *armchair* 1940 (molded plywood with sponge rubber. Purchase). Antonio Bonet, Juan Kurchan and Jorge Ferrari-Hardoy, Argentinians: *sling chair*, c. 1938 (metal and leather. Edgar Kaufmann, Jr. Purchase Fund). Eames: *side chair*, 1951 (metal wire and leather. Gift of Herman Miller Furniture Company). Saarinen: *armchair*, 1948 (molded plastic and foam rubber. Gift of Knoll Associates). Bruno Mathsson, Swedish: *side chair*, 1940 (laminated wood and canvas webbing. Purchase). BOTTOM, LEFT TO RIGHT: Alvar Aalto, Finnish: *armchair*, 1932 (laminated and bent plywood. Gift of Edgar Kaufmann, Jr.). Hans Wegner, Danish: *armchair*, 1949 (wood and woven cane. Gift of Georg Jensen, Inc.). Eames: *armchair*, 1948 (molded plastic and metal wire. Gift of Herman Miller Furniture Company). Eames: *side chair*, 1946 (molded plywood and metal rods. Gift of Herman Miller Furniture Company)

Besides the already classic chairs by Mies van der Rohe, Marcel Breuer and Le Corbusier, the Museum's collection includes examples of two recent solutions to the difficult problem of chair design. The first is the traditional method of hand-shaping wood members and hand-weaving applied seat and back elements, producing fresh variations of traditional themes. The second approach explores the possibilities of new techniques, such as the forming of plywood or plastic into a seat in much the same way that an automobile body is stamped out by a die-press.

Machine-produced objects of complex form, from vacuum cleaners to automobiles, are classified as industrial design. Almost all such design problems are exercises in packaging: a varying number of mechanical components must be protected by an outer casing, the shape of which can sometimes be made to indicate the object's function. In the Olivetti Company's office typewriter (below) the subtly modelled shell partly masks, partly reveals the complex mechanism thereby creating an esthetically satisfactory form.

FROM TOP, LEFT: Emilio Cerri, Italian: *sewing machine*, 1934 (gift of Necchi Sewing Machine Sales Corp.). Marcello Nizzoli, Italian: *printing calculator*, 1946; *portable typewriter*, 1949; *office typewriter*, 1947 (gifts of Olivetti Corporation of America). Raymond Loewy Associates, American: *radio*, 1946 (gift of the Hallicrafters Co.)

TOP ROW, LEFT TO RIGHT: *Crystal bowl*, 1948 (Vera Liskova, Czech. For Lobmeyr. Gift of Van Dugteren & Sons, Inc.). *Champagne glass*, 1924 (Oswald Haerdtl, Austrian. For Lobmeyr. Gift of Van Dugteren & Sons, Inc.). *Teapot*, 1932 (Wilhelm Wagenfeld, German. For Jenaer Glaswerk. Gift of Fraser's, Inc.). *5 stem glasses*, 1920 (Josef Hoffmann, Austrian. For Lobmeyr. Gift of Van Dugteren & Sons, Inc.). *Bowl*, 1930 (A. D. Copier, Dutch. For Leerdam. Gift). *2 tumblers*, 1939-41 (Elis Bergh, Swedish. For Kosta Ltd. Gift of D. Stanley Corcoran, Inc.). *Tumbler*, 1948 (Liskova. For Lobmeyr. Gift of Van Dugteren & Sons, Inc.). *4 stem glasses*, 1911-35 (designed by the manufacturers. Compagnie des Cristalleries de Baccarat. Gift of Baccarat & Porthault, Inc.)

MIDDLE ROW, LEFT TO RIGHT: *Coffee cup and saucer, 3 plates, tea cup and saucer*, 1947 (porcelain. Hermann Gretsch, German. For Schoenwald Porcelain Factory. Gift of Fraser's, Inc.). *4 plates, cream-soup cup and saucer*, 1930-49 (Gretsch. For Arzberg Porcelain Mfg. Co. Gift of H. E. Lauffer Co.). *Tea cup and saucer, plate*, 1929-33 (Trude Petri-Raben. German. For Royal Berlin Porcelain Factory. Gift of Fraser's Inc.). *Pottery bowl*, c. 1951 (William de Vries, Dutch. For Fris. Gift of Foreign Advisory Service Corp.). *Fruit dish and plate* (Petri-Raben. For Royal Berlin Porcelain Factory. Gift of Fraser's, Inc.)

BOTTOM ROW, LEFT TO RIGHT: *Stainless steel flatware*, c. 1929 (German manufacturer's design for Marshall Field & Co. Gift of Marshall Field & Co.). *Pottery salad bowl*, 1947 (Edith Heath, American. For Heath Ceramics. Gift of N. S. Gustin Co.). *Soup ladle, salt dish, pepper mill*, 1949-51 (porcelain and wood. Sitterle and Keith, Americans. Gift of Sitterle Ceramics). *Silver pepper and salt shakers*, 1950 (Allan Adler, American. Gift of the designer). *3 plastic bowls*, 1950 (Charles McCrea, American. Gift of Plastic Productions Co.)

Examples of tableware in the Museum's collection date from 1900 to 1951, ranging through such persistent shapes as Napoleonic cognac glasses and Georgian flatware, to new uses of porcelain and wood in salt and pepper grinders, and the Jena-glass teapot with its curiously 1930 handle. All of these objects depend for their appeal on clarity of forms and relationships, rather than on applied ornament.

Since manufacture by hand allows a variety of shape and finish not necessarily inherent in the machine process, the individual craftsman often enriches the forms of the twentieth century with his particular sensitivity to materials. The craft objects in the Museum's collection illustrate both the formal geometry of the machine and the modeling that retains the mark of the craftsman's hand.

TOP: *Chasuble, burse, stole, chalice veil*, c. 1950 (Henri Matisse, French, born 1869. Silk with velvet and silk appliqués. Les Ateliers des Arts Appliqués, Cannes. Purchase)

RIGHT: *Cherrywood platter* (James Prestini, American. Gift of Philip L. Goodwin). *3 wood bowls and tray*, 1934-45 (Prestini. Edgar Kaufmann, Jr. Fund). *Wood beaker*, 1951 (Reynold G. Dennis, American. Gift of Lemurian Crafts). *Wood cigarette box* (Russian. Gift of Pennsylvania Drug Co.)

LEFT: *Pottery vase* (Laura Anderson, American. Gift of the artist). *Enamelled aluminum platter*, 1950 (Ernst Lichtblau, American. Gift of Joseph Franken). *5 pottery vases and bowls*, 1943-46 (Otto and Gertrude Natzler, Americans. Gifts of Edgar Kaufmann, Jr.). *Jade ashtray* (Austrian. Gift of Georg Jensen, Inc.)

CENTER: *Mother-of-pearl and ebony stamp box*, 1946 (Josef Hoffmann, Austrian. For Künstlerwerkstätten, Vienna—Karl Krehan, craftsman. Purchase). *Stoneware vase*, 1950 (Carl Harry Stalhane, Swedish. Gift of Rorstrand, Inc.). *Glass vase*, 1938 (Paolo Venini, Italian. Edgar Kaufmann, Jr. Purchase Fund). *Blue pottery bowl* (Otto and Gertrude Natzler. Gift of Edgar Kaufmann, Jr.) *Silver ice bucket*, 1950 (Magnus Stephensen, Danish. For Georg Jensen. G. Pedersen, craftsman. Gift of Philip C. Johnson). *Green glass ashtray*, 1935 (Venini. Gift of Lenart Import, Ltd.). *Wood platter*, 1951 (Tapio Wirkkala, Finnish. Gift of Georg Jensen, Inc.). *Silver chess set*, 1927 (Man Ray, American. Mrs. John D. Rockefeller, Jr. Purchase Fund)

BELOW: *White glass vase*, 1949 (Venini. Gift of Georg Jensen, Inc.). *Glass ashtray*, 1944 (Pietro Chiesa, Italian. For Luigi Fontana & Co. Edgar Kaufmann, Jr. Purchase Fund). *Glass bowl*, c. 1946 (Goran Hongell, Finnish. For Karhula. Gift of Finland Ceramics Glass Corp.). *Marble cigarette box*, c. 1952 (Richard Blow, American. For Montici. Purchase)

POSTERS AND TYPOGRAPHY

Graphic design in the twentieth century has been influenced by concepts in painting and architecture. The cubist posters of Cassandre, the photomontages of Lissitzky, and Jan Tschichold's asymmetric compositions of simplified typography all illustrate these concepts. The photograph as a pictorial element, and new mechanical processes of reproduction such as photolithography and silk screen have also contributed to the range and power of visual communication. The Museum's collection of graphic design includes posters for institutional, political, commercial and war themes, as well as for artists' exhibitions. Beginning with the Art Nouveau posters of Toulouse-Lautrec, Chéret, Bonnard, and Steinlen, the collection extends through the *Stijl* movement, the Bauhaus school and surrealism to current posters in which lettering is the sole visual symbol. A few of the posters reproduced have been drawn from the Museum's Print Room, and several pages from books and magazines from the Library.

A. M. Cassandre, French: *Watch the Fords Go By*, 24 sheet billboard poster, 1938.

OPPOSITE LEFT: 1. Raymond Savignac, French: *Air-Wick*, Paris, 1951. 2. A. M. Cassandre, French: *Dubonnet*, 1932. Gift of Bernard Davis. 3. Abram Games, English: *London Transport*, 1949. 4. Max Bill, Swiss: *Vote Yes*, 1940. 5. Herbert Leupin, Swiss: *Die Weltwoche*, c.1950. Gift of Pro-Helvetia. 6. Ben Shahn, American: CIO poster, 1946. 7. W. J.H.B. Sandberg, Dutch: *Ten Belgian Sculptors*. Gift of the Stedelijk Museum, Amsterdam. 8. El Lissitzky, Russian: *USSR Exhibition*, Zurich, 1929. 9. Herbert Matter, American: *Polio*, 1949. Gift of the National Foundation for Infantile Paralysis. 10. Bruno Munari, Italian: *Eco del Mondo* (newspaper), 1949. 11. Jean Carlu, French: World War II poster, 1942. 12. Duda, Misek and Tyfa, Czechs: *International Exhibition of Travel Posters*, 1948. Gift of the Czech Information Service. 13. Otto Aicher, German: Lecture poster, 1950. 14. E. McKnight Kauffer, American: *B. P. Ethyl*, 1933. Gift of Shell-Mex. B.P. 15. G. Klutsis, Russian: *Fulfilled Plan – Great Work*, 1930.

OPPOSITE RIGHT: 1. Jan Tschichold, German: *Exhibition*, Kunsthaus, Zurich, 1929. 2. Henri Matisse, French: *Nice* (tourist poster), 1949. Gift of G.E. Kidder Smith. 3. Jack Levine, American: *Levine Exhibition*, 1950. Gift of Charles Alan. 4. Pablo Picasso, Spanish: *Exhibition, Vallauris*, 1948. Gift of D. H. Kahnweiler. 5. Georges Braque, French: *Braque Exhibition*. Gift of the Galerie Maeght. 6. Joan Miro, Spanish: *Miro Exhibition*, 1949. Gift of the Galerie Maeght. 7. Pablo Picasso, Spanish: *Exhibition, Vallauris*, 1952. Gift of Curt Valentin. 8. David Aronson, American: *Aronson Exhibition*. 9. Yoshio Hayakawa, Japanese: *Department Store Exhibitions*, 1952. 10. Fernand Léger, French: *Léger Exhibition*, 1951.

FIRST ROW—Pierre Bonnard, French: *La Revue Blanche*, 1894. Theophile Steinlen, Swiss: *Pure Milk*. Gift of Pro-Helvetia, Switzerland. SECOND ROW—Max Ernst, American, born Germany: Exhibition, Kunsthaus, Zurich. Max Huber, Italian: *CIAM* 7th International Congress, 1949. Film poster for *Faust*, 1926. Gift of U.F.A.

RIGHT—Paul Rand, American: *Interfaith Day*, 1952. Paul Smith and Kenneth Haak, Americans: *The New York Times*, 1951.

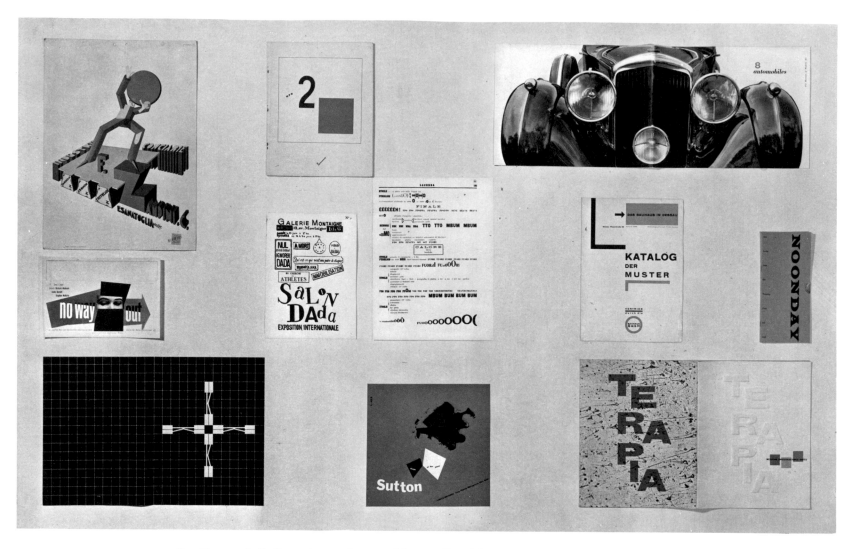

TOP ROW, LEFT TO RIGHT—Ivo Pannaggi, Italian: *show card*, 1924. El Lissitzky, Russian: *book cover*, 1922. Leo Lionni, American: *Museum of Modern Art catalog*, 1951.

MIDDLE ROW, LEFT TO RIGHT—Paul Rand, American: *film advertisement*, 1951. *Catalog cover*, Galerie Montaigne, Paris, 1922. Futurist poem by Francesco Cangiullo, Italian: *Lacerba*, No. 12, 1914. Herbert Bayer, American: *Bauhaus catalog*, 1927. Alvin Lustig, American: *brochure* for Noonday Press, 1953.

BOTTOM ROW, LEFT TO RIGHT—Herbert Matter, American: *catalog* for Knoll Associates, 1951. Rudolph de Harak, American: *album cover*, 1952. Will Burtin, American: *medical magazine*, 1953.

Besides posters, the Graphic Design collection includes work on a smaller scale such as announcements, direct mail advertisements, brochures, book jackets, letterheads, magazine covers and show cards distinguished for their typography and layout.

Early use of typographical liberties for phonetic emphasis is illustrated by Cangiullo's Futurist poem; effective if anarchic freedom of type and symbol, by the Dada catalog cover. By contrast, El Lissitzky's book cover relates the basic form of the numeral to other abstract elements.

More recent examples, such as the design by Matter, show the decorative elaboration of the form of letter. In his catalog cover Lionni cuts a photograph to emphasize the point of the Museum's automobile exhibition, namely, quality of design.

THE MUSEUM COLLECTIONS: COMMITTEES AND DEPARTMENTS

COMMITTEES FOR THE YEAR 1953-54

POLICY COMMITTEE FOR THE MUSEUM'S PERMANENT COLLECTION OF MASTERWORKS: William A. M. Burden, *Chairman*; Stephen C. Clark, Philip L. Goodwin, A. Conger Goodyear, Mrs. Simon Guggenheim, Mrs. David M. Levy, Nelson A. Rockefeller, James Thrall Soby, John Hay Whitney

COMMITTEE ON THE MUSEUM COLLECTIONS: James Thrall Soby, *Chairman*; Philip L. Goodwin, *Vice-Chairman*; Mrs. Simon Guggenheim, Mrs. Sam A. Lewisohn, Mrs. Gertrud A. Mellon, Mrs. John D. Rockefeller, 3rd, John L. Senior, Jr.; *ex officio*: William A. M. Burden, John Hay Whitney. *Advisers*: René d'Harnoncourt, Director of the Museum; Andrew C. Ritchie, Director of Painting and Sculpture

PAST COMMITTEES, 1929-53:

COMMITTEE ON GIFTS AND BEQUESTS, 1929-33: A. Conger Goodyear, *Chairman*; Paul J. Sachs; *ex officio*: Alfred H. Barr, Jr., Director of the Museum

ADVISORY COMMITTEE'S SUB-COMMITTEE ON THE MUSEUM COLLECTION, 1940-41: William A. M. Burden, *Chairman*; Lincoln Kirstein, Mrs. Duncan H. Read, James Thrall Soby, Monroe Wheeler

ACQUISITIONS COMMITTEE, 1934-44

COMMITTEE ON THE MUSEUM COLLECTIONS, 1944-53
(The Acquisitions Committee was superseded in 1944 by the Committee on the Museum Collections, which has similar but somewhat broader responsibilities.)
William A. M. Burden, 1943-50 (succeeding *Chairman*, 1946-47; *Chairman*, 1947-50)
Stephen C. Clark, 1934, 1938-50 (*Chairman*, 1934, 1943-44, 1946-47)
Philip L. Goodwin, 1937-39, 1950-53 (*Vice-Chairman*, 1950-53)
A. Conger Goodyear, 1934-44, 1947-52
Mrs. Simon Guggenheim, 1940-53
Bartlett H. Hayes, Jr., 1944-46
Sam A. Lewisohn, 1934-40, 1945-50 (*Chairman*, 1937-39)
Mrs. Sam A. Lewisohn, 1944-45, 1950-53
Mrs. Charles S. Payson, 1939-40
Miss Agnes Rindge, 1943-46
Mrs. John D. Rockefeller, 3rd, 1950-53
Nelson A. Rockefeller, *ex officio*, 1946-53
John L. Senior, Jr., 1951-53
James Thrall Soby, 1940-53 (succeeding *Chairman*, 1941-42; *Chairman*, 1944-46, 1950-53; *Vice-Chairman*, 1946-50)
James Johnson Sweeney, 1943-46 (*Vice-Chairman*)
Edward M. M. Warburg, 1934-36, 1939-42 (*Chairman*, 1936, 1939-41)
Mrs. George Henry Warren, Jr., 1943-47
John Hay Whitney, *ex officio*, 1946-53
Alfred H. Barr, Jr., 1943-46; *ex officio*, 1934-36

Lincoln Kirstein, *Consultant in Latin-American art*, 1942-43
René d'Harnoncourt, *Adviser*, 1951-53
Andrew Carnduff Ritchie, *Adviser*, 1948-53

THE MUSEUM COLLECTIONS (TO JANUARY 1954)

Alfred H. Barr, Jr., *Director*; Dorothy C. Miller, *Curator*; Betsy Jones, *Secretary*; Sara Mazo, Letitia T. Howe, *Curatorial Assistants*; Marie Alexander, *Secretary to the Director*.

William S. Lieberman, *Curator of Prints*; Dorothy L. Lytle, *Assistant Curator of Prints*.

The Museum Collections, one of Museum's five administrative divisions, established in 1947, embraces all works of art in Museum's possession. Director of the Museum Collections is responsible to Committee on the Museum Collections, Chairman of which reports to Board of Trustees.

Curatorially, staff of Museum Collections directly concerned only with painting, sculpture, drawings and prints; curatorial responsibility for other collections divided among Departments of Photography, Architecture and Design, and Film Library. (Separate Department of Painting and Sculpture has to do only with temporary exhibitions but its director, Andrew Carnduff Ritchie, is also Adviser to Committee on the Museum Collections.)

Proposed before Museum opened in 1929, curatorial departments and their collections took form gradually. In 1945 galleries first set aside for museum collection. Today for lack of space only film and sculpture collections adequately shown, paintings, drawings, prints less so. Photograph and design collections not regularly exhibited but may be studied on request.

SECTION OF PAINTING, SCULPTURE AND DRAWING: collection, begun in 1929, by 1932 numbered 6 paintings, 8 sculptures, 2 drawings, all gifts. Lillie P. Bliss Collection (bibl. 75) conditionally bequeathed 1931, accessioned 1934, gave Museum collection importance. Advisory Committee purchased its first gifts, 1935. Between 1935-37 Mrs. John D. Rockefeller, Jr. gave her collections of painting and sculpture, mostly American. Among early donors of important works were Walter P. Chrysler, Jr., Stephen C. Clark, A. Conger Goodyear, Aristide Maillol, and Edward M. M. Warburg. Director of the Museum, A. H. Barr, Jr., served as Curator of Painting and Sculpture, 1929-43; assisted by Jere Abbott, Associate Director, 1929-32, and Dorothy C. Miller, Assistant Curator, 1935-43.

In 1938 Mrs. Simon Guggenheim made first gift to magnificent collection purchased with her frequently replenished fund (bibl. 101d); Mrs. Rockefeller, aided by Nelson A. Rockefeller, established Museum's first large purchase fund.

First catalog, 1942, listed 693 paintings and sculptures. Inter-American Fund donated, 1942, (bibl. 97).

In 1943, James Thrall Soby became Director of Painting and Sculpture, Miss Miller, Curator. Soby succeeded in 1945 by James Johnson Sweeney who resigned in 1946. In 1947 painting and sculpture collections placed in charge of present Director of newly formed Division of the Museum Collections.

October, 1947, under terms of formal agreement (bibl. 101) Museum sold to Metropolitan Museum of Art a number of works already deemed 'classical,' proceeds to be used for purchase of more 'modern' works. New catalog, 1948 (bibl. 101) listed 797 paintings and sculptures.

February, 1953, important change of policy (bibl. 101d) involved creation of scrupulously chosen permanent nucleus of important works beginning with latter half of 19th century. Policy Committee for the Museum's Collection of Masterworks appointed and 1947 agreement with Metropolitan Museum abrogated.

Among more recent bequests of works of art are those of Anna Erickson Levene in memory of Dr. Phoebus Aaron Theodor Levene 1947, Sam A. Lewisohn 1952 (bibl. 101d) and Katherine S. Dreier 1953 (bibl. 101d). Recent donors of important works include Stephen C. Clark, Allan D. Emil, A. Conger Goodyear, Mr. and Mrs. Alex L. Hillman, Vladimir Horowitz, Mr. and Mrs. William B. Jaffe, Madame Carlos Martins, Mr. and Mrs. John de Menil, Nelson A. Rockefeller, Mr. and Mrs. Peter A. Rübel, Sam Salz, and Mr. and Mrs. Charles Zadok. By 1954 painting and sculpture collection numbered 1145.

PRINT COLLECTION: Paul J. Sachs gave first prints, 1929, followed in 1932 by Mrs. Saidie A. May, J. B. Neumann. Lillie P. Bliss Bequest, 1934, included 50 prints. Mrs. John D. Rockefeller, Jr., collecting for Museum since 1931, gave 1600 prints in 1940, adding others until her death in 1948. Abby Aldrich Rockefeller Print Room opened, 1949, William S. Lieberman, Associate Curator, Dorothy L. Lytle, Custodian. (*M. of M. A. Bul.* XVI, no. 4, 1949.)

Other principal donors of prints or purchase funds include Dr. F. H. Hirschland, Victor S. Riesenfeld, Mrs. John D. Rockefeller, 3rd, Nelson A. Rockefeller, David Rockefeller, Georges Rouault, Curt Valentin and the Spaeth Foundation.

DANCE ARCHIVES established 1939 with Lincoln Kirstein's generous gift (bibl. 78). Paul Magriel, Librarian, succeeded, 1944, by George Amberg, Curator of the Department of Dance and Theatre Design. Suspended in 1948, its modern collections were divided among other departments.

THE DEPARTMENT OF PHOTOGRAPHY

Edward Steichen, *Director*; Wayne Miller, *Assistant to Director*; Kathleen Haven, *Assistant*

Photographs first exhibited in 1932 under Julien Levy's direction in *Murals by American Painters and Photographers*. First photographs acquired 1933, gift of Lincoln Kirstein. First comprehensive exhibition, *Photography 1839-1937*, directed by Beaumont Newhall, Museum Librarian.

Department of Photography formally established 1940, David H. McAlpin, Trustee Chairman, Beaumont Newhall, Curator. (*M. of M. A. Bul.* VIII, no. 2, 1940-41.) By 1943 collection numbered some 2000 prints.

During McAlpin's and Newhall's absence in armed services, 1942-45, James Thrall Soby served as Trustee Chairman, Nancy Newhall as Acting Curator. Photography Center, Willard D. Morgan, Director, 1943-44. (*M. of M. A. Bul.* XI, no. 2, 1943.)

In 1947 Edward Steichen appointed Director, position of curator lapsing. Collection, January 1954, numbered 2500 prints by 650 photographers. (*M. of M. A. Bul.* XIX, no. 4, 1952.)

Among the other most important of 62 exhibitions were: *Photographs from the Collection* '44 (N. Newhall); *Road to Victory* '42 (Steichen, Bayer); *Exact Instant* '49 (Steichen); *In and Out of Focus* '48 (Steichen). Among one-man shows: D. O. Hill, Cameron, Atget, Stieglitz, Strand, Cartier-Bresson, E. Weston.

THE FILM LIBRARY

Richard Griffith, *Curator*; Margareta Akermark, *Circulation Director*; Olga Gramaglia, *Technician*; Joanne Godbout, *Custodian of Motion Picture Stills*. Iris Barry, *European Representative*.

The Museum of Modern Art Film Library founded in 1935 with funds provided by Rockefeller Foundation and several Trustees of the Museum. Original Trustee Committee: John Hay Whitney, *Chairman*, A. Conger Goodyear, Edward M. M. Warburg. (*M. of M. A. Bulletins* III, no. 2, 1935; IV, no. 4, 1937; VIII, no. 5, 1941; XIII, no. 2, 1945)

Films total some 10,000,000 feet, much of merely historical interest. Since 1939, programs of more important films shown in auditorium; (current cycle of 34 films runs for about 7 months). About 350 films a year sent out to other institutions. Film Library is custodian, not owner, of films; ownership resides in original producers or other owners of copyright.

Film Library's first Director, John E. Abbott, served until 1947, its first Curator, Iris Barry, until 1951. Former staff members included G. W. Bitzer, Alistair Cooke, W. L. Jamison, Edward F. Kerns, Arthur Knight, Jay Leyda, and Paul Rotha.

ARCHITECTURE AND DESIGN

Philip Johnson, *Director*; Arthur Drexler, *Curator*; Mildred Constantine, *Associate Curator*; Greta Daniel, *Assistant Curator*.

Department of Architecture established in 1932 following exhibition *Modern Architecture* directed by Philip Johnson, Chairman of Department, 1932-34. First exhibitions of industrial and decorative arts; first poster and typography competitions, 1933. *Machine Art*, 1934, initiated design collection.

In 1935, under Committee headed by Philip L. Goodwin, Ernestine Fantl appointed Curator of Department of Architecture and Industrial Art. John McAndrew, Curator 1937-40: first architecture competitions; *Useful Objects under Five Dollars* (1938) precursor of *Good Design* shows.

Separate Department of Industrial Design set up in 1940; Eliot F. Noyes, Director, organized *Organic Design* competition and show. During war Alice M. Carson in charge of the Department, 1914-43, then Susanne Wasson-Tucker, 1943-46, assisted by Greta Daniel. Edgar Kaufmann, Jr., Curator, then Director, 1946-48, directed *Low Cost Furniture Design* competition; since 1949 Director of annual *Good Design* exhibition. (*M. of M. A. Bul.* XIV, no. 1, 1946.)

Department of Architecture directed by Janet Henrich, 1941-42, then Elizabeth Mock, 1942-46; first *Built in USA, 1932-44*. Philip L. Goodwin, continued Trustee Chairman until 1948.

Two departments reunited 1949 as Department of Architecture and Design. Johnson rejoined staff as Director; Peter Blake, Curator, succeeded by Arthur Drexler, 1950. Design collection, 880 items; posters, 1200. *M. of M. A. Bul.* XVIII, No. 4, 1951.)

Among important shows not mentioned above, with directors, are: *America Can't Have Housing*, '34 (Johnson); *Modern Architecture in England*, '37 (Fantl); Architecture section, *Trois siècles d'art americain*, Paris, '38 (McAndrew); *Bauhaus 1919-1928*, '39 (H. Bayer, W. and I. Gropius); *Brazil Builds*, '43 (Goodwin and Mock); *Architecture of Bridges*, '49 (Mock); *Eight Automobiles*, '51 (Johnson); *Built in USA: 1946-52* (Drexler). Most important one-man shows, 1935-1947: Le Corbusier, H. H. Richardson, Aalto, F. L. Wright, Mies van der Rohe, M. Breuer.

DONORS TO THE COLLECTIONS

PAINTINGS, SCULPTURES, CONSTRUCTIONS, COLLAGES, DRAWINGS

Mrs. Frank Altschul
Jean Arp
Leigh Athearn
Mr. and Mrs. Lee A. Ault
Vico Baer
James W. Barney
Mrs. George E. Barstow, Jr.
Frederic Clay Bartlett
W. B. Bennet
Alexander M. Bing
The Honorable and Mrs.
   Robert Woods Bliss
Richard Blow
Briggs W. Buchanan
Mrs. Wendell T. Bush
Alexander Calder
Carroll Carstairs
Walter P. Chrysler, Jr.
Stephen C. Clark
Mr. and Mrs. Erich Cohn
Mr. and Mrs. Ralph F. Colin
Mme Sibylle Cournand
Mrs. W. Murray Crane
Frank Crowninshield
Mrs. Charles Suydam Cutting
Mme Eve Daniel
Bernard Davis
Richard Davis
Mr. and Mrs. Richard S. Davis
Marcel Duchamp
H. S. Ede
Mr. and Mrs. Allan D. Emil
Eric Estorick
Mrs. Marjorie Falk
Mrs. Marie L. Feldhaeusser
Marshall Field
Myrtil Frank
Dr. Román Fresnedo Siri
Naum Gabo
A. E. Gallatin
The Estate of George Gershwin
Mme Nathalie Gontcharova
Philip L. Goodwin
General A. Conger Goodyear
Mr. and Mrs. Jan de Graaff
Peggy Guggenheim
Mrs. Simon Guggenheim
Mrs. Vahan Hagopian
August Hannibal, Jr.
Mrs. Meredith Hare
Mr. and Mrs. Alex L. Hillman
Dr. F. H. Hirschland
Mr. and Mrs. Walter Hochschild
Vladimir Horowitz
Mrs. O'Donnell Iselin
Mr. and Mrs. William B. Jaffe
Edward James

Philip C. Johnson
T. Catesby Jones
Emilio del Junco
Mr. and Mrs. Hugo Kastor
Edgar Kaufmann, Jr.
Mrs. Edgar J. Kaufmann
Lincoln Kirstein
Auguste Klipstein
Mrs. Alfred A. Knopf
Belle Kogan
Mr. and Mrs. Edward F. Kook
Michael Larionov
Albert D. Lasker
Loula D. Lasker
Lucien Lefebvre-Foinet
Mrs. David M. Levy
Mr. and Mrs. Albert Lewin
Mr. and Mrs. Sam A. Lewisohn
Colonel and Mrs.
   Charles A. Lindbergh
Mr. and Mrs. Leo Lionni
Jacques Lipchitz
Pierre M. Loeb
Henry R. Luce
Earle Ludgin
John McAndrew
Mrs. Charles McKinley
Aristide Maillol
Sra. Carlos Martins
Pierre Matisse
Mrs. Saidie A. May
Mrs. Gertrud A. Mellon
Paul Mellon
Mr. and Mrs. John de Menil
Charles E. Merrill
Mrs. Alma Morgenthau
George L. K. Morris
Mr. and Mrs. Gerald Murphy
Mrs. Ray Slater Murphy
Mrs. Elie Nadelman
Mr. and Mrs. Roy R. Neuberger
J. B. Neumann
Mrs. Silvia Neumann
John S. Newberry, Jr.
Ben Nicholson
Amédée Ozenfant
Frank William Packard
William S. Paley
Stamo Papadaki
Antoine Pevsner
Duncan Phillips
George Poindexter
Luis Quintanilla
Dr. C. M. Ramírez Corría
Mrs. Stanley Resor
Jeanne Reynal
Mrs. John D. Rockefeller, Jr.

Mrs. John D. Rockefeller, 3rd
Nelson A. Rockefeller
Alexander Rodchenko
Edward W. Root
Mr. and Mrs. Peter A. Rübel
Mme Helena Rubinstein
Harry J. Rudick
Paul J. Sachs
Sir Michael Sadler
Sam Salz
Mr. and Mrs. Ansley W. Sawyer
Mr. and Mrs. Norbert Schimmel
Wolfgang S. Schwabacher
Mrs. Wallace M. Scudder
John L. Senior, Jr.
Ben Shahn
Charles Sheeler
Mario da Silva
Mrs. Kenneth Simpson
Mr. and Mrs. James Thrall Soby
Mr. and Mrs. David M. Solinger
Mrs. Maurice J. Speiser
Renée Spodheim
Edward Steichen
Leopold Stokowski
J. van Straaten
Mrs. Arthur L. Strasser
Mrs. Cornelius J. Sullivan
Justin K. Thannhauser
G. David Thompson
Tristan Tzara
Curt Valentin
Abraham Walkowitz
Edward M. M. Warburg
Mrs. Felix M. Warburg
Mrs. George Henry Warren
Edith Wetmore
John Hay Whitney
Dr. Nathaniel S. Wollf
Mr. and Mrs. Charles Zadok
Dr. Gregory Zilboorg
Harry Zolotow

The Advisory Committee of
   the Museum of Modern Art
The American Academy and
   National Institute of Arts
   and Letters Fund
The American Tobacco
   Company, Inc.
The United States of Brazil
Comisión Cubana de Cooperación
   Intelectual, Havana
The Contemporary Art Society,
   London
French Art Galleries, Inc.
The Griffis Foundation

The New York World's Fair 1939
Time, Inc.

BEQUESTS

Lillie P. Bliss
Richard D. Brixey
Katherine S. Dreier
Mary Flexner
Rose Gershwin
Anna Erickson Levene
Sam A. Lewisohn
Mrs. John D. Rockefeller, Jr.
Grace Rainey Rogers

PURCHASE FUNDS

The Advisory Committee Fund
Funds realized through
   the Lillie P. Bliss Bequest
Francis Brennan Fund
Mrs. Wendell T. Bush Fund
Katharine Cornell Fund
Frank Crowninshield Fund
van Gogh Purchase Fund
A. Conger Goodyear Fund
Mrs. Simon Guggenheim Fund
Vladimir Horowitz Fund
Inter-American Fund
Aristide Maillol Fund
Mrs. Saidie A. May Fund
Matthew T. Mellon
   Foundation Fund
Mr. and Mrs. Roy R. Neuberger
   Fund
Mrs. John D. Rockefeller, Jr.
   Purchase Fund
James Thrall Soby Fund
Mrs. Cornelius J. Sullivan Fund
Edward M. M. Warburg Fund

LENDERS OF WORKS
FOR AN EXTENDED PERIOD

Baroness Napoléon Gourgaud
Adelaide M. de Groot
Dr. Franz Meyer
Henri Pierre Roché
John Hay Whitney

The Metropolitan Museum of
   Art, Alfred Stieglitz Collection
The Miller Company's
   Painting Toward Architecture
   Collection
U.S. Department of the Interior,
   Indian Arts & Crafts Board
U.S. Public Works of Art Project
U.S. WPA Art Program

PRINT COLLECTION

Larry L. Aldrich
Irving Amen
Dr. W. Andrew Archer
L. A. Arkus
Kenneth Armitage
Mr. and Mrs. R. Kirk Askew, Jr.
Leo Auerbach
R. Maxil Ballinger
Walter Bareiss
B. A. Barkai
J. N. Bartfield
Leonard Baskin
Willi Baumeister
Heinz Berggruen
Mrs. Cornelius N. Bliss
Mrs. Theodore Boettger
Enrico Bordoni
C. Philip Boyer
Patti Garnell Cadby
Albert Carman
Leo Castelli
Gordon Chadwick
Marc Chagall
Ludwig Charell
Jean Charlot
James Raphael Cherry
Samuel Chotzinoff
Walter P. Chrysler, Jr.
Henry Church
William Cohn
Mrs. Lovis Corinth
Gerald Cramer
Frank Crowninshield
Peter Deitsch
Jean Delmas
Jean Deniau
Martha Dickinson
Mrs. Lewis Eldridge

Erwin Eliel
Lyonel Feininger
Rose Fried
Pola Gauguin
Bernard Gheerbrant
Hubert de Givenchy
Philip L. Goodwin
General A. Conger Goodyear
Mrs. L. H. Grunebaum
Seymour Hacker
Mrs. Edith Gregor Halpert
Paul Herzog
Dr. F. H. Hirschland
Henry-Russell Hitchcock, Jr.
Mr. and Mrs. Alfred Jaretzki, Jr.
Philip C. Johnson
Robert Edmond Jones
Henri Jonquières
D. H. Kahnweiler
Mme Wassily Kandinsky
Edgar Kaufmann, Jr.
Mr. and Mrs. Sheldon Keck
Mr. and Mrs. David Keppel
Lincoln Kirstein
Frau Paul Klee
François Lachenal
James Laughlin, 4th
Susy Laytha
Dr. Arthur Lejwa
Mrs. Sam A. Lewisohn
James Lord
Mrs. Hazel McKinley
M. and Mme Amédée Maeght
Paul Magriel
Henri Matisse
Mrs. Saidie A. May
Guy Mayer
A. Hyatt Mayor

Henry Moore
Rolf Nesch
J. B. Neumann
Sarah Newmeyer
Karl Nierendorf
Pablo O'Higgins
Harry C. Oppenheimer
Sr. and Sra. Felipe Orlando
Mrs. Alice Paalen
Mrs. Theresa Parker
Paul P. Piech
Allen Porter
Cândido Portinari
André Racz
Mrs. Frances Raftery
James William Reid
Bernard Reis
John Rewald
John Richardson
Victor S. Riesenfeld
Mrs. John D. Rockefeller, Jr.
Mrs. John D. Rockefeller, 3rd
Cary Ross
Georges Rouault
William Rubin
Paul J. Sachs
Mr. and Mrs. Jack Schenberg
Karl Schrag
Lasar Segall
Mrs. Bertha M. Slattery
James Thrall Soby
Mrs. Muriel Stokes
Mr. and Mrs.
   Justin K. Thannhauser
Eugene Victor Thau
Tristan Tzara
Curt Valentin
Jacques Villon

Ambroise Vollard
Edward M. M. Warburg
Fru Pepi Weixlgartner
Edith Wetmore
John Hay Whitney
D. H. Xochitiotzin
Albert E. Yersin
Adja Yunkers
Georges de Zayas

Guilde Internationale
   de la Gravure, Geneva-Paris
National Serigraph Society
The Printmakers
School Prints Ltd., London
The Weyhe Gallery

BEQUESTS

Lillie P. Bliss
Katherine S. Dreier

PURCHASE FUNDS

The Advisory Committee Fund
Larry L. Aldrich Fund
Funds realized through
   the Lillie P. Bliss Bequest
Henry Church Fund
Frank Crowninshield Fund
A. Conger Goodyear Fund
Mrs. Simon Guggenheim Fund
Inter-American Fund
Philip C. Johnson Fund
Mrs. John D. Rockefeller, Jr.
   Purchase Fund
James Thrall Soby Fund
Spaeth Foundation Fund
Edward M. M. Warburg Fund

PHOTOGRAPHY COLLECTION

Ansel Adams
Mrs. Ralph Seward Allen
Merle Armitage
Albert M. Bender
Albert Boni
Harry Callahan
Henri Cartier-Bresson
Alvin Langdon Coburn
Frank Crowninshield
Dr. Harold E. Edgerton
Eliot Elisofon
Arthur Fellig
Philip L. Goodwin
General A. Conger Goodyear
Philip C. Johnson
Consuelo Kanaga
Yousuf Karsh
Edgar Kaufmann, Jr.
Gyorgy Kepes
Lincoln Kirstein
Samuel M. Kootz

Mrs. Bella C. Landauer
Dorothea Lange
Dudley Lee
Helen Levitt
Mrs. Charles J. Liebman
George Platt Lynes
David H. McAlpin
John McAndrew
T. J. Maloney
Paul Martin
Gjon Mili
László Moholy-Nagy
Mrs. Jane K. Murray
Arnold Newman
Dorothy Norman
Georgia O'Keeffe
Leo Pavelle
Eliot Porter
Dr. and Mrs. Henry Ritter
Mrs. John D. Rockefeller, Jr.
Nelson A. Rockefeller

Arthur Rothstein
Carl Sandburg
August Sander
Charles Sheeler
Adrian Siegel
Aaron Siskind
James Thrall Soby
Edward Steichen
Alfred Stieglitz
Paul Strand
Luke Swank
James Johnson Sweeney
M. T. Talbot
Milton Halsey Thomas
William Vandivert
Abraham Walkowitz
Edward M. M. Warburg
Edward Weston
Monroe Wheeler
Mrs. Clarence H. White
Cedric Wright

The Boston Post
Condé Nast Publications, Inc.
Connecticut Valley Boys' Schools
Fortune
Life
Magnum Photos, Inc.
The Museum of the
   City of New York
The Nebraska State
   Historical Society
The New York Times
   Wide-World Photos
The Philadelphia
   Commercial Museum
The Photo League
Rapho-Guillumette Pictures
U.S. Farm Security
   Administration

BEQUEST

Katherine S. Dreier

THEATRE ARTS COLLECTION

Walter Allner
George Balanchine
Eugene Berman
Briggs W. Buchanan
Walt Disney Productions
Karl Free
Antonin Heythum

Robert Edmond Jones
Mrs. Sally Kamin
Mrs. Patricia B. Kerns
Lincoln Kirstein
Michael Larionov
Paul Magriel
Donald M. Oenslager

John Pratt
Mrs. John D. Rockefeller, Jr.
Savely Sorine
Ettie Stettheimer
Pavel Tchelitchew
Abraham Walkowitz
Edward M. M. Warburg

Mrs. George Henry Warren

PURCHASE FUNDS

Funds realized through the
Lillie P. Bliss Bequest
Mrs. Simon Guggenheim Fund
Victor Roudin Fund

FILM LIBRARY

Neil Agnew
Harry Aitken
Fred Astaire
Richard Barthelmess
Vincent Bejtman
Thomas J. Brandon
Luis Bunuel
Irene Castle
Alberto Cavalcanti
Charles Chaplin
Walt Disney
Marcel Duchamp
Thomas A. Edison-R. L. Giffen
Douglas Fairbanks
J. S. Fairfax-Jones
Robert J. Flaherty
Walter Futter
I. G. Goldsmith
Samuel Goldwyn
D. W. Griffith
William S. Hart
André Heymann
Alfred Hitchcock
Mrs. Thomas H. Ince
Joris Ivens
Buster Keaton
Mrs. Edwin Knopf
Fernand Léger

Jean Lenauer
Jean A. LeRoy
Peter S. Levine
Robert M. Levine
Harold Lloyd
Louis Lumière
Mrs. Philip Manson
R. W. McCay
Georges Méliès
Erno Metzner
Gabriel Pascal
Mary Pickford
Edwin S. Porter
J. Arthur Rank
Man Ray
Lotte Reiniger
Hans Richter
Hal Roach
Louis de Rochemont
Henwar Rodakiewicz
Arthur M. See
David O. Selznick
Stella Simon
Ralph Steiner
Gloria Swanson
Walter Wanger
Gösta Werner
Christopher Young

Amkino
Biograph (R. H. Hammer)
The British Film Institute,
   London
The British Gas, Light
   & Coke Company, London
British Information Services
The Carnegie Corporation
   & Civic Films
La Cinémathèque de Belgique,
   Brussels
La Cinémathèque Française,
   Paris
Cineteca Italiana, Milan
Columbia Pictures Corp.
Eastman Kodak Company
Federation of Jewish Charities
Film Polski, Warsaw
Ford Motor Company
Gaumont-Franco-Film-Aubert,
   Paris
GPO Film Unit, London
Guaranteed Pictures Company
Harvard University
   Film Foundation
Krimsky & Cochran
Loew's, Inc.
The March of Time

Arthur Mayer &
   Joseph Burstyn, Inc.
Montclair Public Library
NIS — The Scientific-Research
   Institute, Moscow
Paramount Pictures, Inc.
Prestige Pictures
Reichsfilmarchiv, Berlin
RKO Radio Pictures, Inc.
Rochester Civic
   Music Association
Schweizerisches Filmarchiv,
   Basel
Svensk Filmindustri, Stockholm
Twentieth Century-Fox
   Film Corp.
Ufa, Berlin
United Artists Corp.
U.S. Department of Agriculture
U.S. Farm Security
   Administration
U.S. Office of Coordinator
   of Inter-American Affairs
U.S. Office of War Information
U.S. Resettlement Administration
U.S. War Department
Universal Pictures Company, Inc.
Warner Brothers Pictures, Inc.

ARCHITECTURE AND DESIGN COLLECTION

Allan Adler
Mrs. Anni Albers
Laura Anderson
Dr. Anny Baumann
Herbert Bayer
Joseph Binder
Mrs. J. F. Byers
Greta Daniel
Jane Dickerman
Charles Eames
Marli Ehrman
R. Buckminster Fuller
Philip L. Goodwin
General A. Conger Goodyear
Walter Gropius
Mme Hector Guimard
René d'Harnoncourt
Philip C. Johnson
Edgar Kaufmann, Jr.
Richard Kelly
Frederick Kiesler

Mr. and Mrs. Sam A. Lewisohn
John McAndrew
Thomas D. Mabry, Jr.
Peter Muller-Munk
Virginia Nepodal
Eliot Noyes
Davis J. Pratt
Antonin Raymond
Mrs. Stanley Resor
Gerrit Rietveld
Mrs. John D. Rockefeller, Jr.
The Family of
   Mrs. John D. Rockefeller, Jr.
Mrs. V. Henry Rothschild
Eero Saarinen
Dr. Peter Schlumbohm
Ulla of Ugglas
Frank Lloyd Wright
Eva S. Zeisel

Abercrombie & Fitch Company

Aluminum Company of America
Aluminum Cooking Utensil Co.
American Steel & Wire Company
Anchor Tool Company
Artek-Pascoe, Inc.
Baccarat & Porthault, Inc.
Baker Furniture, Inc.
Robert Barber, Inc.
Blenko Glass Company
Bloomingdale Bros., Inc.
BMC Manufacturing Corporation
Bonniers, Inc.
Brazilian Ministry of Education
   & Health, Rio de Janeiro
Charles D. Bridell, Inc.
Arthur Brown & Bros., Inc.
Brown & Sharpe of New York
Burchard, Inc.
Busch-Reisinger Museum
   of Germanic Culture,
   Harvard University

Café Nicholson
Carrollton Manufacturing Co.
Castleton China, Inc.
Chase Brass & Copper Company
Club Aluminum Products Co.
Coors Porcelain Company
D. Stanley Corcoran, Inc.
Corning Glass Works
Eugene Dietzgen Company, Inc.
Henry Disston & Sons, Inc.
Dunbar Furniture Corporation
   of Indiana
Eimer & Amend
Ekco Products Company
Electric Boat Company
Evans Products Company
Federal Tool Corporation
Fifth Avenue Cutlery Shop, Inc.
Finland Ceramics & Glass Corp.
Foreign Advisory Service Corp.
Joseph Franken

Fraser's, Inc.
Martin Freeman Company
Gerber Legendary Blades
Gump's
Gunn & Latchford, Inc.
N. S. Gustin Company
The Hallicrafters Company
Hammacher Schlemmer & Co.
The Heifetz Company
Heywood-Wakefield Company
A. L. Hirsch & Company
House of Italian Handicrafts
Hudson Studios
Georg Jensen Inc.
J. G. Furniture Company, Inc.
Kensington, Inc.
Alfred E. Knobler & Company
Knoll Associates, Inc.
Konwiser, Inc.
Kromex Industries, Inc.
Lalance & Grosjean
   Manufacturing Company
Landers, Frary & Clark
Langbein-Giftwares Division

H. E. Lauffer Company, Inc.
Lemurian Crafts
Lenart Import Ltd.
Lenox, Inc.
Lever Brothers Company
Lewis & Conger
The Lighthouse, New York
   Association for the Blind
Louisville Tackle Company
R. H. Macy & Company
Mardigian Corporation
Markle Products Corporation
Marrell Studios
Marshall Field & Company
Mayhew-Copley Ltd.
Menlo Textiles
Middletown Manufacturing Co.
Herman Miller Furniture Co.
Necchi Sewing Machine
   Sales Corporation
Olivetti Corporation of America
Orrefors Galleries
Ovington's
Pennsylvania Drug Company

Le Petit Mouchoir
Plas-Tex Corporation
Plastic Productions Company
Revere Copper & Brass, Inc.
Rorstrand, Inc.
Rena Rosenthal, Inc.
St. Regis Paper Company
Saks Fifth Avenue
Max Schling Seedsmen, Inc.
Scovill Manufacturing Company
Sculpture House
Seneca Glass Company
Singer Sewing Machine Company
Sitterle Ceramics
SKF Industries, Inc.
Alexander Smith, Inc.
L. C. Starrett Company
Stede, Inc.
Steubenville Pottery Company
Sullivan Shipyards, Inc.
Sweden House, Inc.
Sylvania Electric Products, Inc.
Telex Electro Acoustic Division
Thonet Industries, Inc.

Thyco Electric Products, Inc.
Tupper Corporation
A. J. Van Dugteren & Sons, Inc.
Kurt Versen Company
Victor Tool Company
Vollrath Company
Waldron Associates
Watertown Manufacturing Co.
George E. Weigl Company
Widdicomb Furniture Company.
Willoughby Camera Stores, Inc.
Yale & Towne Manufacturing Co.
Carl Zeiss, Inc.

PURCHASE FUNDS

The Advisory Committee Fund
Funds realized through
   the Lillie P. Bliss Bequest
Mrs. Simon Guggenheim Fund
Inter-American Fund
Edgar Kaufmann, Jr.
   Purchase Fund
Mrs. John D. Rockefeller, Jr.
   Purchase Fund

GRAPHIC ARTS COLLECTION

Otto Aicher
Charles Alan
Walter Allner
Jean Arp
Willi Baum
Herbert Bayer
Lester Beall
Mrs. Max Beckmann
Max Bill
Joseph Binder
Lino Bo Bardi
Will Burtin
Jean Carlu
Mrs. John Carter
Jean Colin
Paul Colin
Bernard Davis
Dick Elffers
Hans Erni
Max Ernst
Rose Fried
Abram Games
Bernard Gheerbrant
Rudolph De Harak
Peter Hatch
Ashley Havinden
F. H. K. Henrion
Philip C. Johnson
E. McKnight Kauffer
Frederick J. Kiesler
Oskar Kokoschka
Le Corbusier
Fernand Léger
Herbert Leupin
Jack Levine
Jan Lewitt & George Him
Jay Leyda
Matthew Liebowitz

Leo Lionni
Alvin Lustig
John McAndrew
Noel Martin
Henri Matisse
Pierre Matisse
Bruno Munari
Jacques Nathan
J. B. Neumann
Beaumont Newhall
Erik Nitsche
Isamu Noguchi
Celestino Piatti
Henry Proskauer
Paul Rand
Manfred Reiss
Mrs. Stanley Resor
John Rewald
Mrs. John D. Rockefeller, Jr.
Nelson A. Rockefeller
Jessie Rosenfeld
Dr. W. J. H. B. Sandberg
Raymond Savignac
Mme Galka E. Scheyer
José Luis Sert
Ben Shahn
Slechinsky
David Smith
G. E. Kidder Smith
S. S. Spivack
J. Srokowski
Paul Standard
Alexander Steinweiss
Georg Trump
Jan Tschichold
Curt Valentin
Carl Van Vechten
Monroe Wheeler

Christian Zervos

American Overseas Airlines
   Company
The Arts Council
   of Great Britain, London
British Ministry of Information,
   Display & Exhibition
   Division, London
Columbia Records, Inc.
C.I.O. Political Action
   Committee
Container Corporation
   of America
Czechoslovak Information Office
Danish Information Office
Decca Records, Inc.
Doyle, Dane & Bernbach
French National Railroads
General Post Office, London
The Institute of
   Contemporary Art, Boston
Institute of Contemporary Arts,
   London
Kunsthaus, Zurich
London Passenger
   Transport Board
R. H. Macy & Company
Maeght Gallery, Paris
Boris Mirski Gallery
Museu de Arte Moderna,
   São Paulo, Brazil
National Foundation
   for Infantile Paralysis
National Savings Committee,
   London
George Nelson Associates
Netherlands Information Bureau

New York Subway
   Advertising Company
The New York Times
Office Suisse d'Expansion
   Commerciale, Zurich
Olivetti Corporation of America
Oxford University Press
Pan American Union
Polish Research & Information
   Service
Royal Society for the Prevention
   of Accidents, London
Shell-Mex B P, London
Stedelijk Museum, Amsterdam
Time, Inc.
U.S. Civil Aeronautics
   Administration
U.S. Department of Agriculture
U.S. Department of the Interior
U.S. Federal Security Agency
U.S. Housing Authority
U.S. Office of the Coordinator
   of Inter-American Affairs
U.S. Office of
   Emergency Management
U.S. Office of War Information
U.S. Public Health Service
U.S. Treasury Department
U.S. War Department
U.S. War Production Board
The U.S.S.R. Society for
   Cultural Relations with
   Foreign Countries, Moscow
Workshop School of Advertising
   & Editorial Art

BEQUEST

Katherine S. Dreier

BIBLIOGRAPHY AND INDEX OF ARTISTS

BIBLIOGRAPHY

The bibliography is divided into three sections: 1) monographs and 2) general works published by the Museum; 3) a few books of other publishers referred to in the text. Prepared by Marie Alexander

MUSEUM PUBLICATIONS: MONOGRAPHS

1 *Alvar Aalto*, J. McAndrew, ed.; S. Breines; A. L. Kocher. 1938
2 *Theatre of Eugene Berman* by G. Amberg. 1947
3 *Pierre Bonnard* by J. Rewald. 1948
4 *Georges Braque* by H. R. Hope; J. Cassou. 1949
5 *Marcel Breuer* by P. Blake. 1949
6 *Charles Burchfield, Early Water Colors* by A. H. Barr, Jr. 1930
7 *Alexander Calder* by J. J. Sweeney. 2nd ed., 1951
8 *Photographs by Henri Cartier-Bresson* by L. Kirstein, B. Newhall. 1947
9 *Posters by Cassandre* by E. Fantl. 1936
10 *Marc Chagall* by J. J. Sweeney. 1946
11 *Giorgio de Chirico* by J. T. Soby, in preparation
12 *Salvador Dali* by J. T. Soby. 2nd ed., 1946
13 *Stuart Davis* by J. J. Sweeney. 1945
14 *Charles Demuth* by A. C. Ritchie. 1950
15 "Charles Despiau" by A. Rindge. *M. of M. A. Bul.* XI, no. 4, 1944
16 *James Ensor* by L. Tannenbaum. 1951
17 *Walker Evans: American Photographs* by L. Kirstein. 1938
18 *Douglas Fairbanks* by A. Cooke. 1940
19 *Lyonel Feininger*, D. C. Miller, ed.; A. J. Schardt; A. H. Barr, Jr.; and *Marsden Hartley* by M. Wheeler; the artist. 1944
20 *Gabo-Pevsner* by R. Olson; A. Chanin; H. Read. 1948
21 *Vincent van Gogh*, A. H. Barr, Jr., ed. 1935
22 *Vincent van Gogh Letters to Emile Bernard*, D. Lord, ed. 1938
23 *Juan Gris*, in preparation
24 *D. W. Griffith* by I. Barry. 1940
25 "George Grosz", *M. of M. A. Bul.* IX, no. 1, 1941
— *Marsden Hartley*: see no. 19
26 "Hayter and Studio 17" by J. J. Sweeney; the artist. *M. of M. A. Bul.* XII, 6, 1944
27 *Edward Hopper* by A. H. Barr, Jr.; C. Burchfield; the artist. 1933
28 *Posters by E. McKnight Kauffer* by A. Huxley; the artist. 1937
29 *Paul Klee*, M. Miller, ed.; L. and J. Feininger; J. J. Sweeney; A. H. Barr, Jr. 1945

30 "Aspects of the Art of Paul Klee", a symposium, *M. of M. A. Bul.* XVII, no. 4, 1950 (M. Breuer; B. Shahn)
31 *Prints of Paul Klee* by J. T. Soby. 1947
32 *Paul Klee* by A. H. Barr, Jr. 1930
33 *Oskar Kokoschka* by J. S. Plaut. 1949. (The Chanticleer Press, New York, for the Institute of Contemporary Art, Boston, the M. of M. A., *et al.*)
34 *Gaston Lachaise* by L. Kirstein. 1935
35 *Léger* by Katharine Kuh. 1953. (The Art Institute of Chicago in collaboration with the M. of M. A., *et al.*)
36 "Fernand Léger versus Cubism" by G. L. K. Morris. *M. of M. A. Bul.* III, no. 1, 1935
37 *Wilhelm Lehmbruck, Aristide Maillol* by J. Abbott. 1930
38 *Jacques Lipchitz* by H. R. Hope. 1954
— *Aristide Maillol*: see no. 37
39 *John Marin* by E. M. Benson; H. McBride; M. Hartley. 1936
40 "John Marin, Yankee Artist" by L. Mozley. *M. of M. A. Bul.* IV, no. 1, 1936
41 *Matisse, His Art and His Public* by A. H. Barr, Jr. 1952
42 *Joan Miro* by J. J. Sweeney. 1941
43 *Modigliani* by J. T. Soby. 1951
44 *Mondrian* by J. J. Sweeney. 1948
45 *Henry Moore* by J. J. Sweeney. 1946
46 *Edvard Munch* by F. B. Deknatel. 1950, with Institute of Contemporary Art, Boston
47 *Sculpture of Elie Nadelman* by L. Kirstein. 1948
48 "Orozco Explains", *M. of M. A. Bul.* VII, no. 4, 1940
— *Pevsner*: see no. 20
49 *Picasso: Fifty Years of his Art* by A. H. Barr, Jr. 1946
50 "Picasso: His Graphic Art" W. S. Lieberman. *M. of M. A. Bul.* XIX, no. 2, 1952
51 "Portinari of Brazil" by F. Horn, R. C. Smith. *M. of M. A. Bul.* VII, no. 6, 1940
52 "Redon: Drawings and Lithographs" by W. S. Lieberman. *M. of M. A. Bul.* XIX, no. 2, 1952
53 *Diego Rivera* by F. F. Paine; J. Abbott. 1931
54 *Mies van der Rohe* by P. C. Johnson. 2nd ed., 1953
55 *Georges Rouault* by J. T. Soby; C. Schniewind. 2nd ed., 1947
56 *Prints of Georges Rouault* by M. Wheeler. 1938
57 *Georges Rouault: Miserere* by M. Wheeler; the artist. 1952

58 *Georges Rouault Retrospective Exhibition*, M. Wheeler, ed.; J. Maritain; W. S. Lieberman. 1953
59 *Henri Rousseau* by D. C. Rich. 2nd ed., 1946
60 *Ben Shahn* by J. T. Soby. 1947, with Penguin Books Ltd., England
61 "Ben Shahn" by J. T. Soby. *M. of M. A. Bul.* XIV, nos. 4-5, 1947
62 *Charles Sheeler*, D. C. Miller, ed.; W. C. Williams; the artist. 1939
63 "Skidmore, Owings & Merrill, Architects, U.S.A.", *M. of M. A. Bul.* XVIII, no. 1, 1950
64 *Paul Strand: Photographs 1915-1945* by N. Newhall. 1945
65 *Tchelitchew* by J. T. Soby. 1942
66 "Jacques Villon: His Graphic Art" by W. S. Lieberman. *M. of M. A. Bul.* XXI, no. 1, 1953
67 *Edouard Vuillard* by A. C. Ritchie. 1954
68 *Max Weber* by A. H. Barr, Jr. 1930
69 *Photographs of Edward Weston* by N. Newhall. 1946

MUSEUM PUBLICATIONS: GENERAL

69a "The Abby Aldrich Rockefeller Print Room: Master Prints from the Museum Collection" by W. S. Lieberman; A. H. Barr, Jr. *M. of M. A. Bul.* XVI, no. 4, 1949.
70 *Abstract Painting and Sculpture in America* by A. C. Ritchie. 1951
71 *American Folk Art* by H. Cahill. 1932
72 *American Realists and Magic Realists*, D. C. Miller and A. H. Barr, Jr., eds.; L. Kirstein. 1943
73 *Americans 1942*, D. C. Miller, ed. 1942
74 *Bauhaus, 1919-1928* by H. Bayer; W. Gropius; I. Gropius. 1938
75 *Lillie P. Bliss Collection*, A. H. Barr, Jr., ed. 1934
76 *Contemporary Painters* by J. T. Soby. 1948
77 *Cubism and Abstract Art* by A. H. Barr, Jr. 1936
78 "The Dance Archives", *M. of M. A. Bul.* VIII, no. 3, 1941
79 "De Stijl" by A. H. Barr, Jr. *M. of M. A. Bul.* XX, no. 2, 1952
80 "Eleven Europeans in America" by J. J. Sweeney. *M. of M. A. Bul.* XIII, nos. 4-5, 1946 (Masson, Ozenfant, Seligmann, Léger, Ernst, Duchamp, Tanguy, Lipchitz, Hélion, Chagall, Mondrian)
81 *Fantastic Art, Dada, Surrealism*, A. H. Barr, Jr., ed.; G. Hugnet. 3rd ed., 1947
82 *Les Fauves* by J. Rewald. 1952
83 *Fifteen Americans*, D. C. Miller, ed. 1952

INDEX OF ARTISTS

THIS BOOK WAS PRODUCED IN THE NETHERLANDS FOR THE
TRUSTEES OF THE MUSEUM OF MODERN ART IN SEPTEMBER, 1954

PRINTING: JOH. ENSCHEDÉ EN ZONEN, HAARLEM,

COLOR ENGRAVING: 43 PLATES BY CHEMEZ, HAARLEM,
15 BY REPRODUCTIE COMPAGNIE, ROTTERDAM,
AND 14 BY KONINGSVELD, 'S-GRAVENHAGE

BINDING: J. BRANDT & ZOON, AMSTERDAM

COLOR PHOTOGRAPHY: FRANK LERNER, NEW YORK

BOOK DESIGNED BY EDWARD L. MILLS;
COVER PAPER DESIGNED BY CHARLES OSCAR